The Political Economy of Local Government

STUDIES IN FISCAL FEDERALISM AND STATE–LOCAL FINANCE

General Editor: Wallace E. Oates, *Professor of Economics, University of Maryland and University Fellow, Resources for the Future, USA*

This important series is designed to make a significant contribution to the development of the principles and practices of state–local finance. It includes both theoretical and empirical work. International in scope, it addresses issues of current and future concern in both East and West and in developed and developing countries.

The main purpose of the series is to create a forum for the publication of high quality work and to show how economic analysis can make a contribution to understanding the role of local finance in fiscal federalism in the twenty-first century.

Titles in the series include:

Financing Federal Systems
The Selected Essays of Edward M. Gramlich
Edward M. Gramlich

Local Government Tax and Land Use Policies in the United States
Understanding the Links
Helen F. Ladd

Fiscal Federalism and State–Local Finance
The Scandinavian Perspective
Jørn Rattsø

The Challenge of Fiscal Disparities for State and Local Governments
The Selected Essays of Helen F. Ladd
Helen F. Ladd

The New Democratic Federalism for Europe
Functional, Overlapping and Competing Jurisdictions
Bruno S. Frey and Reiner Eichenberger

Taxes, Public Goods and Urban Economics
The Selected Essays of Peter Mieszkowski
Peter Mieszkowski

Fiscal Federalism in Russia
Intergovernmental Transfers and the Financing of Education
Kitty Stewart

The Political Economy of Local Government
Leadership, Reform and Market Failure
Brian E. Dollery and Joe L. Wallis

Tax Policy in the Global Economy
Selected Essays of Peggy B. Musgrave
Peggy B. Musgrave

The Political Economy of Local Government

Brian E. Dollery, and Joe L. Wallis

School of Economics, University of New England, Armidale
Department of Economics, Otago University, Dunedin

STUDIES IN FISCAL FEDERALISM AND STATE - LOCAL FINANCE

Edward Elgar
Cheltenham, UK • Northampton, MA, USA

Published by
Edward Elgar Publishing Limited
Glensanda House
Montpellier Parade
Cheltenham
Glos GL50 1UA
UK

Edward Elgar Publishing, Inc.
136 West Street
Suite 202
Northampton
Massachusetts 01060
USA

A catalogue record for this book
is available from the British Library

Library of Congress Cataloguing in Publication Data
Dollery, Brian.
    The political economy of local government : leadership, reform, and market failure / Brian Dollery and Joe Wallis.
        p. cm. — (Studies in fiscal federalism and state-local finance)
    Includes bibliographical references and index.
    1. Economic policy. 2. Political planning. 3. Policy sciences. 4. Local government. I. Wallis, Joe. II. Title. III. Series.

    HD87 .D65 2001
    320.8—dc21   2001023717

ISBN 1 84064 451 6
Printed and bound in Great Britain by MPG Books Ltd, Bodmin, Cornwall

Contents

List of figures

List of Tables

Preface

Despite a voluminous literature, the role of the state in advanced market economies and the concomitant problems of appropriate policy formulation and implementation remain unsettled questions. Various factors may explain this unsatisfactory state of affairs. For instance, the complexities and dynamic nature of policy making in contemporary developed economies may preclude any single 'general theory'. Thus Christopher Hood's (2000) 'art of the state' may simply be too labyrinthine to be amenable to any overarching theoretical analysis. Similarly, the fact that until fairly recently social scientists have approached these questions largely from within the paradigmatic confines of their own particular disciplines has surely not helped. Indeed, as economists we have often been constrained by our own disciplinary boundaries and have consequently felt the need to stray well beyond the analytical tools traditionally available to economists.

If the problem of the proper role of the state has yet to be satisfactorily resolved for higher levels of government, then this problem is certainly much more acute in the realm of local government, which has attracted far less attention in the literature. The comparative lack of interest in local government may perhaps best be explained on institutional grounds. For example, local government is often seen as the 'poor relation' of higher tiers of governance both in terms of size and autonomy and thus as less deserving of intensive study. Moreover, specialist scholarly journals devoted to local government, such as the leading publication *Local Government Studies*, are often obliged to appeal to practitioners and scholars alike, and thus carry a high proportion of articles on matters of topical relevance rather than theoretical significance. Furthermore, many of the published books in the area, including D.E. Wildasin's (1986) classic text *Urban Public Finance* and David King's (1984) *Fiscal Tiers: The Economics of Multi-level Government*, are now somewhat dated. Although more recent work, especially Stewart Bailey's (1999) excellent *Local Government Economics* and George Boyne's (1998) authoritative *Public Choice Theory and Local Government,* represents a most welcome and insightful addition to the relatively limited literature on local government, it typically focuses on the institutional characteristics of particular systems of local governance, particularly those of Britain and the United States. Accordingly, there is an urgent need for a text which incorporates and extends current thought on the proper role of the state in policy making into a generic local government context rather than in some specific national institutional milieu. This is what we have attempted to do in the present book.

In this book we have sought to move beyond conventional disciplinary boundaries in order to advance the understanding of local government. We begin with conventional economic approaches to the problem of policy making in local government, including the theory of fiscal federalism, the market failure paradigm and the literature on government failure, and attempt to augment these arguments to make them more applicable to the special circumstances of local governance. We then try to comprehend the shift from 'government to governance' that tends to follow a process of local government modernization with theoretical tools derived from the 'New Institutional Economics'. In particular we use the comparative institutional approach associated with this school of thought to analyze the deployment of markets, hierarchies and networks as alternative governance mechanisms at this level. Local government reform is then examined against the background of the paradigm shift that is often involved with the organizational restructuring and management reform that have occurred in many countries at all levels of government during the last two decades. With particular reference to local government reforms in the UK and New Zealand we explore the extent to which 'minimalist' and 'activist' approaches to matching local functions to local capacity can be related to the different styles of policy leadership that may be required to advance a paradigmatic reform process through its distinct phases.

This book represents yet another product of an ongoing research collaboration between the authors which stretches back almost two decades to the Department of Economics at Rhodes University in Grahamstown, South Africa, where we were both employed. A mutual interest in cricket, rugby and beer soon led to fruitful research discussions and a steady flow of papers and books which continues to the present day. Joe Wallis's move to the Department of Economics at the University of Otago in Dunedin, New Zealand in 1987 and Brian Dollery's subsequent relocation to the Department of Economics at the University of New England in Armidale, New South Wales, Australia, a year later allowed us both to observe at first hand the astonishing policy reversals associated with 'Rogernomics' in New Zealand and 'microeconomic reform' in Australia. A good deal of our thinking on the nature of policy making and implementation in local government derives from a close scrutiny of these policy changes and their associated policy paradigms.

We are grateful to a number of individuals and organizations for the assistance they have rendered towards the successful completion of this book. In particular, we would like to thank Craig 'Hitman' Lawlor of the School of Biological Sciences at the University of New England for his amazing technical expertise and extraordinary diligence in preparing a 'camera-ready' draft of the manuscript. We would also like to thank the editorial staff of Edward Elgar Publishing Limited for their helpful assistance with the book. Moreover, we acknowledge the kind permission granted us by Frank Cass Journals to use parts of Andrew Worthington and Brian Dollery (2000b), 'An Empirical Survey of Frontier Efficiency Measurement in Local Government', *Local Government Studies*, 26 (2), in the preparation of Chapter 4. We are also very grateful to Dr A.C. 'Wortho' Worthington of the School of Economics and Finance at the Queensland University of Technology for co-authoring this chapter of the book. We also acknowledge the kind permission given us by Basil Blackwell to use some sections of Joe Wallis and Brian Dollery (2001), 'Local Government Policy Evolution in New Zealand: Radical Reform and the Ex Post Emergence of Consensus or Rival Advocacy Coalitions', *Public Administration* (forthcoming).

Brian Dollery would like to express his personal appreciation to collaborator Joe Wallis for an invigorating and productive research partnership. He would also like to thank various colleagues for their help and encouragement in the preparation of the book, especially Dr G.O. 'Fair Go' Smith and Dr M. 'Kortto' Kortt of the School of Economics at the University of New England. Most of all, he would to thank his wife Therese Burton for her love and support.

Joe Wallis would like to thank Brian Dollery for the leadership, encouragement and humor he brings to their research collaboration. Long may it continue 'ouboet'. He would also like to thank his colleagues in the Department of Economics at the University of Otago for providing a congenial and supportive work environment. Most of all, Joe would like to thank his wife, Kim, and daughters, Caitlin and Jessica, for their love and the fun times they share together.

1. Introduction

1.1 INTRODUCTION

In many respects local government can be said to be the poor handmaiden of its more august state and federal counterparts in terms of the attention it has traditionally attracted from scholars. Various reasons can be advanced to account for this state of affairs. For instance, in contemporary developed economies local government expenditure typically comprises a relatively small proportion of total public sector outlays and may thus be deemed to warrant less scrutiny. Secondly, even when municipal expenditure in absolute terms constitutes substantial sums of money, the fact that local governments are usually statutory creatures of higher levels of government means that their actions are often rigidly manipulated and constrained by state and central governments. This has led many writers to focus on these higher tiers of governance to try to explain local government behavior. Furthermore, local governments often have an amorphous and mutating nature. For example, commenting on British local government, Bailey (1999, p. 4) observes that 'the ill-defined status of local government combines with changing perceptions of local autonomy, accountability, equity and the need for macroeconomic control, causing the relationship between central government and local government to be in a state on continuous change'.

Although the terms 'local government', 'municipality', 'council' and 'local authority' are used synonymously in this book to describe democratically elected sub-central governments with jurisdiction over spatially limited areas, they nevertheless all describe a tier of government in both unitary and federal states which is characterized above all else by diversity. After all, whereas some local governments deliver a complex array of goods and services, including education, health and social services, especially in the European context, other municipal systems, particularly in Australia and New Zealand, focus much more narrowly on 'services to property', like roads, sewage and water. Similarly, while some councils serve large populations in big cities with budgets measured in billions of dollars, their more modest cousins may attend jurisdictions with a mere handful of citizens.   Moreover, local government systems also differ drastically in their relationships with higher levels of government.   In many cases municipalities may enjoy only limited autonomy in terms of both service delivery and financial independence whilst others may exercise wide discretion and be largely self-financing.   This diversity and complexity evident in real-world systems of local governance may also go some way towards explaining the comparative neglect which local government has suffered in the scholarly literature.

The traditional economic approach to local government is to locate it within a broader context of a multi-tiered or federal system of governance and then tackle the problem of assigning the various functions of the state amongst the different levels of government in the most economically efficient manner possible (Oates 1972).   But at best this is a partial view of the role of local government within a federation.   Inman and Rubinfeld (1997, p. 44) have identified three 'alternative principles' or 'models' of federalism since those 'who value a federal system typically do so for some mix of three reasons: it encourages an efficient allocation of national resources; it fosters political participation and a sense of democratic community; and it helps to protect basic liberties and freedoms'.   All federal arrangements must decide on the number of sub-national governments, the representation these governments are accorded in the central government, and the assignment of policy responsibilities between the different tiers of government.   The actual arrangements which are selected will have significant implications for economic efficiency, political participation and the protection of basic rights.   Moreover, trade-offs may exist between these objectives of federal constitutions.   Inman and Rubinfeld (1997, p. 54) put this argument as follows:

> [T]here are good reasons to think that efficiency, participation, and the protection of individual rights may at times conflict.   For example, a strong federal government built on the principles of economic federalism or democratic federalism with a small legislature is likely to be the relatively more efficient for the provision of public goods and spillovers.   However, such a structure may shortchange the valued goal of political participation which is typically best served by giving small local governments stronger central government representation and more policy responsibilities.

With its emphasis on efficiency, the traditional economic approach to the appropriate role for local government in a federation, epitomized by the theory of fiscal federalism (Oates 1972), thus focuses on only one dimension of the problem to the exclusion of participation and individual liberty.   Since this book falls squarely within the conventional economic approach, it is important to bear this limitation in mind at the outset.

Although the theory of fiscal federalism was formulated to design, explain and evaluate real-world federations, and relied heavily on American federalism as its quintessential example, it has been extended by King (1984) and others to include unitary states such as New Zealand and the United Kingdom. However, despite its generality to all systems of multi-level government, the application of fiscal federalism has focused almost exclusively on the comparatively narrow question of how to assign responsibility for public goods between the different tiers of government. But policy makers are concerned with how local and higher levels of government should cope with all kinds of market failure and not just the problem of public goods. In this book we seek to remedy this shortcoming by extending the analysis to all forms of market failure which confront local governments.

A major drawback of the theory of market failure resides in the fact that it rests on an idealistic and inflated view of the abilities of governments, including local government, to achieve intended outcomes efficiently. This has often led to excessive and ineffective levels of state intervention. In their exhaustive *Public Spending in the Twentieth Century*, Tanzi and Schuknecht (2000, p. 18) describe the growing skepticism surrounding the ability of governments to enhance social welfare which first arose more than two decades ago: 'the failure of government policies to allocate resources efficiently, to redistribute them in a well-targeted manner, and to stabilize the economy in the stagflation of the 1970s was coupled with the results of studies that highlighted the disincentive effects of high taxes and the growing underground economies'. Consequently, a more realistic view of the capacities of government is necessary to broaden the theoretical vision of the policy maker. Accordingly, we contend that in addition to the market failure paradigm, the literature on the phenomenon of government failure must also be taken into account by local government policy makers. This will enable them to consider both the benefits and costs of government activity.

The hard-headed realism imparted by this government failure perspective does, however, need to be balanced by an appreciation of the opportunities that can arise for local authorities to forge multi-organizational partnerships with other agencies and organizations. Indeed, in countries like the United Kingdom, the emergence of an 'enabling role' for local authorities has been an unforeseen consequence of restructuring designed to reduce the scope for government failure at the local level. We argue that 'New Institutional Economics' (NIE) provides a coherent and parsimonious framework to analyze and compare the transactions costs of markets, hierarchies and networks as alternative governance mechanisms that can be deployed by such enabling authorities.

NIE does, however, tend to focus on the conditions under which informal rules can assure the trustworthiness of the members of networks that are held together by 'structures of resource dependence'. We contend that this neglects the expressive dimension in some forms of network interaction. Accordingly, we draw on Elster's (1998) 'economic theory of the emotions' to develop a concept of a hope-based network that can be distinguished from the concept of an interest-based network (IBN) associated with NIE and the burgeoning literature on policy networks. We also refer to recent developments in the theory of social capital that tend to highlight the impact this form of capital has on the capacity of area-based organizations, such as local authorities, to engage in networking activities so as to exploit their comparative institutional advantage in the supply of local community governance.

A concern with local government capacity does suggest that there are two directions in which the reform of this sector can proceed. On the one hand, it can proceed in a 'minimalist' direction as the reformers seek to close a 'capacity gap' by limiting local authorities to their 'core business' functions and constraining their ability to undertake these functions in a fiscally irresponsible way. On the other hand, it may be recognized that the application of *avant-garde* management principles and financial disciplines at the local level may enable councils to play a more catalytic role in the economic and social development of their communities. A more 'activist' approach to local government reform may therefore seek to build on these developments to enhance the capacity and discretion of local authorities to take on more functions, engage community participation to a greater degree in their decision making and play a more significant role in the delivery of the central government's domestic policy agenda.

It seems to us that these minimalist and activist approaches to local government reform can be related to the styles of policy leadership that tend to succeed one another at different stages of the more encompassing type of paradigmatic reform process that effects a fundamental reshaping of the role of the state in the economy. We make reference to the way the minimalist approach favored by the Thatcher government, which exercised a 'strong' style of policy leadership to overcome various pockets of resistance to its reform initiatives, appears to have been replaced in the UK by the more activist approach the Blair government has undertaken as part of a general shift to the more 'empathetic' leadership style associated with 'Third Way' politics.

We also make reference to the case of New Zealand where central government has usually been more disengaged from the local government policy sub-system. The landmark 1989 reform of local government in this country appears to have been driven through by two key 'policy entrepreneurs' who were able to conceal their activist intentions from 'gatekeepers' in central control agencies who would tend to favor a more minimalist approach. This incoherence in the original reforming coalition seems to have contributed to the eventual emergence in the late 1990s of an 'advocacy coalition structure' that is split along similar minimalist-activist lines to that which divides the local policies of the main political parties in the UK.

These case studies highlight a major theme of this book which is that a theoretical analysis of local government can only be considered to be adequate if it takes into account the complexity that modern local governance exhibits in practice. We would argue that while conventional economic theory can go further than some of its critics may realize in comprehending this complexity, there are occasions where it needs to draw from other disciplines, particularly political science, if it is adequately to grasp the issues involved in reforming this sphere of government.

1.2   THE MEANING OF ECONOMIC EFFICIENCY

Since this book is centrally concerned with the problem of economic efficiency in local governance it seems appropriate at the outset to carefully define the meanings which can be attributed to this term in economic discourse. In economic analysis, the concept of economic efficiency is defined in three principal ways.

Firstly, productive or technical efficiency refers to the use of scarce resources in the most technologically efficient manner. The notion of productive efficiency, or deriving the maximum technically feasible output from a given combination of inputs, was first defined with precision by Farrell (1957) and closely approximates to what lay people commonly think of as 'best practice' or 'benchmarking' in production. Although productive efficiency is a useful means of evaluating economic activity, by itself it is an insufficient measure of economic efficiency since the efficient production of goods and services alone does not take into account the consumption wishes of society. Put differently, it is rather pointless to produce a given combination of goods efficiently if people would prefer to consume some other mix of output. Accordingly, some other measures of economic efficiency are necessary to augment the concept of productive efficiency.

Second, a gauge of economic efficiency, known as allocative efficiency, refers to the efficient allocation of productive resources amongst alternative uses so as to produce an optimal combination of output. In standard economic parlance, in competitive markets or under 'perfect competition', the optimal output mix arises through consumers calibrating their consumption decisions in accordance with the 'true' costs of production or 'marginal costs'. Allocative efficiency thus involves an interaction between the productive capacity and consumption desires of society.

Dynamic or intertemporal efficiency represents the third main method of defining economic efficiency. In comparison with both productive efficiency and allocative efficiency, dynamic efficiency is a much less precise concept with no universally agreed formal definition. Nevertheless, in general terms, dynamic efficiency refers to the economically efficient use of scarce resources through time, and thus embraces allocative and productive efficiency in an intertemporal dimension. The basic idea behind dynamic efficiency may be traced back to the work of Joseph Schumpeter (1943) and his emphasis on continuous innovation and risk taking as the primary engines of economic growth. Schumpeter argued that perfect competition, with its attendant properties of allocative and productive efficiency, was not necessarily the most conducive means of achieving the highest possible long-term growth. Accordingly, dynamic rather than static resource allocation assumed critical importance.

In comparison with both productive and dynamic efficiency, economists have invested far more effort into the establishment and refinement of the properties of allocative efficiency. In essence, two main approaches to the problem of analyzing allocative efficiency have been developed.

In the first place, a partial equilibrium or Marshallian approach has focused on individual markets on the assumption that the prices of all other commodities and factors of production are given. An obvious disadvantage of this approach is that it does not allow for feedback effects between markets. In practice, the Marshallian approach is especially suitable for markets whose output is not a significant item in total expenditure nor highly substitutable or complementary for any other commodities. Arthur Pigou (1920) adapted the positive Marshallian system into a normative method of assessing the degree of allocative efficiency exhibited by a market by specifying the conditions necessary for allocative efficiency. In essence, Pigou argued that allocative efficiency occurred when the benefit to society of consuming some good or service exactly equaled its cost to society. In technical jargon, allocative efficiency for private goods occurs where marginal social benefit equals marginal social cost: that is, no divergence between private and social benefits and costs occurs. At an intuitive level, this means that the resultant price and quantity accurately reflect the degree of relative scarcity for this good or service.

The second main approach to the problem of allocative efficiency is the general equilibrium or Walrasian model which focuses on the simultaneous determination of all factor and commodity prices. With perfect competition in all goods and factor markets, rational maximizing behavior by all economic agents will generate the highest possible national income in aggregate terms. Allocative efficiency under general equilibrium requires the simultaneous satisfaction of three conditions. Firstly, economic efficiency in production must occur so that any intersectoral reallocation of productive resources which increases the output of one commodity must decrease the output of some other economic good. In technical language, this means that the marginal rates of technical efficiency of input factors must be equal in all production sectors at current factor market prices. Secondly, economic efficiency in consumption must occur such that no interpersonal reallocation of commodities can increase the well-being (or utility) of some other consumer. In economic jargon, the marginal rates of substitution for all goods and services must be equal for all consumers at prevailing market prices. Finally, overall economic efficiency in both production and consumption requires an optimal conformity between economic efficiency in production and economic efficiency in consumption, such that a change in the consumption of output cannot increase the utility of some consumer without decreasing the utility of some other consumer. In technical language, a given set of market-determined prices will equal both the marginal rate of transformation in production and the common marginal rates of substitution in consumption. If these three conditions are met, then society is said to have achieved high-level optimality in the sense that allocative efficiency occurs in all spheres of economic activity.

From a normative point of view, Walrasian general equilibrium is regarded as desirable in so far as it is Pareto efficient since it is impossible to improve anyone's welfare by altering production or consumption without reducing someone else's well-being. The idea of Pareto optimality was developed by Vilfredo Pareto (1909) in his *Manual of Political Economy* and now forms the basis of much contemporary welfare economics. A central proposition of neoclassical welfare economics holds that if all prices are determined in competitive markets, then a Pareto efficient general equilibrium will result. In other words, the operation of competitive markets in a capitalist economy through Adam Smith's 'invisible hand' ensures that allocative efficiency will occur in all markets. Accordingly, no government intervention can improve upon this allocative outcome since it is already Pareto efficient.

1.3 PLAN OF THE BOOK

The book is divided into two broad parts. Chapters 2, 3 and 4 revolve around the question of economic efficiency and the various considerations which local government policy makers should take into account when formulating municipal policy. In effect, these chapters draw on conventional economic analysis and extend it to the domain of local government. By contrast, chapters 5, 6 and 7 focus on the political economy of policy formulation and the various influences which act on policy making in local government. The latter half of the book is thus concerned with the process of policy making rather than local government policies themselves.

Chapter 2 begins with an examination of the orthodox theory of fiscal federalism and especially its bearing on the optimal assignment of expenditure functions amongst the different levels of government in a federation. The discussion then moves on to the market failure paradigm and its application to local government beyond simply the problem of local public goods. The chapter provides a detailed critical evaluation of the theory of market failure and emphasizes its deficiencies from the perspective of policy formulation.

Chapter 3 takes up the question of an appropriate model of the state for economic analysis and examines various theories of the state advanced by scholars. The theory of government failure is introduced, together with taxonomic systems of generic government failure which have been developed in the public choice tradition. Discussion then focuses on the nature of government failure in local governance and we examine the models advanced by Bailey (1999) and Boyne (1998) which have been especially designed for local government. We argue that local government is particularly susceptible to government failure and develop a new taxonomy of local government in order to support this claim.

Chapter 4 deals with the question of how efficient local governments actually are in terms of service delivery. In this sense, we test the implicit assumption of the market failure paradigm that municipalities can perform well and the presumption in the government failure literature that in general local governments cannot deliver goods and services effectively by appealing to the empirical literature. In contrast to the other chapters in this book, Chapter 4 is unavoidably technical in parts. However, non-specialist readers can omit this chapter without losing the thread of the overall argument advanced in this book.

Chapter 5 examines the contribution the NIE approach can make to an analysis of networks as an institutional alternative to markets and hierarchies as solutions to the horizontal coordination problems that can arise within the multi-organizational partnerships within which local authorities are increasingly being called upon to play an enabling, facilitative role. The role local authorities can play in both interest- and hope-based networks are considered, as are factors, such as 'social capital', that affect their capacity to play this role.

Chapter 6 explores the relationship between minimalist and activist approaches to local government reform and the strong and empathetic styles of policy leadership that tend to succeed one another over the course of a more encompassing paradigmatic reform process. It examines the extent to which local susceptibility to government failure can be reduced through territorial amalgamation and the extension of the principles of the 'New Public Management' (NPM) to the local level and focuses specifically on some of the minimalist initiatives the Thatcher government undertook to limit the discretion councils have to indulge their propensity for excessive spending. It then considers the extent to which the Blair government has adopted a more activist approach to local government reform as part of its quest to differentiate a 'Third Way' that reflects a more empathetic leadership style.

Chapter 7 examines the claim that, in areas like local government that were subject to radical reform and restructuring, the New Zealand model of strategic reform was more effective than the somewhat reactive approach followed in the UK in overcoming resistance at the implementation stage and in establishing a post-reform consensus on the objectives according to which the reforms should be evaluated. It finds evidence that the local government policy sub-system is becoming increasingly divided along similar minimalist-activist lines to those observed in the UK despite the tendency of central government to adopt a more 'hands-off' approach to organizational development in this sector.

Chapter 8 concludes the book by appraising the scope and limits of economic theory as a framework for understanding the increasingly complex nature of local government in practice.

2. Market Failure and Local Government

2.1 INTRODUCTION

In many developed countries, including Australia, Britain and the United States, local governments are usually creations of state or central government legislation and seldom enjoy explicit constitutional recognition. Accordingly, their roles, functions and autonomy are generally specified in their enacting legislation and can be relatively easily transformed at the whim of these higher governments. In response to changing demands and unforeseen contingencies, state and central governments can and often do modify the powers accorded to local governments, either extending or restricting their range of activities. For example, following the Unemployed Workmen's Act (1905), English local authorities were empowered to set up local labor bureaus to assist unemployed people find work and up to 1929 subsequent legislation entrusted them with numerous further welfare responsibilities. However, with the introduction of the 1934 Unemployment Assistance Board, these responsibilities were progressively eroded and transferred back to the national government under the 'belief that the services were either national in scope, or that the artificial boundaries of local authority areas constrained efficient operation, or that they would be better run by single-purpose organizations' (Henney 1984, p. 23). Similar cyclical patterns are evident in the powers and functions of American local government. It is often observed that a process of 'centralization' has characterized the exercise of government in the United States in the twentieth century. For instance, Wallis and Oates (1988, p. 5) note that 'in 1902, local governments accounted for 82 percent of the tax revenues in the local-state sector; by 1982, this had fallen to 43 percent', although 'the local-state sector exhibits wide variation in the relative roles of state and local government both over time and across states'.

Historical circumstances have also been a decisive factor in determining the functions of local government and their evolution through time. For instance, the relatively narrow focus and minor role of local government in all Australian states and territories, with its emphasis on so-called 'services to property' functions, can be ascribed to both the reluctance of the nineteenth-century British imperial government to devolve powers to then nascent local governments and a concomitant unwillingness on the part of local communities to accept the financial costs involved (McNeill 1997). A comparable pattern of development is also evident in New Zealand local government, which similarly delivers relatively few services. By contrast, the constitutional legacy of ambiguity of functional responsibilities between French local councils and other levels of government has necessitated extensive collaborative 'interlinking of responsibilities', which has made it difficult even to define the role of French local government with any degree of precision (Keating 1988, p. 156).

Although constitutional neglect, political opportunism and historical accident have largely shaped the actual roles and functions of contemporary local government, economists have nevertheless created a voluminous theoretical and empirical literature on developing normative principles that should guide the assignment of expenditure, revenue-raising and regulatory responsibilities between the different tiers of government in a multi-unit state. In the present context, two dimensions of this literature are especially significant.

Firstly, a massive literature has adopted a 'fiscal federalist' approach which holds that a decentralization of expenditure functions within a multi-level system of government can generate substantial efficiency gains and enhance equity outcomes (see, for example, Tiebout 1956; Musgrave 1969; and Oates 1968; 1972). According to this view, each tier of a multi-unit government should deliver only those goods and services, which benefit citizens directly within its jurisdiction. Although this model provides useful prescriptions for assigning functions to different levels of government, it has various limitations. For instance, 'as a practical matter, it is often difficult to define the scope of benefits of a specific service and to determine which specific jurisdiction will reap these benefits' (Dillinger and Fay 1999, p. 20). Similarly, even if benefit regions for particular services can be established, each different service may nevertheless have a different geographic benefit region, indicating that a three - or even four-tiered federal structure could not accommodate all services satisfactorily (King 1984, p. 8–10). Put differently, 'given that there are many public goods at all sorts of levels, and given we cannot have an infinite numbers of layers of government, how do we decide at what level to set up government functions' (Helm and Smith 1987, p. iv). Conversely, economies of scale and scope may outweigh, or at least moderate, the advantages of decentralization. Moreover, efficiency gains attendant upon decentralization can easily conflict with other distributional and stabilization objectives of public policy. Bahl and Linn (1992), Ter-Minassian (1997) and others have also pointed to the organizational complexities of federalism and the increasing recognition that 'theoretical efficiency gains may be negated in practice (or substantially reduced) by administrative weaknesses at the subnational level' (Ter-Minassian 1997, p. 22), especially in developing and transforming societies.

Secondly, the market failure paradigm, and its conceptual analogue in the form of the theory of government failure, can provide further useful guidelines to public policy makers on the question of the optimal assignment of economic and other functions between different tiers of government. These theoretical paradigms, which have proved especially helpful in determining the appropriate economic role for the public sector in a market economy as a whole, as well as in establishing the comparative advantages of the public and private sectors in a system of decentralized economic decision making (see, for instance Wallis and Dollery, 1999), can also assist in defining the optimal economic role for local government.

The application of the market failure and government failure paradigms to the problem of the proper roles and functions of local government in a multi-unit system can be justified in at least two ways. Firstly, Adam Smith's famous doctrine of the 'invisible hand', often referred to as the 'first fundamental theorem' in modern welfare economics, holds that maximizing behavior by individual economic agents in competitive decentralized market relationships will generate a socially rational or Pareto optimal use of scarce resources, under certain defined conditions. But following the efforts of Pigou (1920), Bator (1958) and others, an examination of these conditions led to the systematic identification of generic instances where markets 'failed' to produce allocatively efficient results. Examples of market failure along these lines, including externalities, imperfect markets, information asymmetries, and public goods, thus provided an intellectual case for government intervention aimed at achieving allocative efficiency. An equivalent argument can be developed for the use of the market failure paradigm to guide public policy making in federal societies. According to Tiebout (1956), competition amongst state and local governments in a federal state will not only result in these governments providing local public goods and services efficiently, but also ensure that specific communities with particular tastes in local public goods will be accommodated. In an analogous fashion to 'dollar voting' in the marketplace, local and state government electors as consumers of local public goods can 'vote with their feet' in search of communities that provide their desired mix of local public goods. Local governments thus have an incentive to meet the public good preferences of their constituents. Under certain specific assumptions, the Tiebout model can generate Pareto efficient outcomes in a similar manner to the optimality of private good provision under competitive markets (see, for example, Cornes and Sandler 1996).

However, in general the assumptions necessary to yield Pareto efficiency in the Tiebout model do not hold. Quite apart from the potential problems posed by the distributive outcomes of local government competition, market failure may generate sub-optimality in the provision of local public goods and services. For example, externalities can be a pervasive problem at the level of local government. Municipal abattoirs, sewage treatment plants, zoned industrial areas, and many other local authority facilities situated near demarcated boundaries can impose significant negative externalities on people in neighboring areas. Similarly, migration of individuals between local government and other sub-national jurisdictions can have benefits, like an increased tax base, as well as costs, such as congestion and pollution. It follows that the market failure paradigm, suitably tailored for the analysis of state and local government conditions, can assist policy makers in determining the appropriate role for local governments.

But an appraisal of the literature on the application of the market failure paradigm to the behavior of the lower tiers of government in a multi-tiered state demonstrates that this use of the paradigm is almost always restricted to analysis of local public goods to the exclusion of other kinds of market failure. This may simply be a consequence of the fact that economists schooled in the fiscal federalism tradition have become accustomed to limiting their analyses of the expenditure functions of local government to local public goods and services. Perhaps more complex epistemological reasons can be found to account for the circumscribed application of the market failure paradigm in the context of sub-national government. Whatever the apposite explanation may be, the problem itself has been recognized by at least two other commentators. In his examination of the economic functions of 'subcentral authorities', King (1984, p. 8) focused exclusively on the provision of local public goods, despite explicitly acknowledging the defects of this approach. For example, he observes that while in his exposition 'little will be said about subcentral authorities interfering with local monopolies' even though 'it is probable that the arguments for and against subcentral responsibility for intervention in local monopolies are similar to those for and against the provision of local public goods, but there is perhaps scope for more research in this area' (King 1984, p. 8). Similarly, King (1984, p.8) notes further that the literature:

> gives little attention to the possibility of a role for subcentral authorities in handling the problems created by externalities. This feature of the literature arises, perhaps, because the correction of externalities is generally seen as a matter of devising taxes, subsidies or controls that will result in production occurring where each item's price equals its marginal social cost, and it may be felt that there is little point in assigning to subcentral authorities a function that allows little scope for discretion. It could be argued, however, that some external effects are of primary concern to local citizens ... This line of reasoning might be the chief reason why subcentral authorities are so often given powers over land use and

controls over new buildings ... It appears, therefore, that there is scope for further theoretical analysis of the case for some decentralization of this function. It is likely, though, that such analysis would incorporate many of the arguments raised in discussions of the case for decentralizing the provision of local public goods.

A similar view has been expressed by Tresch (1981) in his well-known textbook on public finance. For instance, in his discussion of Oates's (1972) definition of the principle of 'perfect correspondence', Tresch observes that 'while he (Oates) talks only of public goods, the principle clearly applies to any form of externality, or any decreasing cost industry'. Thus, 'a governmental body must be sufficiently large to capture all decreasing costs from a particular decreasing cost service, or to include all citizens affected by a particular externality generating activity, but it need not be any larger' (Tresch 1981, p. 567).

A second view of the applicability of the market failure and government failure paradigms to the issue of fiscal federalism in general and local governance in particular places a somewhat different emphasis on the roles of these respective literatures. According to this view, whilst the economic theory of federalism as expounded by Oates (1972) and others is instructive in deciding on the appropriate level of government to deliver different public functions, once functions have been assigned to the various tiers of government, the market failure paradigm (and its government failure counterpart) can assist policy makers in determining the optimal manner of delivering these functions. For instance, Helm (1986) identified three ways in which a local authority (or any other level of government) can deal with a purported case of market failure. It can provide (but not produce) some good or service (the 'market solution'), it can produce the service in question (the 'interventionist or state solution'), or it can simply ignore the problem on grounds that intervention will worsen matters (the *laissez-faire* solution). The theory of market failure can thus assist in ascertaining whether market failure has indeed occurred and, together with the theory of government failure, can also help policy makers to decide on the optimum form of policy response. This chapter adopts this view of the role of the theory of market failure in the analysis of the functions of local government.

The chapter itself is divided into four main sections. Section 2.2 is devoted to a synoptic discussion of the theory of fiscal federalism, and especially its bearing on the optimal assignment of expenditure functions amongst the different levels of government in a federation. Section 2.3 defines the phenomenon of market failure in both efficiency and equity terms, and then examines the theory of market failure in the context of local government. Section 2.4 provides a critical evaluation of this paradigm, most notably the so-called 'nirvana fallacy'. The chapter ends with some brief concluding remarks in section 2.5.

2.2 FISCAL FEDERALISM AND THE FUNCTIONS OF LOCAL GOVERNMENT

In his classic treatise entitled *Fiscal Federalism*, Wallace Oates (1972, p. vi) defined the economic analysis of multi-unit government as 'what economic theory implies about the division of fiscal functions among levels of government ... (and) ... the extent to which such a theoretical structure can explain the organization and workings of the public sectors of different countries'. According to this view, the central concern facing the economic theory of federalism revolves around the question of which public functions can best be discharged at the federal, state or local government levels. Following the conceptual taxonomy of the functions of the public sector developed by Musgrave (1959), most literature in the 'optimal federalism' tradition has focused on the most appropriate level of government to deliver the various stabilization, distribution and allocation functions of government. From a policy perspective, an important objective of this line of inquiry is not simply the determination of the optimal assignment of governmental functions per se, 'but rather the vertical restructuring of the government sector so as to enhance its performance' (Oates 1998, p. xiii). In particular, the theory of fiscal federalism assists policy makers in answering four fundamental questions (King 1992). Firstly, which powers should be assigned to state and local authorities rather than federal governments? Second, what is the optimal size of sub-national governments? Third, how should state and local governments be financed? And fourth, to what extent should the activities of state and local governments be controlled by the central government, specifically 'in order to prevent them from frustrating its policies, especially its macroeconomic policies?' (King 1992, p. 23).

The theoretical apparatus of fiscal federalism constructed by Oates (1968; 1972) hinged on the now famous 'correspondence principle' which holds that 'the jurisdiction that determines the level of provision of the public good includes precisely the set of individuals who consume the good' so as to 'internalize the benefits from the provision of each good' (Oates 1972, p. 34). Accordingly, each public good (or, more generally, each function of government) should be provided by the smallest (that is, lowest level) of government consistent with no spatial spillovers into adjacent administrative regions. The concept of a benefit region is thus crucial to the assignment of functions in a federal system. Almost all public goods have limited geographical areas in which they confer benefits on citizens. Some governmental functions are such that the incidence of their benefits is nationwide (like national defense or monetary policy) whereas others are geographically limited (as in the case of fire brigades or street lighting). If the spatial benefit area is limited, then obviously the benefits of some public good will be confined to residents of that area. Moreover, if the costs of provision of the public good are also met by these residents and would be the same for any level of government, then Pareto efficiency will be attained when this good is provided by the lowest possible level of government (that is, Oates's (1972, p. 35 and pp. 54–63) 'decentralization theorem'). As we have seen, Pareto efficient resource allocation in this sense means no conceivable change in the production and distribution of public goods can make one person or group better off without making at least one other person or group worse off. According to Oates (1972, p. 54, original emphasis) the decentralization theorem itself prescribes that:

> in the absence of cost-savings from the centralized provision of a good and of interjurisdictional external effects, the level of welfare will always be at least as high (and typically higher) if Pareto-efficient levels of consumption of the good are provided in each jurisdiction than if *any* single, uniform level of consumption is maintained across all jurisdictions.

This establishes the economic case for multiple jurisdictions in a federation.

An earlier alternative economic rationale for federalism was offered by George Stigler (1957, p. 1) who pursued the question 'if the people in a given community wish to embark on a particular governmental policy, when does the efficient discharge of this policy require that it be imposed by a central authority also on other communities?' In effect, this line of inquiry begins with a presumption that local government is the 'natural' unit of governance and higher levels of government require additional justification. Stigler (1957) argued that local government possesses two main characteristics: local government is more efficient at articulating the demands of voters since it is 'closer' to citizens, and, in a constitutional democracy local communities are entitled to determine what local public goods they consume. It follows that decision making should occur at the lowest level of government consistent with national allocative and distributional efficiency. Higher levels of government are thus only justified where they can achieve superior allocational, distributional or stabilization outcomes.

But the theory of fiscal federalism must also furnish answers to the question of what constitutes the optimum size of a fiscal community. If we introduce the realistic assumption that the benefits of public goods and other functions of government are not precisely contained within specific spatial areas, then the essence of the problem can be expressed as follows: 'the determination of the optimal-sized group to consume jointly the public good involves a trade off between the increased cost-savings from joint consumption in larger groups versus the greater welfare from more responsive levels of consumption in smaller groups' (Oates 1972, pp. 41–42). In theoretical terms, the optimal size of government will occur where the benefits accruing from decreasing per capita costs of providing some public good exactly equal the rising costs associated with more people in a jurisdiction. In the language of the theory of clubs, there is an allocatively efficient size of government, which occurs where the marginal social benefits of consumption equal the marginal social costs associated with congestion.

At its most general, the normative framework offered by the theory of fiscal federalism seeks to prescribe the level of governance most suited to solving the threefold Musgravian allocation, distribution and stabilization problems inherent in a modern market economy. In his seminal work, Oates (1972) sought to determine the comparative advantages of the different levels of government ranging from the extreme of a unitary or perfectly centralized state to its bipolar opposite of a decentralized fiscal system. For instance, since a unitary state can exercise both monetary and fiscal policy, in contrast to local governments, which have fiscal discretion only, it would appear that national governments enjoy a comparative advantage in dealing with the macroeconomic problems of stabilization. Similarly, if government is assigned a role in redistributing income, then a unitary state would seem optimal because migration of relatively poor people between local jurisdictions would both thwart the intentions of local redistribution and add to its costs. Put differently, if the alleviation of poverty is viewed as a national public good then it is best tackled at the national level. It would thus appear that both the stabilization and distribution functions of government should reside at the national level.[1] King (1984, p. 6) has summarized this view as follows: 'The general consensus seems to be that subcentral authorities ... will have little or no part to play in the distribution function, and that they will have no part at all to play in the stabilization function'.

By contrast, the allocation function of government provides much stronger arguments for a multi-level federal system of government. Oates (1972, p. 13) himself identified three 'economically desirable characteristics' of a decentralized public sector. Firstly, multiple jurisdictions are likely to be more responsive to spatial variations in the demand for public goods. Second, competition between different jurisdictions and the potential mobility of citizens along the lines envisaged by Tiebout (1956) should enhance both static productive efficiency and long-term dynamic efficiency. Finally, a system of decentralized governments may promote 'better public decision-making by compelling a more explicit recognition of the costs of public programs'(Oates 1972, p. 13).

Since Oates's (1972) pioneering efforts, an extensive literature has developed which examines the comparative advantages of sub-national governments in the delivery of local public goods (and implicitly other governmental functions with restricted benefit regions). King (1984, pp. 20–24) has identified a number of compelling arguments in favor of 'subcentral provision of local public goods'.

Firstly, echoing Oates, a number of writers have emphasized the abilities of state and especially local governments to cater for geographic variations in tastes by producing services that differ in quantity and quality between jurisdictions. By contrast, it is often observed that central governments are much more likely to provide spatially uniform services for various reasons, including administrative convenience and insufficient information on regional variations in taste. The result would be sub-optimal from a societal perspective since Oates (1972, pp. 11–2) has demonstrated that economic efficiency is maximized by the provision of public goods, which best reflect the preferences of citizens.

A second line of argument pursued by scholars has highlighted the likelihood that local governments are more inclined to meet the wishes of their voters than their national counterparts. For instance, Peacock (1977) and Jones and Stewart (1982) claim that local government politicians are better informed about local tastes since they tend to live in their local constituencies, fight elections on local issues and are demographically more 'representative' of their local areas. Similarly, some commentators contend that in a multi-tiered federal system citizens exercise greater 'control' over the machinery of government because 'decentralization with a number of tiers of government can simultaneously increase the ratio of representatives to officials and reduce the number of fields in which each representative has to operate' (King 1984, p. 23) thereby reducing the degree of discretion of the bureaucracy. Following Oates (1972), it has been argued that local public goods will be provided more efficiently in a federal system since voters are well informed about the costs and benefits of government services in their own residential areas.

A third genre emphasizes the efficiency-enhancing characteristics of multi-tiered government. Oates's (1972) original insight that a decentralized system of government is more likely to invoke greater entrepreneurship and innovation in the provision of local public goods has found subsequent support in the literature. For example, King (1984, pp. 23–4) outlines several reasons why local governments are inclined to be somewhat more adventurous than their central counterparts, not least because innovation in one municipal jurisdiction might compel other local governments to follow course. In the area of administration, Helm and Smith (1987) argue that a devolution of the functions of government to local authorities promotes economic efficiency due to 'informational economies': local governments possess a comparative advantage in the acquisition 'of more and better information'(Helm and Smith 1987, p. ix).

By contrast, powerful arguments also exist against the decentralized provision of local public goods. Several authors have advanced Tiebout-style logic of competitive federalism arguments. Thus it has been claimed that tax exporting, or shifting some of the burden of local taxes onto non-residents, results from decentralized government. Where intergovernmental grants augment the revenues of local governments in proportion to their own tax-raising efforts, the problem of tax-shifting will be compounded since a jurisdiction's total revenues will be further artificially inflated. Similarly, from a competitive federalism perspective, 'beggar-thy-neighbor' policies, in the form of tax rebates, low cost land and so on, often deployed to attract (or retain) firms to specific municipal jurisdictions, can lower aggregate revenues and terminate in sub-optimal levels of service provision (Breton, 1995).

Others have developed public choice arguments against decentralization. For example, fiscal illusion amongst local government voters may result in excessive expenditure. King (1984, p. 25) has observed that 'there is the possibility that overprovision would occur if taxes levied by subcentral authorities were not perceptible to citizens, because they might them underestimate the costs of service provision'. Similar arguments invoking a median voter model also stress the dangers of excessive expenditure. For instance, some writers maintain that where revenues depend on taxes with a limited demographic incidence, attempts to woo median voters can mean excessive expenditure by local governments since these citizens only bear a small fraction of the cost of public expenditure. Alternatively, rapidly populating municipalities, or those with a highly mobile population, might well resort to debt financing and an attendant overprovision of services since current voters know they will bear relatively few future costs. Other public choice arguments focus on the phenomenon of 'bureaucratic failure', which we will examine in detail in Chapter 3. A significant dimension of bureaucratic failure in this context resides in public employees pursuing their own interests rather than those of the municipality.

Various other arguments have been advanced against the decentralized provision of local public goods. For instance, numerous commentators have claimed that local governments cannot reap the full benefits of economies of scale and economies of scope in the delivery of many services, although this remains hotly contested terrain (Boyne 1998). Peacock (1977) has argued that local governments might sometimes provide services, and especially new services, relatively inefficiently due to inexperience or lack of 'learning by doing'. Others have argued that local authorities will ignore positive externalities to non-residents and consequently under-provide local public goods (King 1984). An additional and somewhat more general argument for centralized provision of services may be found in the administrative costs of decentralized provision. For example, in real-world federations local governments typically differ in their revenue-raising capacities and

administratively expensive systems of equalizing intergovernmental grants
become necessary. All of these arguments point to a need for the local public
goods in question to be provided by a more centralized government.

2.3 MARKET FAILURE AND THE FUNCTIONS OF
LOCAL GOVERNMENT

Perhaps the central insight offered by economics can be traced back to Adam
Smith's famous doctrine of the 'invisible hand' in his *The Wealth of Nations*
in 1776.   According to Smith, the pursuit of individual self-interest by
citizens engaged in the exchange of property rights through competitive
market institutions results in socially desirable outcomes. In one of many
comments on this characteristic of pure voluntary exchange in a market
economy in *The Wealth of Nations* (and indeed in his earlier *Theory of Moral
Sentiments*, 1759) Smith (1776, p. 421) observed that:

> Every individual is continually exerting himself to find out the most advantageous
> employment for whatever capital he can command. It is his advantage, indeed,
> and not that of society, which he has in view. But the study of his own advantage
> naturally, or rather necessarily leads him to prefer that employment which is most
> advantageous to that society.

The notion of *homo economicus*, or the idea that self-interest is the
predominant human motive in economic relationships, has made many of
Smith's successors in the economics profession somewhat uneasy (Hollis and
Nell 1975). Modern economists are often much more tentative than Smith on
the status of the *homo economicus* assumption and instead construe 'profit
maximization' or 'utility maximization' as 'working hypotheses'.   By
contrast, for Smith self-interest 'was more than an assumption ... it was
stated boldly as fact' (West 1976, p. 97).

However, the invisible hand doctrine that individual maximization in
market relationships can enhance societal welfare rests much more easily
with contemporary economists. In the context of a dynamic market economy
entrepreneurs are customarily modeled as risk-taking innovators who pursue
excess profits or quasi-rents. Given the assumption of maximizing behavior
on the part of *all* economic agents, and an absence of constraints on resource
mobility, in the stylized world of neoclassical economic theory, competitive
forces will ensure the dissipation of this quasi-rent in a manner which
produces socially desirable outcomes. Indeed, it merely serves to reinforce
'the original contributions of the classical economists themselves, whose
great discovery was that individuals acting in the pursuit of their own
interests may unintentionally generate results that serve the overall "social

interest"' (Buchanan 1986, p. 24).

Nevertheless, both Adam Smith and his contemporary disciples recognized that the socially benevolent consequences of the individual pursuit of self-interest, which can characterized as a 'positive sum game' in the language of game theorists, only occurs under defined institutional circumstances. For instance, once we adjust the social mechanisms in which the pursuit of excess profit or quasi-rent occurs, then its consequences may be quite different viewed from the perspective of society at large. Suppose barriers to entry in an industry characterized by excess profits prevent new firms from entering the industry and dissipating these excess profits through competition. Under these circumstances excess profits metamorphose into permanent rent. Economic rent of this kind is defined as a return in excess of opportunity cost. Buchanan (1980, p. 4) has outlined the socially malevolent consequences of self-interested behavior in this alternative institutional setting: 'The term rent-seeking is designed to describe behavior in institutional settings where individual efforts to maximize value generate social waste rather than social surplus.'

Pure voluntary exchange through competitive markets is of course only one method of coordinating human endeavor. Kenneth Boulding (1978) distinguished between three groups of social organizers. Firstly, the threat system, which is based on interaction of the type 'you do something I want or I will do something you do not want' underlies the existence of organized government which provides for the existence and enforcement of property rights and other legal obligations. Second, the integrative system, which embraces such things as altruism, affection and so forth, and embodies social structures like the family, community and nation which serve to foster and legitimize the operations of the threat and exchange systems. Finally, the market or exchange system, which is based on the possibility of mutual gain epitomized by interaction of the type 'you do something for me and I will do something for you'. Exchange or market relationships are thus premised on the principles of voluntarism and mutual benefit.

An interesting theme developed in the literature on game theory (Rubinstein 1990) explores the possibility that in contrast to the threat and legitimacy systems, which generally seem to possess the characteristics of negative sum Prisoner's Dilemma games, or at the very least zero sum games, the market system usually results in a positive sum outcome. However, whilst this may represent a general theoretical property of market relationships, it is by no means a ubiquitous outcome. An important reason for the incapacity of exchange systems to maximize positive sum outcomes resides in the existence of the phenomenon of market failure.

In generic terms market failure may be defined as the inability of a market or system of markets to provide goods and services either at all or in an economically optimal manner. It is of course possible to define market failure more precisely in terms of the two approaches to allocative efficiency we discussed in Chapter 1. For instance, from a Pigouvian perspective, market failure occurs when marginal social costs do not coincide with marginal social benefits for a particular good or service. Put differently, market failure occurs when market prices do not equate with marginal social costs. This means that market prices as signaling devices will not accurately reflect the full social costs of producing the economic good in question and so producers will either under or over-produce the good.

Although this way of defining market failure exclusively in terms of allocative efficiency represents the conventional wisdom in standard neoclassical economics, it is regarded by many as far too narrow. Numerous critics have observed that even if markets yield allocatively efficient outcomes, these outcomes may still be unsatisfactory viewed from a wider ethical or distributional perspective. In other words, if we broaden the definition of market failure to include equity as well as efficiency, then the full societal consequences of the operation of markets can be considered. Some commentators have indeed sought to provide a more comprehensive definition of market failure. For example, Charles Wolf (1989, pp. 19–20) has developed a more complete definition of market failure which embraces both efficiency and equity elements; that is, '...markets may fail to produce economically optimal (efficient) outcomes or socially desirable (equitable) outcomes'.

Needless to say, the introduction of equity or 'fairness' issues into economic analysis brings with it complex considerations, not least the fact that a virtually inexhaustible range of plausible ethical standards for evaluating equity exist (Kolm 1993). Weimer and Vining (1999, p. 134) have posed the problem as follows:

> As individuals we turn to philosophy, religion, and our moral intuition to help ourselves develop systems of values to guide our assessments. Absent a consensus on the values to be considered and their relative importance when they conflict, our political institutions must unavoidably play a role in selecting the specific values to guide our assessments.

For these and other reasons, economists have (perhaps understandably) been reticent about the specific introduction of ethical yardsticks into economic analysis. But from the pragmatic perspective of real-world policy making, it seems impossible to avoid equity issues no matter how much they complicate policy formulation. After all, as Wolf (1989, p. 30) has observed, 'most public policy decisions are usually even more concerned with distributional issues (namely, who gets the benefits and who pays the costs) rather than efficiency issues (namely, how large are the benefits and costs)'.

If we concern ourselves exclusively with market failure narrowly defined in terms of Pareto efficiency, then it is possible to identify six main types of market failure typically examined in textbooks on the topic; namely, non-competitive markets, externalities, public goods, asymmetric or uncertain information, incomplete or missing markets, and macroeconomic business cycles. Much more comprehensive taxonomies of market failure have been developed (see, for instance, Weimer and Vining 1999, table 6.1). Indeed, various cynics have declared that instances of real or perceived market failure are only limited by the imaginations of economists!

As we noted earlier, in accordance with the normative prescriptions of the theory of fiscal federalism, the various functions of government should be assigned to the different levels of government by virtue of the correspondence principle. The literature dealing with this question has focused almost entirely on market failure arising from public goods, even though, as we have seen, no substantive reasons exist to limit the analysis to public goods to the exclusion of other forms of market failure which meet the correspondence principle and should thus be dealt with by local government. Accordingly, we will examine other forms of market failure which are also best addressed by local governments, beginning with market failure narrowly defined in terms of allocative efficiency, and then broadening the discussion to include the wider concept of market failure by adding equity considerations.

Externalities

A ubiquitous form of market failure resides in so-called externalities. Externalities are variously known as external effects, external economies and diseconomies, spillovers and neighborhood effects. In essence, externalities stem from an interdependence between consumption and/or production activities and result in a divergence between private and social benefits and costs. The problem posed by externalities is that the resource allocation generated by markets will not be efficient because market prices do not reflect the 'full' or social costs involved, and accordingly will not yield socially efficient levels of consumption and production. A myriad of externalities exist in the real world. For instance, if a manufacturing plant discharges industrial effluent into a lake thereby poisoning fish and harming the local fishing industry, then this would constitute a negative production externality. By contrast, industrial agglomeration along the lines of Silicon Valley represents a positive production externality where separate economic activities reinforce one another and lower production costs. Similarly, drinkers in a pub listening with enjoyment to a music juke box exemplify a positive consumption externality whereas tired neighbors attempting to sleep adjacent to a riotous late night party signify a negative consumption externality.

In all cases of externalities, the problem can be resolved by equating marginal social costs and benefits with market prices thus obliging consumers and producers to take into consideration the full costs and benefits of their activities. At all levels of government, conventional policy responses to externalities have typically resulted in government intervention. Two generic forms of intervention have usually been adopted. In the first place, direct intervention has sought to supersede markets by embracing direct government production and regulation. Thus governments often impose standards of food hygiene, air and water pollution, and provide vaccination and other medical services in the event of epidemics. Secondly, indirect intervention attempts to work through the market mechanism by means of taxes and subsidies. For example, because formal education is believed to confer benefits on society at large in addition to the benefits bestowed on the individual recipients of education, it receives large subsidies from the fiscus.

However, the problems imposed by externalities need not necessarily require resolution through government intervention, at least in principle. The 'Coase Theorem', which derived from Nobel Laureate Ronald Coase's (1960) insights, holds that if nothing obstructs efficient bargaining between parties affected by an externality, then people will negotiate a Pareto efficient outcome themselves. Government intervention is thus rendered superfluous. However, the successful operation of the Coase Theorem rests on several heroic assumptions, not least costless bargaining with no transactions costs.[2]

The problems posed by market failure induced through externalities impinge on local government policy making in at least two ways. Firstly, interjurisdictional externalities often arise when the revenues and expenditures of one particular local government spill over into some other local authority's jurisdiction. For instance, if a specific jurisdiction undertakes to remove water pollution from a river located within its boundaries, then municipalities downstream may also benefit from this expenditure on pollution control without bearing any cost. Interjurisdictional externalities of this kind can lead to a misallocation of scarce resources. In this example, the local government in question has no incentive to take into account the marginal social cost of river pollution outside its own geographic area and may thus under-supply pollution control from a societal perspective.

Market failure resulting from interjurisdictional externalities may be ameliorated by three alternative forms of government intervention. Firstly, the jurisdiction dealing directly with the externality can be subsidized so that it will consider the external benefits of its anti-pollution policies on other affected local government areas and instigate a socially efficient level of pollution control. This raises the issue of intergovernmental grants and the most efficient methods of designing such grants (see, for example, Bailey (1999) for a detailed discussion of this problem). In real-world federations intergovernmental grants are the most important policy instrument for tackling interjurisdictional externalities at the local government level. Second, the externality could be 'internalized' by enlarging the size of a local government jurisdiction so that all of the benefits of its pollution program fall within its own boundaries and it thus has an incentive to produce the optimal level of pollution control. This option is not often feasible in real-world fiscal federations since boundary changes may be subject to constitutional constraints. However, actual examples of internalization are by no means entirely uncommon. For instance, in Australia where local government is not a creature of the constitution, the 1990s were characterized by large-scale 'amalgamation' programs whereby adjacent small municipalities formed bigger consolidated local government units. Finally, affected jurisdictions could negotiate directly with each other in order to reach agreement on the socially optimal level of pollution control. Australian local government provides another example of this kind of behavior with 'resource sharing' agreements between municipal councils which entailed joint expenditures on projects of mutual benefit.

The second concern for local government policy makers resides in externalities whose area of influence falls entirely within their benefit region. Numerous examples of this kind of externality exist. For example, almost all local governments in advanced economies promulgate noise abatement regulations, many provide fire protection services, municipal health inspection agencies, animal pounds, 'alcohol-free' public spaces, and so forth. In cases of this kind local governments can produce services themselves, finance the private production of services, or regulate economic and other potentially externality-generating activities directly through local legislation.

Non-competitive Markets

Perhaps the most important assumption underpinning Adam Smith's famous doctrine of the invisible hand is the existence of a competitive market which forces prices to equal marginal costs over the long-term and only allows firms to earn a 'normal' profit, although more recently it has been recognized that potential competition as well as actual competition can both fulfill this function, if markets are 'contestable' (Baumol et al. 1982). By contrast, if output markets are not contestable but nevertheless characterized by monopoly, oligopoly, bilateral monopoly or some other market imperfection, then the invisible hand may fail to allocate resources efficiently. Several factors can prevent competition from occurring in some defined market. For instance, governments often create monopolies through the legal system, licensing regulations, patent laws, import restrictions and the like. Similarly, geographic circumstances such as isolated locations and great distances can serve to limit competition. Thus the vast outback of Australia contains numerous small communities usually serviced by a single supplier. Technological barriers to entry also facilitate the formation of monopolies. Economies of scale, which result in falling average costs over large volumes of output, provide an economic rationale for so-called natural monopolies to develop. In general, substantial economies of scale typically occur in production processes characterized by very high capital or fixed costs and low marginal or variable costs. A further complicating aspect of natural monopolies resides in the fact that where average costs are falling slowly over the relevant range of output, marginal costs will be below average costs. This means that marginal cost pricing necessarily implies firms will incur losses and can only survive if governments subsidize them accordingly. At the local government level, it is possible to identify numerous industries with this characteristic: sewage systems, water reticulation systems, electrical power distribution systems, transportation systems and fire protection services are only some examples of typical natural monopolies in municipal areas.

Since the cost structure underlying natural monopolies precludes Pigouvian marginal social cost pricing and thus generates market failure and its concomitant outcome of allocative inefficiency, this means that a case for government intervention exists. Three possibilities can be identified. In the first place, governments can produce the service itself, set prices equal to marginal social cost and finance the resultant deficit out of general tax revenue. Second, the service could be provided by a private firm, prices regulated to equal marginal social cost, and the firm subsidized to the extent of its losses. Finally, the private firm could be allowed to charge a price sufficient to cover the average costs of production thereby removing the need for a subsidy, but at the cost of output falling short of Pigouvian allocative efficiency.

The question naturally arises as to which level of government in a federal system should operate or regulate a natural monopoly. The answer to this question once again centers on Oates's (1972) correspondence principle and depends on the extent of economies of scale: that is, the greater the extent of economies of scale, the larger should be the political jurisdiction to allow for the realization of economies of scale associated with the specific service under examination. Accordingly, local governments should be responsible for those services where economies of scale are exhausted within their benefit region. Real-world observation indicates that this is indeed often the case, with local governments frequently providing sewage systems, water reticulation, transportation systems and many other services with the characteristics of a natural monopoly.

Public Goods

As we have argued earlier, the literature on fiscal federalism has hitherto focused largely on public goods in its assignment of governmental functions to the different tiers of government in a multi-level system of government. The significance of public goods as a source of market failure derives from the inability of private markets to deliver public goods as a consequence of their peculiar characteristics. In general, public goods may be distinguished from private goods on two main counts. Firstly, pure public goods are said to be nonrival in consumption; that is, one person's consumption does not reduce the availability of the good for consumption by others as, for instance, in the case of television viewing. Nonrivalrous consumption is sometimes also referred to by the synonymous term joint consumption, where everyone can consume the same good simultaneously. By contrast, if the enjoyment of consumption by one consumer is inhibited by the concurrent consumption of large numbers of other consumers, such that the good is semi-rivalrous, then it is described as an impure or congestible public good. Examples of this kind of public good include popular beaches over summer, public parks during fine weather, and city streets during rush hour. An important economic implication of nonrivalry is that each extra consumer can consume the good at zero marginal cost to society. Secondly, pure public goods, in addition, possess the twin characteristic of nonexcludability in consumption; that is, producers of the good are technologically, politically and/or economically unable to prevent individuals from consuming the good as, for example, in the case of national defense. A significant economic consequence of nonexcludability is that because no individual can be prevented from consuming the good every consumer has an incentive to avoid paying for the good: that is, the problem of 'free-riding' means that the good cannot be provided through markets. From the perspective of local governments, pure public goods possess the additional characteristic of 'localness', where the benefits of the good are limited to a specific benefit region or geographical area. For example, residents of a particular city reap most of the benefits of street lighting or the local fire brigade.

The problem of market failure stemming from the attributes of public goods is much more intractable for local governments than their national counterparts due to the comparative 'openness' of municipal areas. Wildasin (1986, pp. 2-3, original emphasis) has put the issue thus:

[I]t is evident that all of the basic issues of public economics that arise at the level

of the (closed) national economy will be present in the local context as
well...What one naturally wants to emphasize, however, are those issues that are
unique to the local public sector. Perhaps the most novel feature that needs to be
taken into account is the *openness* of local jurisdictions.

Important ramifications of the openness of local economies include the
migration of households on the one hand and commodities and factors of
production on the other. Decisions taken about the kinds and levels of local
government public expenditure can thus induce either in- or out-migration
and significantly affect resource allocation in the private sector, both
spatially and economically.

Given these complexities, determining optimal public expenditure at the
local level is bound to be difficult, regardless of which tier of government in
a federation makes the relevant decisions. Pigouvian welfare economics
provides the basic rule for ascertaining the allocatively efficient level of
public good provision, which will occur where the marginal social benefit of
the good or service equals its marginal social cost. From the point of view of
public policy making, this rule is always difficult to apply in practice in any
purported instances of market failure owing to the complexities involved in
gathering the requisite information, but in the case of public goods this
exercise is made even more onerous due to the problem of free-riding. In
essence, non-exclusion means that consumers as taxpayers have an incentive
to understate the intensity of their demand for public goods in the belief that
they can free-ride on those public goods which are provided regardless of
their personal contribution. Since all taxpayers face similar incentives, the
problem of demand revelation takes on the properties of a Prisoner's
Dilemma game, and it is consequently difficult to estimate the marginal
social benefits of any particular public good. Public opinion surveys,
contingent valuation studies, and numerous other systems have been
developed to try to circumvent this problem of demand revelation with
limited success.

Notwithstanding these problems, in the real-world responsibility for
determining the optimal quantities of local public goods must nevertheless
still be assigned to some tier of government in a federation. Once again,
Oates's (1972) correspondence principle can be invoked to deal with this
problem. According to this principle, the appropriate jurisdictional level will
depend on the 'localness' of the public good in question: that is, if the
benefits fall primarily within the jurisdiction of a given local government,
then it should be assigned responsibility for providing the good. Conversely,
where some of the benefits of the public good spill over into adjacent
jurisdiction, then compensatory intergovernmental grants or other
arrangements along the same lines as externalities discussed earlier should be
invoked.

Once the assignment problem has been resolved, the designated local government still has to decide on the optimal quantity and quality of a specific public good to provide. Given the difficulties involved in the application of the Pigouvian rule, in practice the municipal political processes must determine optimum outcome. This usually means local government electors vote for candidates advocating their own desired mix of local public goods, although in some cases local government referenda may be held to determine popular sentiment on specific projects.

When municipal politicians have decided on the quantity of public goods, the question still remains of how best to provide the requisite public goods. Various options can be canvassed. For instance, local governments can, and often do, both finance and produce the services themselves. Fire protection services, police services and sewerage often fall into this category. Alternatively, municipalities can finance provision but private companies can produce the service. 'Outsourcing' along these lines often include maintenance of public buildings, open spaces and public vehicles. Finally, and somewhat more rarely, subsidies can be paid directly to households to provide the service themselves, as in the case of the upkeep of verges in suburban streets. Obviously, given the characteristics of pure public goods, privatization is not a policy option under these circumstances.

Asymmetric and Uncertain Information

Market failure can also arise under conditions where economic agents on one or both sides of the market possess incomplete information on the nature of the transaction, or where available information is asymmetrically concentrated on either sellers or buyers. Akerlof's (1970) famous analysis of the market for used cars is a good illustration of this latter source of market failure. Developing the concept of 'adverse selection', where individuals on the 'informed' side of the market self-select in a way that harms the 'uninformed' side of the market, Akerlof (1970) proposed that in used car markets, sellers typically possess more information than buyers on the quality of vehicles for sale. Since sellers are more adept at picking 'duds' or 'lemons' than buyers, buyers will realize that the possibility that they may inadvertently purchase a dud is high and consequently only offer discounted prices to reflect this perception. As a result, sellers will be unwilling to part with quality used cars and will sell only duds or 'lemons'. The final outcome will be an adverse selection process where 'lemons' crowd out quality used cars. In Pigouvian terms, this represents an instance where more uncertainty exists in buyers' minds over marginal private benefits than equivalent uncertainty on the part of sellers over marginal private cost. Allocative efficiency is thus unlikely to occur providing a rationale for government intervention on grounds of market failure.

By contrast, it is also possible that a good deal of uncertainty can coexist simultaneously on both sides of the market, a situation described as incomplete information. Under these circumstances, buyers have difficulties computing their marginal private benefits and sellers experience similar problems with their marginal private costs, with the likely outcome of socially sub-optimal prices and quantities prevailing in market exchanges. Government intervention is thus warranted to generate the Pigouvian equation of marginal social cost with marginal social benefit.

In common with the earlier sources of market failure, the allocation of responsibility for prescribing policies to deal with the problems of incomplete and asymmetric information should be assigned under federal constitutional arrangements in accordance with Oates's (1972) correspondence principle. Thus where the incidence of either incomplete or asymmetric information falls within the jurisdictional benefit region of local government, then it should be assigned the appropriate policy formulation role. For example, the power to zone land within their jurisdiction between residential, industrial and other uses is usually accorded to local governments, which typically assess the geological, hydrological and other properties of the land in question in making their decisions. This information is then made publicly available to potential buyers and sellers, thereby reducing the problem of incomplete information and enhancing the prospects of allocatively efficient property markets. Similarly, housing construction is typically subject to municipal regulations on quality, size, safety standards and the like, and local governments enforce these regulations through authorized compulsory building inspections. Accordingly, buyers of new houses can be reasonably assured that the dwellings they purchase meet certain specified minimum standards. This serves to remove fears of 'jerry-built' homes by alleviating the degree of asymmetrical information in a situation where builders would otherwise be much better informed than homebuyers. The resultant amelioration of the problem of asymmetrical information thus assists in reducing market failure from this source.

By contrast, where the benefit region stretches beyond municipal jurisdictions, then following Oates's (1972) correspondence principle, the power to address the problem should be assigned to a higher level of government. For instance, regulations concerning the introduction of new medical pharmaceuticals usually fall under the authority of federal governments given their nationwide benefit region. Similarly, food labeling laws are also typically a federal matter.

Incomplete and Missing Markets

The efficient operation of Adam Smith's doctrine of the invisible hand implies that markets will provide all goods and services where consumer demand is sufficient to cover the costs of supplying these goods and services. Where this does eventuate, market failure due to incomplete markets is said to have occurred. It is often argued that this form of market failure is especially prevalent in insurance markets and capital markets, where farmers and small businesses experience difficulties in securing loans and other forms of financial services. As a consequence, governments often intervene to provide credit or guarantee loans in an attempt to alleviate market failure.

A related form of market failure stems from an absence of complementary markets, where the necessary markets for interdependent economic activities simply do not exist. Complementarity between markets exists when activity in one market is entirely dependent on the existence of related markets. For instance, equestrian bookmakers require regular horse races in order to service the betting market in this 'sport of kings'. Without a racing industry they would have to deal in other forms of gaming.

For both incomplete and missing markets as sources of market failure, the assignment of policy responsibility to a particular tier of government once again depends on the correspondence principle, with local authorities liable for correcting market failure within their benefit regions. For example, in depopulating towns in rural Australia in the 1990s, the critical mass of people often fell below the threshold level required to sustain a local branch of a commercial bank. To provide their communities with ongoing banking services, municipalities sometimes acted as agents for private banks and thus averted market failure due to incomplete markets in the banking services sector in their limited jurisdictions. Similarly, in small Australian country towns in beef ranching and lamb producing areas, local governments have often constructed and managed abattoirs, in the absence of privately-run facilities, in order to assist the pastoral industry on which their prosperity depends by providing the requisite missing market. In both instances, the extent of intervention should be guided by Pigouvian social benefits and costs calculus.

Business Cycles

Market economies have always experienced macroeconomic business cycles in the form of periodic upswings and downswings in economic activity. Macroeconomic fluctuations of economic activity create a *prima facie* case for government intervention intended to flatten the business cycle. Since macroeconomic policies affect an entire economy, their formulation and implementation are typically assigned to the federal government rather than state and local governments. Indeed, the need for macroeconomic stability is sometimes employed as an argument to transfer other expenditure powers away from lower tiers of government in favor of the central government so that they do not thwart macroeconomic policies.

Equity Arguments

The arguments we have presented thus far have considered the case for local government policy intervention based on a narrow conception of market failure conceived exclusively in terms of allocative efficiency. But as we indicated earlier, public policy questions often embrace ethical or equity dimensions which go far beyond economic efficiency. This is true not only of federal and state governments, but also for local governments. Consequently, a broader definition of market failure is required to encapsulate issues of fairness arising out of the workings of the market economy. In this section, we adopt a definition along the lines of that developed by Charles Wolf (1989) cited above, and examine the case for government intervention on equity grounds.

The introduction of explicit ethical norms into economic analysis creates at least two forms of complexity. Firstly, and as we argued earlier, it is difficult to identify moral values outside of the Pareto principle on which there exists widespread consensus. Needless to add, reasonable people often disagree on the content of 'universal' values and these disagreements cannot be resolved through logical disputation or any other intellectual process. A second and related source of difficulty resides in selecting from the almost unlimited range of potential ethical claims a manageable number of equity arguments likely to command popular assent.

In their influential text on policy analysis, Weimer and Vining (1999, p. 146) identify three main 'rationales for some of the more important substantive values that often compete with efficiency'. The first of these is 'human dignity' which has implications for public policy in terms of income transfer schemes to ensure minimum consumption levels or 'floors on consumption', participation in public decision-making processes along the lines of the universal franchise, and 'paternalistic' intervention on behalf of children and mentally impaired adults. A second rationale involves 'increasing the equality of outcomes' in a relative sense of considering the 'aggregate wealth of society'. Finally, 'preserving institutional values' requires an adherence to existing constitutional frameworks, which engender 'perceptions of fairness'. By contrast, Wolf (1989, p. 82, original emphasis) has proposed a more extensive (but by no means exhaustive) list of possible equity standards:

Equity evaluated as equality of opportunity; equity as equality of outcome; equity as perfect equality of outcome unless departure from equity is an essential precondition for securing advantages for those who are least favored; equity as a categorical imperative specifying that no personal or individual action is fair *unless* it can be applied as a general maxim to govern the behavior of others; equity in the sense of horizontal equity (treating equally situated people equally); equity as vertical equity (treating unequally situated people in appropriately unequal ways); equity as Marxian equity ('from each according to ability, to each according to nee'); equity according to the Old Testament ('an eye for an eye'); or equity according to the New Testament ('turn the other cheek').

Apart from the formidable problems posed by the existence of alternative equity criteria, further complications arise when different methods of approaching ethical questions are adopted. For example, it is possible to distinguish between ethical frameworks which may emphasize distributive processes or distributive opportunities or distributive outcomes (New Zealand Treasury 1987). Thus if a distributive outcomes approach is followed aimed at equality of income, then this could conflict with the prescriptions offered by a distributive processes model or the opportunities *modus operandi*. For instance, it is entirely conceivable that unequal distributions may be fair if they result from fair processes of exchange. It is thus evident that the adoption of any one of these generic approaches to equity involves trade-offs between processes, opportunities and outcomes, not to mention more general trade-offs between equity and efficiency.

Despite these complications, following Wallis and Dollery (1999), three common ethical propositions are often invoked to guide government policy intervention, including municipal policy. In the first place, it is often argued that distributive outcomes of allocatively efficient markets can generate extremes of wealth and poverty, which do not meet socially accepted norms of equity and thus create a case for redistributive government intervention. As we have seen in Section 2.2, according to the correspondence principle, in a federal system of government Musgravian redistributive functions should be assigned to the central government (King 1984, p. 6) since their delegation to lower tiers of government would be hampered by interjurisdictional migration by poor people. In many modern welfare states, including Australia and New Zealand, this is indeed the case, although lower levels of government often implement welfare policies formulated and financed by central governments.

A second equity argument for state intervention in the face of allocatively efficient markets rests on the concept of merit and demerit goods developed by Musgrave (1959, p. 13). Richard Musgrave defined the nature of merit goods as follows:

Such wants are met by services subject to the exclusion principle and are satisfied by the market within the limits of effective demand. They become public wants if considered so meritorious that their satisfaction is provided for through the public budget, over and above what is provided for by private buyers.

Underlying the idea of merit goods is the notion that people do not always behave in their own best interests. For example, citizens might not wear seatbelts or send their children to school, unless compelled to do so by law. Moreover, private markets may fail to provide socially desirable levels of particular services, like 'high culture' in the form of opera or art museums. In these and other instances, government intervention through legal compulsion, subsidies to the arts and so on can often be justified on merit good or 'paternalistic' grounds. On the basis of the correspondence principle, the merit and demerit argument can easily be adduced in the local government milieu. War memorials, sports fields, civic parades, zoning restrictions on liquor outlets and brothels, and many other examples of municipal activity clearly fall under the merit good umbrella.

Thirdly, the contentious notion of equal economic opportunity represents an additional ethical rationalization for government intervention in a market economy. Thus, it is sometimes claimed that ethnic, disability, gender, racial and sexual orientation stereotypes may be consciously and/or even unconsciously adopted in employment, housing and other markets which serve to disadvantage members of these various groups. Exponents of this argument contend that market outcomes are systematically biased against 'minority' groups and demand government intervention in the form of equal opportunity programs, affirmative action laws and the like to correct perceived discrimination. In most federal countries, statutory responsibility for regulating labor markets is usually invested in central or state governments and not local governments, although obviously as significant employers local authorities are obliged to adhere to any legislation of this kind.

Although it would be impossible to determine with any degree of precision the specific impacts of the multifarious economic, demographic, intellectual, social and other forces which propelled the massive expansion of public expenditure at all levels of government in the post-World War II era in advanced western countries, it seems reasonable to presume that the market failure paradigm, with its enormous influence on public policy makers over this period, played a decisive role. Not only was government activity in public utilities, such as electricity and transportation, drastically expanded, but the state also sometimes participated directly in other sectors, like banking and insurance. Moreover, under the additional influence of various ethical theories purporting to advance 'social justice', government regulation of private economic activity became extensive. One consequence has been the growth of the 'welfare state', with its attendant policy tentacles now affecting virtually all spheres of social life. In common with higher tiers of government, the local government sector has not been immune from these influences.

2.4 CRITICISMS OF THE MARKET FAILURE PARADIGM

Although the market failure paradigm provides a useful conceptual apparatus for thinking about the appropriate role of government in a market economy and can greatly assist policy makers in designing policy interventions and selecting suitable policy instruments, it has nevertheless been criticized in the literature on at least four counts. We shall briefly examine these criticisms here since they have a bearing on the efficacy of the market failure model for local government.

First and foremost, the market failure theory has been attacked by numerous writers on the grounds that it implicitly embodies an idealized conception of the state. Chang (1994, p. 25) has described the problem in the following graphic terms: 'it is (implicitly) assumed the state knows everything and can do everything'. More specifically, critics have identified three heroic and untenable assumptions in the model of government invoked by the market failure paradigm. Firstly, it presumes that policy makers can accurately determine the degree of market failure; that is, the extent to which actual markets diverge from a theoretical allocatively efficient optimal outcome. Secondly, it presupposes that armed with this knowledge governments can intervene efficiently to restore allocative efficiency. And finally, it assumes that politicians and bureaucrats involved in framing public policy are motivated by altruism rather than self-interest. All of these assumptions have been questioned and the subsequent rejection of the descriptive accuracy of the market failure paradigm has led to the development of an alternative government failure approach. We shall examine this approach and its implications for local government in detail in Chapter 3.

A second and a more general argument aimed at all forms of policy intervention is contained in the theory of the 'second best' advanced by Lipsey and Lancaster (1956). This theory holds that even if policy makers know the extent of market failure, they intervene efficiently and they are motivated by entirely altruistic motives, the outcome of policy intervention may nonetheless not achieve Pareto optimality. In essence, the theory of the second best demonstrates that if market failure is present in one sector of the economy, then it is conceptually possible to achieve a higher level of social welfare by deliberately violating Pareto efficiency conditions in some other sector, rather than by intervening to restore Pareto efficiency in the original instance of market failure.

A third and much more recent critique of the market failure paradigm has been developed by Zerbe and McCurdy (1999) and draws on the notion of transactions costs. In broad terms, a transaction can be defined as an agreed exchange or transfer of goods and services between distinct parties and the costs involved in reaching such an agreement and which facilitate such a transfer are collectively known as transactions costs. Zerbe and McCurdy (1999, p. 561) summarize the basic problem with the market failure paradigm as follows:

> A fundamental problem with the concept of market failure, as economists occasionally recognize, is that it describes a situation that exists everywhere. While the ubiquity of market failures seems well accepted, the consequences of this observation are not. Some people believe this dooms the concept as an analytical tool; others disagree.

They argue further that all market exchanges involve transactions costs, which simply represent the costs of the operation of the price system, and these costs are typically not priced. It follows that 'since unpriced transaction costs are ubiquitous, this gives rise to a situation in which externalities and hence market failures can be found wherever transactions occur' (Zerbe and McCurdy 1999, p. 563). Government intervention on the basis of market failure is thus misplaced: instead, 'anytime government can reduce private transaction costs or its own costs of provision, it should do so regardless whether or not an externality exists' (p. 565).

Perhaps the most damaging attack on the market failure model focuses on its methodological underpinnings. In essence, this line of argument holds that the market failure paradigm embodies a methodology which compares actual economic arrangements against some idealized theoretical norm (that is, allocative efficiency) thereby violating the fundamental concept of opportunity cost, which constrains economists to evaluate existing situations against the next best alternative, and not some abstract idealized hypothetical norm. Harold Demsetz (1969, p. 1), the architect of this view, termed this procedure the 'nirvana problem' and contrasted it with an alternative 'comparative institutions' approach. Demsetz compared these two approaches as follows:

> This nirvana approach differs considerably from a comparative institutions approach in which the relevant choice is between alternative real institutional arrangements. In practice, those who adopt the nirvana viewpoint seek to discover discrepancies between the ideal and the real and if discrepancies are found, they deduce the real is inefficient. Users of the comparative institution approach attempt to assess which alternative real institutional arrangements seem best able to cope with the economic problem; practitioners of this approach may use an

ideal norm to provide standards from which divergences are assessed for practical alternatives of interest and select as efficient that alternative which seems most likely to minimize the divergence.

These sentiments appear to reinforce Coase's (1964, p. 195) dictum that 'until we realize we are choosing between social arrangements that are more or less all failures, we are not likely to make much headway'. As we shall seek to demonstrate in Chapter 3, when the theory of government failure is used to augment the market failure paradigm, the nirvana argument is somewhat blunted.

2.5 CONCLUDING REMARKS

Although the functions of real-world local governments in advanced countries are largely the outcome of a myriad of historical happenstance and constitutional evolution, we have sought to show that economic theory can nevertheless play a useful role in shaping the behavior of contemporary local authorities. In the first place, the assignment of responsibilities for the various functions of government amongst the different tiers of government in a federal system can be both positively explained and normatively examined using the economist's analytical tools. Thus, the theory of fiscal federalism, and especially Oates's (1972) correspondence principle, can act as guides to policy makers in determining how to assign the multifarious activities performed by the state between the different levels of government. However, since it is difficult to determine the benefit regions for public goods and all the other services provided by government and since these benefit regions will differ for different services, at best the correspondence principle can only be used as a benchmark in the determination of actual assignments.

Similarly, the theory of market failure can provide a diagnostic instrument for local government policy makers. Extant literature on the application of the market failure paradigm to the problems of local government has invariably focused on local public goods to the exclusion of other kinds of market failure. In this chapter, we have sought to extend the analysis to services beyond simply local public goods and, invoking a narrow or 'efficiency only' definition of market failure, we examined externalities, non-competitive markets, including so-called natural monopolies, asymmetric and uncertain information, and incomplete markets. We also expanded the notion of market failure to include equity issues and looked at various examples of this sort of market failure, including income inequalities, merit goods and equal economic opportunities.

Notwithstanding its undoubted usefulness as a coherent intellectual framework for assisting policy formulation, as we have seen, the market failure paradigm is not without its problems. However, in Chapter 3 we will argue that despite these problems, if the market failure model is used in tandem with its government failure counterpart, then it can still provide useful insights into designing public policies, including local government policies.

NOTES

1. This line of argument is advanced by Joseph Stiglitz (2000) in the third edition of his well-known textbook *Economics of the Public Sector*.
2. Coase (1992, p. 717) himself has eschewed any practical significance for the Coase Theorem

   The significance to me of the Coase theorem is that it undermines the Pigouvian system. Since standard economic theory assumes transactions costs to be zero, the Coase theorem demonstrates that the Pigouvian solutions are unnecessary in these circumstances. Of course, it does not imply, when transactions costs are positive, that government actions (such as government operation, regulation or taxation, including subsidies) could not produce a better result than relying on negotiations between individuals in the market. Whether this would be so could be discovered not be studying what imaginary governments but what real governments actually do. My conclusion: let us study the world of positive transactions costs'.

3. Government Failure and Local Government

3.1 INTRODUCTION

Despite the impressive intellectual achievements embodied in both the theory of fiscal federalism and the market failure paradigm, and the valuable guidance they provide to public policy makers in general and local government analysts in particular, it is clear from the discussion in Chapter 2 that, by themselves, these conceptual frameworks are by no means sufficient to enable us to design, implement and evaluate efficient local government policies. For instance, we have seen that although the theory of fiscal federalism and its correspondence principle (Oates 1972) can direct the assignment of functions between the different tiers of government, difficulties in determining benefit regions mean that it needs to be augmented by additional conceptual criteria. Similarly, we have indicated that in spite of its undoubted usefulness as a diagnostic tool in the analysis of the optimal role of municipal governments, the theory of market failure alone cannot prescribe rational interventionist public policies, given its various deficiencies, not least the 'nirvana problem'.

In Chapter 3 we argue that a more realistic view of the abilities and capacities of government is necessary to amplify the theoretical armory of the policy maker. In so doing we contend that in addition to a more descriptively satisfactory theory of the state, the literature on the phenomenon of government failure must also be taken into account by local government policy makers. This will enable policy makers to consider not only the benefits of government intervention, but also its costs. In an analogous fashion to market failure, government failure can be generically defined as the inability of a governmental agency or agencies in a given tier of government or in a federal system of multi-tiered governments to intervene optimally in a market economy to achieve allocative and productive efficiency. If we broaden the definition of government failure to include equity as well as efficiency, then the full social consequences of government intervention can be considered. Wolf's (1989) earlier definition

of market failure can be employed *mutatis mutandis* to read: governments
may fail to produce economically optimal (efficient) outcomes or socially
desirable (equitable) outcomes.

The chapter itself is divided into four main parts. Section 3.2 examines the
question of an appropriate model of the state for the economic analysis of
government and argues that the naive idealized conception of the state
employed by the market failure paradigm cannot form the basis of a theory
of government failure. We outline various theories of the state developed by
scholars, especially Breton's (1995) comprehensive typology, and contend
that the basic building blocks of methodological individualism and *homo
economicus* are required in conjunction with a conception of the state along
the lines of Breton's (1995) 'self-interest doctrine' and North's (1976)
'predatory state'. Section 3.3 focuses on public choice approaches to the
problem of government failure and on the taxonomic systems of generic
government failure which have been developed in the literature, including
O'Dowd (1978), Dollery and Wallis (1997), Weisbrod (1978) and Wolf
(1989), as well as typologies of government failure specifically developed for
local government by Boyne (1998) and Bailey (1999). We argue that
although this literature is indeed extremely useful for the analysis of
government failure, it does not recognize that the peculiarities of the
institutional milieu of local government make it particularly susceptible to
government failure. Accordingly, section 3.4 seeks to construct a new
taxonomy of local government failure which explicitly acknowledges this
susceptibility and attempts to explain its causes in terms of received
theoretical approaches, including the public choice analysis of voting
behavior (Aldrich 1997), agency theory (Jensen and Meckling 1976), the
economic theory of bureaucracy (Bendor 1990), rent-seeking (Tollison
1997), the theory of interest groups (Olson 1965; Buchanan et al. 1980;
Magee et al. 1989), and the theory of fiscal illusion (Dollery and
Worthington 1996a). The chapter ends with some brief concluding remarks
in section 3.5.

3.2 ALTERNATIVE MODELS OF GOVERNMENT

As we have seen, the market failure paradigm rested on an idealized
conception of the state in modern polity. According to this view, the state is
an essentially benevolent entity not only motivated by a singular desire to
maximize social welfare, but also possessed with the requisite knowledge and
ability to achieve this noble aim. This definition of the state drew vociferous
criticism from opponents of the market failure model, largely on the basis
that it is descriptively false. But if this naive conception of the state is

rejected, then what alternative theories of government could replace it?

Numerous theories of the state have been developed by political philosophers, economists and others. It is possible to classify these theories in various ways. For instance, North (1979, p. 250) contends that all theories of the state may be categorized as either 'contractarian' theories, which examine the conditions under which rational individuals would enter into a 'social contract' with each other, or 'predatory' theories, which focus on the redistributive struggles engendered by a centralized authority. Similarly, Chang (1994, p. 18) has distinguished between three main conceptions of the state, namely '[the] autonomous-state approach, the interest-group approach and the self-seeking bureaucrats approach'. Writing from a specifically local government perspective, Bailey (1999, pp. 13–14) has developed a fourfold typology of the state: that is, the 'despotic benevolent model' in which 'government knows best and its actions take account of market failure in maximizing economic welfare', the 'fiscal exchange model' where the 'government provides services solely in accordance with voters' willingness to pay taxes', the 'fiscal transfer model' in which 'the provision of public sector services is used to pursue social policy objectives', and the 'leviathan model' where 'despotic self-serving bureaucrats and politicians maximize their own welfares, rather than those of national and local citizens'.

But perhaps the most comprehensive taxonomy of theories of the state has been created by Albert Breton (1995). Breton (1995, p. 10) suggests that all 'models of government' stem from either a 'common-good doctrine', which assumes 'that governments are the embodiment of the common will', or its polar opposite, a 'self-interest doctrine', premised on the notion that 'governments are nothing but the embodiments of the interests of those who inhabit the halls of power or of those with whom they collude, or both'. It is possible to identify seven models of government within these two broad genres. Figure 3.1 summarizes these seven models.

Under the common-good doctrine, the 'organicist' model 'recognizes no autonomous preferences or demands of individuals different from those that are ascribed to the collectivity' whereas the benevolent despot model 'recognizes the preferences and demands of individual persons but proceeds on the supposition that these preferences and demands can somehow be aggregated into a collective welfare or utility function that is given expression by a body or institution' (Breton, 1995, pp. 10–11). By contrast, the self-interest doctrine has spawned two distinctive traditions; a 'monolithic structure' government and a 'composite structure' government.

The monolithic structure tradition subsumes four specific models of government. 'Bureaucratic capture models' conceive of the state as a monolith under the exclusive control of public sector bureaucrats whilst 'interest group capture models' depict the state as simply a producer and supplier of economic rents to dominant interest groups. In contradistinction, the second subset of monolithic structure models is based on the idea that 'governments are monopolies'.

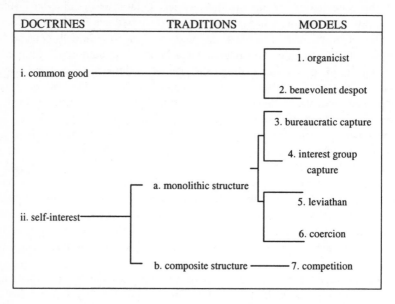

Figure 3.1   Source: Breton (1995, p. 10) seven models of government

Thus 'leviathan models' treat the state as an entity which seeks to maximize its own surplus whereas in 'coercion models' the government monopolizes 'compulsion' or coercion rather than economic surplus or rent. Finally, the composite structure tradition has spawned the 'competition model' which assumes 'that governments are inhabited by self-interested individuals' and 'in which powers are divided between a multiplicity of autonomous and quasi-autonomous centers of power' (Breton 1995, pp. 13–14). This latter model clearly underpins the Tiebout hypothesis outlined in Chapter 2.

The question naturally arises as to how we should choose among these models of the state? In part the answer to this question depends on the purposes for which we intend using the model. This in turn will depend on the descriptive realism of the model for the kind of government we wish to analyze.

In contrast to the market failure paradigm, which is essentially a normative or prescriptive approach to public policy making, models of government failure may be classified as either positive theories, like the Chicago school of regulation and public choice theory, or normative theories, such as Wolf's (1989) theory of non-market failure. Positive theories of government failure seek to explain how governments actually work whereas the market failure paradigm and normative theories of government failure are concerned with how governments should operate. It is thus not surprising that positive theories require a different conception of the state in comparison with their normative counterparts.

Positive theories of government failure, in common with positive economics in general, are founded on methodological individualism as their engine of analysis. Methodological individualism holds that the rational maximizing individuals are at the center of economic analysis; that is, only individuals and not groups have interests. Buchanan (1994, p. 82) underscores this point as 'Individuals in a community may, of course, share values in common and they may agree on specific goals or objectives for policy directions to be taken by their political organization. But this very organization, like others, exists only for the purpose of furthering individual values.'

Given the emphasis placed on rational maximizing economic agents by methodological individualism, it evidently requires a theory of the state taken from Breton's (1995) 'self-interest doctrine' genre or North's (1976) 'predatory' category.

In addition to their reliance on methodological individualism, positive theories of government failure also embody the *homo economicus* (or 'economic man') assumption as a heuristic device for modeling human behavior. According to the reductionist *homo economicus* postulate, people can be viewed as rational self-interested maximizers with stable preferences for the purposes of economic analysis, even though it is recognized that actual human motivations may be much more multi-faceted and conflicting.

Many theorists in the positive government failure tradition, and especially public choice theorists, argue that the standard tools of economic analysis, encompassing *inter alia* methodological individualism, the *homo economicus* postulate and an appropriate model of the state, which have been so successful in explaining market relationships, can be fruitfully extended to other areas of human endeavor, including political behavior. Although this contention can be justified on numerous counts (see, for instance, Mueller 1989), and has been challenged on similarly multifarious grounds (see, for example, Stretton and Orchard 1994), perhaps the most persuasive argument in its favor is the so-called 'symmetry argument' advanced by Brennan and Buchanan (1985, pp. 48–50). They observe that:

On the basis of elementary methodological principle it would seem that the same model of human behavior should be applied across different institutions or different sets of rules. If, for example, different models of human behavior were used in economic (market) and political contexts, there would be no way of

isolating the effects of changing the institutions from the effects of changing
behavioral assumptions.... The symmetry argument does nothing to establish
homo economicus as the appropriate model of human behavior. Alternative
models may be introduced. The symmetry argument suggests only that whatever
model of behavior is used, that model should be applied across all institutions.

3.3   PUBLIC CHOICE THEORY

We have seen that positive theories of government failure require a theory of
the state within Breton's (1995) 'self-interest doctrine' and approximating
Bailey's (1999) 'leviathan' model of local government.   The earliest
contemporary positive theory of government failure is the so-called Chicago
School or 'capture theory of regulation' developed by Stigler (1971) and
extended by Peltzman (1976). According to this view, state regulation of
private economic activity is subject to 'capture' by the industries under
regulation and the process of regulation simply becomes an exercise in the
distribution of monopoly profits between politicians, bureaucrats overseeing
regulation and the regulated industries themselves.   The outcome of
government regulation thus depends on the relative strengths of the interest
groups involved rather than any concept of social welfare.

But by far the most important positive theory of government failure
resides in public choice theory. As we have indicated earlier in this chapter,
public choice theory follows methodological individualism as its analytical
approach and rests heavily on the *homo economicus* postulate. In essence,
public choice theory seeks to apply the tools of economics to non-market or
political processes underlying public policy formulation and implementation,
and in so doing has developed a comprehensive critique of government
intervention in a market economy. In stark contrast to the market failure
paradigm, public choice theorists have rejected the 'common good doctrine'
(Breton, 1995) implicit in this approach and instead have developed models
of decision making in advanced representative democracies on the
assumption '...that people should be treated as rational utility maximisers in
all of their behavioral capacities' (Buchanan 1978, p. 17). In other words,
politicians, public servants, voters, and members of special interest groups
involved in public policy formulation and implementation are presumed to
use the resources and opportunities available to them to pursue their own
objectives rather than the 'common good'. Crain and Tollison (1993, p. 3)
have summarized the public choice approach as follows:

At the most basic level public choice is founded on the idea that human behavior
in governmental settings is motivated by the same self-interested forces that guide
human behavior in private settings. This does not mean that behavior is the same

in the two environments – the constraints on self interest will differ between government and the private sector. But people acting in both sectors are the same sort of people, whatever the context in which they work, and public choice hypothesizes that private interest will dominate decision making in a large number of cases.

The application of the public choice approach to the public sector has generated various taxonomic systems of government failure. For example, perhaps the earliest typology of government failure was developed by O'Dowd (1978, p. 360) who argued that all forms of government failure fell into a generic tripartite classification containing 'inherent impossibilities', 'political failures' and 'bureaucratic failures'. 'Inherent impossibilities' referred to instances where the state 'attempts to do something which simply cannot be done'. By contrast, 'political failures' described cases where the objectives of government intervention are conceptually feasible but '...the political constraints under which the government operates make it impossible in practice that they should follow the necessary policies with the necessary degree of consistency and persistence to achieve their stated aim.' And finally, 'bureaucratic failure' covers examples of state intervention where 'the administrative machinery at their disposal is fundamentally incapable of implementing policy in accordance with their intentions'.

A somewhat more recent and closely related taxonomy of government failure has been advanced by Dollery and Wallis (1997). They argue that it is possible to identify three main forms of government failure. In the first place, legislative failure refers to the 'allocative efficiency [which] arises from the excessive provision of public goods as politicians pursue strategies designed to maximize their chances of re-election rather than policies which would further the common good' (Dollery and Wallis 1997, p. 37). Secondly, 'even if socially beneficial policies were enacted, bureaucratic failure will ensure that these policies are not efficiently implemented ...[since] public servants lack sufficient incentives to carry out policies efficiently' (p. 360). The third form of government failure resides in rent-seeking because government intervention virtually always creates wealth transfers and 'people thus devote scarce resources which could have been employed in wealth creation towards redistributing existing wealth in their favor' (p. 360).

Perhaps the most comprehensive typology of government failure has been developed by Weisbrod (1978), who has advanced a fourfold classification. 'Legislative failure' refers to excessive public expenditure attendant upon the vote maximizing behavior of politicians. Secondly, 'administrative failure' derives from the observation that the 'administration of any law inevitably requires discretion, and the combination of information and incentives acts to affect the manner in which the discretion is exercised' (Weisbrod 1978,

p. 36). Thirdly, 'judicial failure' occurs when the legal system does not yield economically optimal outcomes. And finally, 'enforcement failure' is defined as the sub-optimal 'enforcement and non-enforcement of judicial, legislative, or administrative directives [which] can thus vitiate the effectiveness of actions of these other stages' (p. 39).

Although not strictly in the tradition of positive theories of government failure, Charles Wolf (1979; 1987; 1989) has nevertheless also developed an extremely useful typology of government or 'non-market' failure. Wolf identified various peculiarities in the nature of nonmarket demand and supply which form the foundation of his theory of government failure and the resultant taxonomy of nonmarket failure. Wolf (1979 p. 115) outlines his methodology as follows:

> The supply and demand characteristics of the non-market sector are fundamental to the theory of non-market failure. They provide a basis for formulating a typology of non-market failure analogous to that which already exists for market failure. In both cases, the 'failures' – whether market or non-market are evaluated against the same criteria of success: allocative efficiency and distributional equity judged according to some explicit social or ethical norm.

Wolf constructed a fourfold taxonomy of non-market failure. Firstly, and evidently by far the most important form of non-market failure resides in 'internalities and private goals'. These refer to intraorganizational allocation and evaluation procedures which determine distributional outcomes for agencies and agency personnel alike, and accordingly constitute part of their respective utility functions. Although both market and non-market firms must perforce employ an 'internal version of the price system' for intrafirm resource allocation, market pressures ensure that the 'internal standards' of market organizations are strongly linked to the 'external price system', whereas non-market organizations may have internalities largely unrelated to optimal performance. This may mean that the actual behavior of some public firm may diverge from its intended or ideal role. Thus, just as the problem of externalities in market failure arises from a predominance of private costs in private sector decision making, so the problem of internalities in non-market failure stems from the ascendancy of private motives in public sector decision making. Examples of internalities are easy to find within the public bureau milieu, and include the 'more is better' approach and the 'more complex is better' yardstick both instances of Wolf's (1989) contention that 'Cadillac quality' is encouraged in public agencies.

Secondly, 'redundant and rising costs' represent another kind of non-market failure. In essence, Wolf argues that while market processes impose a relationship between production costs and output prices, this relationship is generally absent in non-market activity since revenues derive from non-market sources, like government tax income. Consequently, Wolf (1989, p. 63) observes that:

> where the revenues that sustain an activity are unrelated to the costs of producing it, more resources may be used than necessary to produce a given output, or more of the nonmarket activity may be provided than is warranted by the original market-failure reason for undertaking it in the first place

As an example, Wolf (1989) cites the case of government agencies trying to provide 'dignified' employment for retarded people by attempting to train them to unrealistically high levels.

The third type of non-market failure in the Wolfian taxonomy is termed 'derived externalities'. Derived externalities are the unintended and unanticipated side effects of government intervention designed to ameliorate perceived instances of market failure. Just as externalities generated in market relationships represent costs and benefits not considered by economic agents, so too derived externalities in the non-market sphere 'are side effects that are not realized by the agency responsible for creating them, and hence do not affect the agency's calculations or behavior' (Wolf 1989, p. 77). In common with market externalities, derived externalities may be both positive and negative. A good contemporary example of negative derived externalities can be found in child allowances paid to single mothers. The intended outcome of these payments is the prevention of child poverty in single parent families, but an unanticipated result is the increase in the number of children born by single mothers in their quest for higher welfare payments from governments.

Finally, Wolf incorporates adverse distributional consequences as his last category of non-market failure. Whilst hypothesizing that 'there is an identifiable process by which inequities can result from nonmarket activities' similar to inequalities flowing from market outcomes, Wolf (1989, p. 84) nevertheless argues that non-market inequities characteristically occur in terms of power and privilege, whereas distributional market failures typically appear in income and wealth differences. Instances of distributional inequities include 'corrupt practices', like 'bribery to obtain contracts with foreign governments for sales abroad of weapons or other controlled imports, and import licenses or preferential exchange rates conferred on the relatives, friends, or associates of officials and politicians who exercise discretionary authority' (Wolf 1989, p. 84).

The literature contains comparatively few instances of the application of public choice theory to a specifically local government context in the sense of developing a taxonomic theoretical system of government failure, with some exceptions, most notably Boyne (1998) and Bailey (1999). Of these authors, Boyne is undoubtedly the most ambitious in his approach. In his

Public Choice Theory and Local Government, Boyne (1998, p. 1) attempts to assess the 'empirical validity of the core public choice proposition that competitive pressures lead to superior performance in the public sector'. He develops a taxonomy of competitive categories in local government that can influence the degree of government failure at this level of government. He distinguishes between 'three distinct forms of competition' in the local government arena.   Firstly, there is 'competition between public organizations for a share of tax revenues and service responsibilities' (p. 1). Following Schneider's (1989) public choice analysis in which local government is essentially an industry for local services in which buyers, made up of households and businesses, make location decisions and pay local rates and taxes to sellers, comprising municipal politicians and council bureaucrats, who either purchase or produce the requisite services, Boyne argues that public choice theory holds that municipalities engage in two kinds of competition. On the one hand, 'geographical competition' occurs between local governments 'in different areas for a share of the market in households and businesses', and on the other hand, there is 'competition between different tiers of local government for a share of local tax revenues in the same geographical areas' (p. 16). However, in common with many other industries, producers are subject to various regulatory constraints on their behavior. Accordingly, Boyne argues that for effective Tiebout-style competition to occur in local government, at least three conditions must be met which are often ignored by public choice theorists.   Firstly, governmental structures providing local public goods and services must be 'horizontally fragmented' in the sense that a large number of local governments at a given level of government must be providing the same kinds of services and competing for the same spatially mobile customers. Moreover, 'vertical fragmentation' must also be present in which several tiers of government compete over the finite tax revenue base and consumers can judge the relative efficiency with which each level of government delivers its services and allocate their political support and taxation payments accordingly. Just as consumers of local government must be able to migrate towards more efficient service providers, so too local governments must be legislatively capable of relocating scarce resources between existing local governments and the establishment of new municipal structures.

But fragmentation and flexibility alone are not sufficient to ensure vigorous competition between local governments. Boyne (1998. p. 22) argues that 'substantial local autonomy' is also an essential prerequisite for intergovernmental competition, which has generally been neglected by exponents of public choice theory. He puts the argument thus:

Local communities should have the discretion to innovate, experiment and develop distinctive policies. In other words, the center should encourage localities to compete on service and quality. This condition for competition has been ignored in the public choice literature, perhaps because most authors have written from an American perspective...[where] there is a much stronger tradition of local autonomy.

Finally, even if local government is fragmented, flexible and autonomous, vertical fiscal imbalance may nevertheless prevent the emergence of Tiebout-style competition. High levels of central or state government funding to local governments can constrain competition and impede efficiency in various ways which have been overlooked by public choice theorists. For instance, large subsidies allow local governments to 'externalize' their costs by shifting them on to higher levels of government (Dye 1990). Similarly, when most of the cost of local government services is born by national and state taxpayers, little incentive exists for households and businesses to migrate away from inefficient municipalities and this erodes the nature of competition itself (King 1984).

The second form of local government competition identified by Boyne (1998, p. 1) as a feature of the public choice approach refers to 'competition between political parties for the power to determine policy choice'. Drawing on the theory of contestable markets, Boyne argues that party competition in this context has two basic characteristics. Firstly, where no significant barriers to entry are present, the threat as well as the actual existence of opposition parties which could oust the incumbent party, may be sufficient to induce even a monopoly governing party to behave 'as if' it faced electoral competition. Policy selection, formulation and implementation under these conditions will embrace public preferences and consequently lead to better governance. Secondly, where uncertainty over election results prevails, with the possibility of changes in party control a distinct prospect, electoral competition may result in the adoption of popular policy platforms by both incumbent and opposition parties. This should also enhance the performance of governing parties and their competitors as they pursue the 'median voter', a topic we shall investigate in more depth later in this chapter.

The final form of competition which can prevail in local government has been described by Boyne (1998, p. 1) as 'competition between governmental and private organizations for control over the production of public services'. In many respects this dimension of competition represents the core of the public choice model in so far as it deals with the comparative advantages of markets as opposed to governments in the production of local government services. In essence, public-choice type arguments in favor of competition emphasize 'bureaucratic failure' as outlined earlier and can be summarized as follows (Boyne 1998, p. 91):

[I]n the absence of competition, officials pursue their own interests and the result is services that are inefficient, oversupplied, and unresponsive to public demands. Moreover, public choice theory predicts that bureaucrats will not voluntarily transfer service responsibilities to private providers, and that where competition is thrust upon them, they will strive to keep production in-house.

The import of this argument from a policy perspective is that where alternative suppliers of some good or service are available, policy makers can compare relative prices and make rational decisions on this basis. Although Boyne (1998) does not raise the point, a key distinction should be drawn here between the provision and production of local government services. Given the public good characteristics of many local public services, government provision is often unavoidable. However, with public funding there are seldom strong arguments for avoiding private production if it is demonstrably more efficient than public production.

Drawing on the work of Albert Hirschman (1970 and 1976), Bailey (1999) approaches the question of government failure at the municipal level from a somewhat different perspective. Hirschman (1970) developed the concepts of 'exit' and 'voice' as alternative means by which consumers of public services can influence the provision of these services and thereby decrease the degree of government failure they experience. In generic terms exit refers to the capacity of citizens to choose between alternative producers of some specified service. In a market mechanism the existence of many competing firms makes exit a simple method of changing suppliers in the absence of prohibitive transaction costs, whereas in a local government context exit deals with the ability of consumers to move from one municipal jurisdiction to another to experience a more desirable form of public service provision. By contrast, voice refers to the ability of consumers to express their preferences for a different mix or quality of public services through various administrative mechanisms, like electoral voting, complaints to public service managers and customer surveys, without migrating away from their municipal jurisdictions. Hirschman (1970) saw exit as falling primarily within the economic sphere of activity whereas voice was manifest most often in the political realm.

The exit-voice taxonomic approach to the problem of government failure in local government provides an extremely useful conceptual framework for policy makers, especially in so far as it implicitly subsumes many of the other analytical perspectives which have been developed. Bailey (1999, p. 60) has described the strengths of this approach as follows:

Although developed separately from fiscal federalism theory, and from the other areas covered by local government economics, in effect it underpins them. Voice is implicit in Oates' decentralization theorems and exit in Tiebout's 'voting with the feet hypothesis. The differing financing arrangements for local government, reform of its internal structure, privatization of its activities, and other reforms, can all be analyzed by making use of the exit-voice typology to a greater or lesser extent.

As methods by which citizens can influence the extent of government failure at the local government level, both exit and voice have various limitations. Bailey (1999, pp. 47–8) identifies five main characteristics of local public services which can inhibit the effectiveness of voice in municipal affairs. 'Legal and institutional barriers' in the form of diluted political representation, electoral and procedural irregularities, inadequate public hearings, and so forth, can all serve to impede political attempts aimed at improving public services. 'Information asymmetries' between public bureaucrats and citizens concerning the nature and costs of public service delivery can also constrain the efficacy of voice. Where services are highly differentiated as, say, in the case of the quality of education provided by different schools, voice by some citizens may only influence the behavior of a particular school rather than the whole school system, in contrast to undifferentiated services where voice will have more general effects. The socioeconomic characteristics of the population in a particular jurisdiction may be a decisive factor, with better educated, affluent groups more likely to express voice than their poorer, less educated counterparts. Finally, the greater the relative importance of some public service to the perceived welfare of a population, the more important voice will be as a means of addressing government failure.

Exit is also subject to a number of constraints which are spelt out by Bailey (1999, p. 48). The non-excludability characteristic of public goods may preclude exit altogether when these are national public goods, and even for some local public goods, like poor environmental protection legislation, may involve expensive relocation. Natural monopolies similarly preclude exit where they cover large geographical areas. Legislative impediments to entry by alternative suppliers of a service may negate exit possibilities, as in the case of national telecommunication providers. In large countries with uneven concentrations of population, such as Australia, Canada and the United States, large local government jurisdictions with small numbers of people may generate spatial barriers to exit. And lastly, imperfect information available to consumers may mean they are unaware of relatively unattractive service provision they are currently receiving, and thus induce them to underestimate the benefits of exit.

Hirschman (1970) considered various public policy options for improving the efficacy of both exit and voice. From the perspective of local government, Bailey (1999) argues that two distinct approaches can be adopted: 'piecemeal measures' or a more drastic 'radical reorganization of local government'. We will briefly review these strategies.

In general, Bailey (1999, p.56) contends that 'exit can be made easier by measures which serve to liberalize the supply-side of public service provision, enabling service users to choose between alternative suppliers'. He identifies six different strategies which can facilitate exit. Fragmenting existing large local governments into smaller units can reduce the costs of migration and thus enhance the mobility of the citizenry. Financing local public service provision through user charges rather than compulsory local rates and taxes allows individual consumers to 'opt out' of specific services they do not want to avail themselves of even if they remain within the same municipal jurisdiction. Vouchers exchangeable both within and without the jurisdiction, like school vouchers, enable citizens to select the public service in question from a range of alternatives. Competitive tendering of particular local public services for specified contract periods to different private producers will allow consumers to choose between alternative providers of the same service within the same jurisdiction. Deregulation of public service provision away from single statutory service providers may also increase consumer choice. Finally, privatization may result in the introduction of several new public service producers, provided it is designed to avoid the transformation of public monopolies into private monopolies.

Similarly, Bailey (1999, p. 57) argues that 'voice can be made easier by measures which amplify the demand side', apart from voters simply electing local government politicians at periodic elections. For example, institutional changes can be introduced to give consumers of local public services a greater opportunity to participate directly in decision making concerning the quantity and quality of such services, including the use of referenda and the appointment of citizens to management boards. Moreover, municipal managers can also encourage public consultation through opinion surveys, public hearings, and other consultative practices. 'Complaints procedures', like legally prescribed minimum service standards and ombudsmen, can be instituted to garner further information on public perceptions of service provision. Lastly, scope should be created for citizens to launch legal challenges on grounds of inadequate service provision.

Following Hirschman (1970), Bailey (1999) urges caution in redesigning local government institutions to facilitate greater exit and voice since trade-offs may exist. For instance, if exit is easy, then this may undermine any incentives consumers have to engage in voice. Conversely, should exit be costly, this could weaken voice, in so far as self-interested local government policy elites may realize that disgruntled citizens cannot back voice initiatives with the ultimate threat of exit. Accordingly, some optimal 'mix' of exit and voice should be sought by policy makers. But Bailey (1999, p. 56) argues that in a changing world it is unlikely that such a mix would be static: 'even if an optimal (in terms of public interest) mix of exit and voice could be specified for a particular organization at any point in time, that mix is not forever fixed, since forces will be instigated which, by design or default, change the scope for exit and/or voice'.

On the other hand, exit and voice may be complementary rather than competing mechanisms under plausible circumstances. For example, Bailey (1999, p. 60) notes that 'in particular, the ultimate sanction of exit can increase the effectiveness of voice – provided always that the providers of public services lose revenue as a consequence of exit and that appropriate structures of hierarchical control are in place'. Thus threats of exit may strengthen rather than weaken voice and policy measures which facilitate exit can enhance the credibility of these threats.

3.4 THE SUSCEPTIBILITY OF LOCAL GOVERNMENT TO GOVERNMENT FAILURE

The various taxonomic systems of government failure which we have examined shed considerable light on the numerous ways in which this phenomenon can manifest itself in market economies characterized by representative democracy. Moreover, it would appear that not only are the generic forms of government failure ubiquitous in the sense that they apply to governance systems in all advanced countries, but that they also occur at all levels of governance in these countries. Needless to add, the weight of evidence suggests that government failure is much more severe in developing societies than in their developed counterparts (Grindle 1996), but either the fragility or absence of democratic institutions in these nations would seem to imply that the origins of government failure in the developing world are due to institutional incapacity and dictatorship rather than the functioning of a sophisticated democratic process. Nevertheless, with the significant exceptions of Boyne (1998) and Bailey (1999), the extant taxonomies of government failure discussed earlier are designed to apply to all tiers of governance and contain no explicit suggestion that some levels of government may be more susceptible to government failure than others. Moreover, even though both Boyne (1998) and Bailey (1999) direct their attention exclusively at municipal governance, there is no indication that they believe local governments are especially predisposed towards government failure in comparison with higher levels of government. Indeed, both authors seem to think the relative ease of exit from local government jurisdictions should make municipalities rather less prone to government failure than their more august counterparts.

In contrast to this literature, we contend that cogent reasons exist which suggest that local governments are much more susceptible to government failure than higher levels of government. Furthermore, drawing on the existing taxonomic literature contributed by public choice theorists, we develop a new fourfold typology of government failure in order to sustain this claim. In essence, we argue that at the level of municipal governance, it is possible to identify four main forms of government failure which, although they might also afflict federal and state governments, are nonetheless especially evident in the operations of local government. These kinds of government failure can be termed 'voter apathy', 'asymmetric information and councilor capture', 'iron triangles', and 'fiscal illusion'. We shall examine each of these proposed taxonomic categories in turn.

Voter Apathy

A fundamental proposition of public choice theory holds that, in general, voting by citizens in political elections is an irrational activity since the process of voting is costly whereas the benefits associated with voting are negligible (Aldrich 1997). After all, the act of voting involves various expenses in terms of both time and money while the vote of a single individual has virtually no effect on the outcome of elections. Accordingly, if voting is perceived as an investment activity, then it is irrational to vote since the costs of voting clearly outweigh its benefits, even if the costs of voting are low in absolute terms. On the basis of this kind of hedonistic calculation no one would vote. Yet obviously in the real world people do vote, although in many instances participation rates are low. This so-called 'paradox of voting' can be resolved if voting is viewed as a consumption activity. Moreover, in western societies the socialization process strongly emphasizes the civic virtues associated with political participation. Stiglitz (2000, p. 178) has put this argument as follows:

> This paradox is resolved, in a somewhat tautological manner, simply by assuming that individuals get utility out of voting, or more generally, out of participation in the political process. More to the point, considerable time and energy are devoted to inculcating into our children notions of civic responsibility, and among these civic responsibilities the responsibility to be an informed voter.

Although the conception of voting as a consumption activity may thus explain why people vote in elections, it cannot predict how voters will choose between alternative options once they are inside the polling booth. The conventional analysis of this question focuses on the economic dimensions of the choice; voters weigh up the costs and benefits of competing policy options and select the policy which maximizes their net benefit in terms of outcomes (Mueller 1989). However, more recent literature on 'expressive voting' seems to indicate that the actual choice of electors depends more on preferences for options rather than outcomes, where options do not consider the costs involved in outcomes (Brennan and Buchanan 1984; Faith and Tollison 1993).

Despite the undeniable fact that the right to vote plays a decisive role in democracy, together with related constitutional rights, including free speech and freedom of association, the act of voting in democratic elections is fraught with ambiguities. For instance, the substantial costs of gathering and digesting information on competing candidates, alternative policies, the costs and benefits of policy platforms, and the like, together with the fact that the vote of an individual elector cannot realistically influence electoral outcomes, means that most voters choose to remain 'rationally ignorant' on many of the issues involved. Similarly, voters typically play dual roles in the political process, acting both as potential beneficiaries of public policies and as prospective financiers of these policies in their capacities as taxpayers. The phenomenon of 'decoupling' has been identified by Wolf (1989, p. 41) as a further complicating ingredient of these ambiguities. Decoupling refers to the 'decoupling between those who receive the benefits, and those who pay the costs, of government programmes'. Wolf argues that decoupling occurs in two different forms. On the one hand, 'microdecoupling' arises when the benefits of collective action accrue to a particular group, whereas the costs of such action are dispersed amongst all groups. On the other hand, 'macrodecoupling' occurs where the benefits of collective action are shared by all groups, but the costs of this action are concentrated on some specific group. As a consequence of this dual role voting takes on some of the characteristics of a Prisoner's Dilemma game. Mitchell and Simmons (1994, p. 47) have summarized the problem as follows:

> As a taxpayer, the citizen is interested in the aggregate size of the budget and supports reduced spending, reduced taxation, and increased economic growth. As a beneficiary of governmental spending, the same citizen supports an increase in subsidies or favors for his company or employer and governmental regulation of his profession: he or she has little interest in the size of the budget. Predictably, these latter interests are generally apt to be more intensely felt than taxpayer commitments.

Moreover, additional factors further complicate the voting process. Electors are usually faced with policy platforms combining widely disparate elements and must choose candidates who espouse policies both favorable and unfavorable to them. Thus a voter may be obliged to stomach a range of social policies he does not like in order to support economic policies he does like.

Despite the centrality of voting in the democratic process, it is by no means the only element in collective decision making. Numerous other mechanisms exist, which we examined earlier in our discussion on Hirschman's (1970) 'voice' concept, which range from formal voting procedures to opinion polls, protest meetings, petitions, 'talkback' radio shows and the like. These alternatives to voting serve to diminish its significance in elector's eyes and contribute towards low political participation rates, ill-informed voters, and the various other problems associated with elections under representative democracy.

Although the difficulties arising from voter apathy undoubtedly afflict both the electoral process and its subsequent 'responsiveness' to the preferences of citizens at all levels of government, the problem seems to be most acute in local government. It is possible to identify several factors that may account for this observation. Firstly, and perhaps most importantly, in many local government systems, voters do not perceive periodic municipal elections as politically significant events because the behavior of local governments is severely constrained and manipulated by state and national governments. Local governments simply 'don't matter in the scheme of things'. For example, Bailey (1999, p. 265) notes that in Britain 'by the early 1990s, central government directly controlled about two-thirds of local government income and also had powers to cap local rates as well as having a significant influence on other revenue sources such as rents for municipal housing'. It is thus hardly surprising that not only were voter turnouts low in British local government elections, but voters also seemed to view them 'as little more than opinion polls on the popularity of central government' (Boyne 1998, p. 69). Similarly, with respect to New Zealand local government, Kerr (1999, p. 4) has observed that 'there is a low turnout at elections, usually no more than 50 percent, despite postal voting'. By comparison, in state and national elections voter participation rates have generally been substantially higher (Loughlin 1986), except in countries with compulsory voting, like Australia.

A second reason for greater voter apathy in local government elections resides in the fact that in many countries these elections are not contested along party political lines, and even in those nations where political parties do participate, many candidates do not have a party affiliation and party affiliations may in any event be much weaker than at the state or federal levels of government. Accordingly, voters do not have the informational benefits of party platforms to assist them in making informed choices. For instance, in the United States, political parties often play little formal role in municipal elections largely because in many jurisdictions they are debarred from participation as a consequence of the earlier 'reform movement' aimed at removing corruption from American urban politics (Hawley 1973). Along similar lines, in many parts of Australia, including regional and rural New South Wales, long-standing convention usually precludes municipal candidates from adopting explicit partisan platforms.

Media reporting of local government elections is typically much less comprehensive and unquestioning than for comparable federal and state ballots and consequently affords voters much less opportunity to become well acquainted with the policy platforms of individual candidates standing for election. Whether this is a cause or simply an effect of voter apathy is a moot point, but it nevertheless surely accounts for a greater degree of ill-informed voting in municipal elections than their counterparts at higher levels of government.

Because of their lower public profiles and complicated interface, governance and management roles in municipal government are often confused in the eyes of many citizens, who cannot readily distinguish between elected representatives and professional public servants. Thus, perceived responsibility for past policy successes and failures is difficult to assign between the councilors and managers. Moreover, the committee systems characteristic of numerous local governments serve to further confuse the question of responsibility (Kerr 1999).

Finally, the nature of local government activities itself makes any evaluation difficult. Municipalities typically deliver a vast range of services, even where their focus is on the relatively narrow 'services to property' dimension of delivery. Under these circumstances, not only is monitoring of service delivery an onerous task, but accountability is extremely difficult to establish. It is thus little wonder that citizens remain apathetic towards the operations of local government.

The relatively high degree of voter apathy in local government, in comparison with its national and provincial counterparts, provides greater scope for government failure at this level of governance. In general, it can be argued that apathetic voters might not only elect inadequate representatives, but also fail to scrutinize their performance with a sufficient degree of rigor. For example, where voters are comparatively ill-informed about the election platforms of councilors they are in a poor position to judge whether subsequently elected candidates have indeed met expectations or carried out their mandates. Similarly, given accountability and monitoring difficulties, citizens may experience difficulties in ascertaining how well municipalities are performing and who is responsible for any noteworthy problems that may arise. This seems to provide local government legislators with greater scope for opportunistic behavior than their colleagues at higher levels of government and accordingly makes local government more prone to what both Dollery and Wallis (1997) and Weisbrod (1978) classify as legislative failure. This may explain why in many real-world jurisdictions, state and federal governments sometimes retain statutory powers to override the decisions of local governments or even suspend local governments and arrange new elections.

Asymmetric Information and Councilor Capture

Given the comparative lack of scrutiny afforded elected local government representatives by apathetic municipal voters, relationships between these councilors and senior professional managers in the local government bureaucracies take on even greater significance than comparable relationships between politicians and public servants at higher levels of government. Ronald Wintrobe (1997, p. 430) has posed the central question in this context by asking 'how much influence does the bureaucracy have over what (and how much) governments do?'. One way of understanding the nature of these relationships is through agency theory.

The literature on agency theory is primarily concerned with the ways in which one economic agent (the principal) can design and implement a contractual system to motivate another economic agent (the agent) to act in the principal's interests. Accordingly, agency theory is chiefly focused on the problem of economic incentives. By contrast, conventional neoclassical economics, with its reductionist construct of the organization as simply a production function converting inputs into outputs in the most productively efficient manner, assumed away principal-agent problems and the associated question of incentives. In the orthodox tradition, principals were perfectly informed on the nature of the tasks agents were hired to perform and their subsequent actions could be costlessly monitored. Agency theory can thus be viewed as the extension of the neoclassical theory of the firm to embrace 'the problems posed by limited information and goal conflict within organizations' (Levinthal 1988, p. 154).

A principal-agent relationship comes into being whenever a principal delegates authority to an agent whose behavior has an impact on the principal's welfare. Numerous principal-agent relationships exist across virtually the entire spectrum of human endeavor. For example, principal-agent relationships include voters and their elected representatives, governing politicians and the bureaucrats hired to implement policies, patients and physicians, employers and employees, shareholders and corporate managers, and so forth. The essence of all these principal-agent relationships involves a trade-off for the principal. By delegating authority to an agent, the principal economizes on scarce resources by adopting an informed and able agent, but simultaneously takes on the risk that since the interests of the principal and agent will never be identical, the agent may fail to carry out the wishes of the principal. For instance, despite being paid a proportionate commission, real estate agents may wish to sell a property quickly at a lower price than could otherwise be obtained for the owner of the property. Since the interests of principals and agents are likely to diverge in most real-world relationships, agency theory focuses on the costs attached to such relationships and the efforts that both principals and agents will take to economize on these costs. In their seminal contribution, Jensen and Meckling (1976) identified three categories of agency costs. Firstly, monitoring costs arise from the resources principals invest in monitoring the behavior of agents and creating incentives for desirable behavior. Secondly, bonding costs will derive from resources invested by agents to guarantee successful outcomes to their principals. And thirdly, residual loss costs consist in the losses to their well-being suffered by principals due to a divergence between their interests and those of their agents. According to Jensen and Meckling (1976), total agency costs are thus comprised of the aggregate of monitoring costs, bonding costs and residual loss costs.

The extent of total agency costs are postulated as dependent on the characteristics of particular principal-agent relationships. For example, in a typical agency relationship agents almost always possess more information about both the task assigned and the relative efficacy of their own performance. Agents often take advantage of this asymmetry of information by engaging in shirking or opportunistic behavior antipathetical to the interests of principals, and clearly the greater the extent of this behavior the higher will be the level of total agency costs.

Although in its initial stages agency theory was applied exclusively to the firm, and especially the modern corporation with its separation of ownership from control characteristic of a principal-agent relationship, it was soon used more widely once its explanatory powers were recognized. Jensen and Meckling (1976 p. 309) recognized the generality of agency theory:

> The problem of inducing an agent to behave as if he [or she] were maximizing the 'principal's' welfare is quite general. It exists in all organizations and in all cooperative efforts at every level of management in firms, in universities, in mutual companies, in cooperatives, in governmental authorities and bureaus, in unions, and in relationships normally classified as agency relationships such as are common in the performing arts and the market for real estate.

Although the problems identified by agency theory are thus endemic to all human organizations, they nevertheless manifest themselves in different ways in divergent institutional settings. Economists have approached the question of principal-agent relationships in bureaucracies formally controlled by elected politicians by seeking to model their behavior. The first rigorous economic model of bureaucracy was developed by Niskanen (1971), whose work provoked much subsequent modeling activity (see, for example, Bendor 1990), and Niskanen's budget-maximizing model still represents the mainstream position of American public choice theorists (Mueller 1989).

In his classic analysis, William Niskanen (1971) argued that bureaucrats sought to maximize the size of their budgets, since larger budgets implied increased salaries, power and prestige. Bureaucrats can increase the size of their budgets by oversupplying output, or by inefficiently supplying output, or both. Bureaucrats are said to bear an agent-principal relationship to politicians who in turn bear an agent-political relationship to voters. Bureaucrats benefit directly from large governmental budgets and thus have intense preferences for high levels of expenditure. By contrast, taxpayers typically only benefit indirectly from government expenditure, and have preferences for low taxation levels. The objectives of agents and principals thus diverge. But because bureaucrats have greater per capita incentives to increase expenditure than the corresponding incentives of taxpayers to decrease taxes, public sector expenditure may be higher than desired.

Chang and Rowthorn (1995, p. 9) have outlined the general significance of the arguments underlying bureaucratic failure as follows:

> These models saw the root of many problems of the contemporary capitalist countries – for example, the over-extension of the bureaucracy, the waste of resources in government administration, the inefficiency of the public enterprises – in the inability of the principals (the public) to monitor the self-seeking behavior of their agents in public affairs (the bureaucrats). These models were usually presented as neutral efficiency arguments, but have had much deeper political impacts. By arguing that the same assumption of self-centered behavior should be applied both to the private sector agents and the public sector agents, they not only questioned the public's trust in the benign paternalism of the welfare state but also undermined the self-confidence of government officials and their commitment to a public service ethos.

If we conceive of the public sector in a representative democracy as being constituted by an interlocking series of principal-agent relationships, then the importance of agency failure becomes apparent. For example. Moe (1984, p. 65) observes that 'the whole of politics can be seen as a chain of principal-agent relationships, from citizen to politician to bureaucratic superior to bureaucratic subordinate and on down the hierarchy of government to the lowest-level bureaucrats who actually deliver services directly to citizens'. This view leads to an approach to public sector reform that seeks to reduce the scope for agency failure in these relationships.

We contend that the agent-principal problems between elected representatives and professional bureaucrats in the local government milieu are likely to be much more acute than in their federal and state counterparts. Various arguments can be advanced in support of this contention. For instance, outside large metropolitan local governments, elected municipal representatives typically hold part-time positions and are remunerated accordingly. In the majority of cases they are thus obliged to have alternative full-time employment not only to sustain themselves economically in the short run, but also as a form of longer-term insurance against the possible failure of re-election in the future. They are thus unable to devote their full attention to the duties of their elected office. One consequence is often an inability to master the complexities and minutiae of local government finances and service delivery. This leads to a strong reliance on the advice and information provided by professional managers. Following the economic theory of bureaucracy, these managers may be motivated to pursue objectives in conflict with those espoused by elected representatives. Moreover, in accordance with agency theory and the lack of capacity for elected representatives to monitor principal-agent relationships with managers adequately, managers are well placed to exploit the resultant agency failure. Put differently, since the 'hands-on' nature of their jobs means managers are bound to be much better informed than councilors, and since managers are the chief policy advisers to councilors, it seems likely that by manipulating the asymmetry of information to their advantage, managers can 'capture' councilors and thereby achieve the policy outcomes they desire. Although analogous problems clearly exist at higher levels of government, because elected representatives in national and state governments serve in a full-time capacity, they can devote much more time and energy to mastering the complexities of the bureau they oversee and are thus not as badly disadvantaged by problems of asymmetrical information and attendant capture as their colleagues in local government.

A similar and related argument derives from the fact that elected municipal councilors seldom have access to policy advisers at all, never mind advisers with a detailed knowledge of the workings of local government. By contrast, it is commonplace in state and federal governments for elected representatives to have constant access to professional advisers and researchers well-versed in the intricacies of policy formulation and implementation who can assist them in evaluating and 'filtering' information from public service managers. Whilst the presence of such policy advisers and researchers obviously cannot completely nullify the problem of asymmetric behavior in the interactions between politicians and public sector executives and thus altogether remove capture, it surely goes some way towards overcoming these problems.

Agenda control represents an additional means by which well-informed bureaucrats hold a comparative advantage over their relatively ill-informed political masters and can thus out-maneuver them in agent-principal terms. In their 'setter model', Romer and Rosenthal (1978) have shown how bureaucrats can control the outcomes of votes by elected councilors (or actual citizens in referenda) by specifying the alternatives which are voted upon. More specifically, councilors may be called to vote on a particular budget proposal. If a majority favor the proposal, then it is accepted. If a majority reject the proposal, then expenditure is set at a predetermined 'reversionary level'. In essence, 'the lower the reversion level, the higher the budget the bureaucratic setter is able to extract from voters' (Wintrobe 1997, p. 438), and if the reversionary level of expenditure is set higher than the pre-vote expenditure, then this also allows for budget growth.

Finally, strategies of 'selective behavior' (Breton and Wintrobe 1982), especially 'selective efficiency' (Wintrobe 1997) can be embarked upon by bureaucrats using their advantage of asymmetric information. Wintrobe (1997, p. 431) describes selective efficiency as a means by which 'bureaucrats control their masters' choices by being efficient at the things they want to do, and inefficient at those they do not'. Thus when elected representatives oblige public managers to implement policies against their will, these can be confounded by deliberate inefficiency until they are withdrawn. Conversely, in areas where bureaucrats wish to expand operations, they can ensure efficient delivery and bring this to the attention of politicians. Given the greater degree of asymmetric information in municipal governance, it can be argued that selective efficiency is likely to prove a more potent weapon than at higher levels of government.

Iron Triangles

Whereas some of the earlier taxonomies of government failure we have examined made explicit reference to citizens attempting to divert scarce resources from governments to themselves, like Dollery and Wallis' (1997) rent-seeking category, most of these typologies nevertheless at least implicitly recognized that individuals and interest groups seek to influence both policy formulation and implementation in self-interested ways. Mitchell and Simmons (1994, p. 62) provide an intuitively appealing description of the rationale behind the formation of interest groups in politics:

> Rational citizens in pursuit of private desires quickly learn the superiority of organized groups over individual pursuit of welfare through the ballot box. By organizing into an interest group, voters can pursue their goals with greater efficiency. The interest group provides a division of labor, specialization, and the power of concentrated passion and incentives.

The analysis of interest groups in redistributing wealth and power through the political process has been approached by economists from at least three main theoretical directions. Firstly, and perhaps most importantly, the theory of rent-seeking tries to explain the ways in which citizens as wealth maximizers seek to use government intervention to create economic rents for themselves. The resultant burgeoning literature has provided fascinating insights into the interplay between state intervention and maximizing economic agents (Buchanan et al. 1980). In orthodox economic theory the concept of economic rent has traditionally been defined in terms of opportunity cost. Thus rent is simply that part of the reward accruing to the owner of a resource over and above the payment the resource would receive in any alternative employment. Given the customary assumption of maximizing behavior on the part of economic agents, and an absence of constraints on resource mobility, in the stylized world of neoclassical theory competitive forces will ensure the dissipation of rent in a manner which produces socially desirable outcomes. The existence of positive rent in a competitive market will attract resources in the same way as the existence of potential profits, and consequently result in the erosion of such rent through a socially desirable reallocation of resources. However, once we adjust the social mechanisms in which this process occurs, the consequence of maximizing behavior motivated by the possibility of economic rent may be quite different viewed from the perspective of society at large. Buchanan (1980, p. 4) has neatly summarized the nature of rent-seeking in this alternative setting:

> The term rent-seeking is designed to describe behavior in institutional settings where individual efforts to maximize value generate social waste rather than social surplus...The unintended consequences of individual value maximization shift from those that may be classified as 'good' to those that seem clearly to be bad not because individuals become different moral beings and modify their actions accordingly, but because institutional structure changes. The setting within which individual choices are made is transformed. As institutions have moved away from ordered markets toward the near chaos of direct political allocation rent-seeking has emerged as a significant social phenomenon.

The theory of rent-seeking is thus appropriate for the analysis of the origins of, and competition for artificially created rent, and not for short-lived rents (or quasi-rents) which characterize dynamic market processes. The existence of contrived rent implies the possibility of wealth transfers between individuals and groups in society, and rent-seeking behavior encompasses attempts by economic actors at creating and competing for these wealth transfers. Given the massive extension of state intervention in modern times, and its ability to affect the redistribution of property rights and hence generate wealth transfers, the primary source and focus of rent-seeking activity has, not surprisingly, been the political process.

In addition to rent-seeking aimed at capturing the benefits generated by existing state intervention, in a society where severe constitutional limitations on state involvement are absent, rent-seeking by interest groups (and individuals) will also occur with the object of attaining intervention and its attendant advantages. It is thus possible to identify at least two further forms of rent-seeking behavior.   Firstly, rent-seeking directed at securing initial state intervention which will induce contrived rent through the artificial limitation of market processes thus allowing for wealth transfers to occur. And secondly, rent-seeking aimed at capturing the resultant rent and maintaining a position of capture.

A second theoretical perspective on the role of interest groups in the political process derives from Mancur Olson's (1965) pioneering work on distributional coalitions. Olson sought to provide a generalized analysis of 'the problem of collective choice, the prisoner's dilemma, the free-rider problem and the conditions of common fate, depending on the context (or discipline) in which it arises' (Barry and Hardin 1982, p. 19) by invoking the economic paradigm of rational choice in group or collective behavior. Distributional coalitions comprise single or multiple interest groups that seek to further the material interests of their members. Olson (1965) distinguished between successful or 'privileged' and unsuccessful or 'latent' interest groups, where the former were capable of overcoming the ubiquitous problem of free-riding while the latter were not.   In broad terms, Olson (1982) argues that group interaction in complex, stable societies over time leads to socially inferior outcomes given the asymmetric organizational capacities of different interest groups, their group-specific maximands and their attendant ability to affect distributional outcomes.

Finally, endogenous policy theory, first developed by Magee et al. (1989), can also shed light on the manner in which interest groups can manipulate the political process to secure their desired distributional outcomes. In essence, this theoretical perspective investigates the nature of economic and social policy formulation and tries to explain why welfare-reducing policy distortions exist since they are not rational from the point of view of society as a whole.   Magee et al. (1989) distinguish between the concepts of economic efficiency and political efficiency. They argue that 'economically efficient policies create greater gains than losses whereas inefficient policies do the reverse' (Magee et al. 1989, p. 1). By contrast, politically efficient policies are those which increase the probability of election of parties and candidates.   Moreover, a trade-off generally exists between economic efficiency and political efficiency. Magee et al. (1989, p. 51) put the argument as follows:

> Economic agents take all actions that increase their welfare; political parties take all actions that increase their electoral welfare. It is obvious that a movement toward political efficiency involving an increase in redistributional policies usually lowers economic welfare. At the same time, a movement toward economic efficiency that dismantles economically inefficient redistributive policies would lower political efficiency (because their reinstitution would enhance the electoral success of one or more parties).

Magee et al. (1989) argue that in politics policies play much the same role as prices in an economy: that is, both are equilibrating variables that adjust until opposing forces are in balance. In the determination of redistributive economic and social policies, competing demands for and against a particular policy will determine the ultimate nature of the policy. For instance, in the case of tariff protection, if strong groups favor tariffs and comparatively weak groups oppose tariffs, then we would anticipate the outcome to be relatively high tariffs. Policies are thus entirely 'endogenously' determined in the sense that no single individual or group can determine their shape. Even politicians cannot control policy formulation since their vote-maximizing behavior makes them dependent on interest groups – a phenomenon termed the 'powerless politician effect'. The upshot of this model of policy determination is a bleak view of the potential for policy reform; namely, 'there is no solution to the economic waste caused by competitive redistribution' (Magee et al. 1989, p. 2) since any remedial policies will themselves be endogenously determined in the political process.

Although policy formulation and implementation at all levels of government will be characterized by rent-seeking distributional coalitions maximizing self-interest in a process of endogenous policy development, it seems likely that powerful interest groups may be particularly successful in the local government sphere. We have argued earlier that municipal politicians generally without strong party affiliations are often elected on ill-defined policy platforms by apathetic and ill-informed voters and their activities are typically not subject to the same degree of media and other scrutiny as their colleagues at higher levels of government. Similarly, professional bureaucrats enjoy far greater discretion as a consequence of the acute asymmetry of information between them and their part-time political masters. Moreover, outside of the American political system, with its strong emphasis on congressional committees and other delegated powers, and in contrast to Westminster style parliamentary democracy, local government relies much more on standing committees to oversee its operations. For instance, municipal councils usually have 'parks and gardens' committees to run its public open spaces programs, 'roads and maintenance' committees to direct its public thoroughfare operations, and so forth. Interest groups can thus readily identify specific politicians with powers over particular aspects of municipal activity and target these individuals accordingly. They can also form alliances with municipal managers in charge of the various programs and attempt to influence the advice these bureaucrats give to committee members. In this way 'iron triangles' made up of elected committee councilors, professional managers and interest groups can arise which dominate policy making in specific areas. Often these interest groups will be made up of sub-contractors who undertake operations for municipalities, suppliers who provide goods and services to councils, property developers who build and renovate residential and other areas, and businesses that enjoy preferential zoning arrangements and licensing agreements. The tripartite composition of these confluent colluding associations or 'triangles' and the difficulty of penetrating them or their 'iron' nature mean that these iron triangles will tend not only to be dominant for considerable periods, but also stable through time.

Rent-seeking in this situation will aim at the formation and protection of iron triangles and countervailing rent-seeking by individuals and groups outside of triangles will consist of attempts to join existing triangles or replace extant triangles with new ones. Olson's (1965) categorization of interest groups as either potentially successful ('privileged') or inherently unsuccessful ('latent') will determine the outcome of rent-seeking activity. Resultant policy formulation and implementation can be characterized as endogenous in the sense that it represents the interplay of the interests of the politicians, bureaucrats and interest groups who form the iron triangle in question.

Bailey (1999), argues that distributional coalitions are likely to have a greater deleterious effect on resource allocation in local government than at higher levels of government in a federation. He contends that a high proportion of local tax payments are fixed by various rules, not least property taxes which depend on land value, and do not vary significantly with the consumption of local government services. Under these circumstances, distributional coalitions have an incentive to attempt to change the level of service provision in their favor or to modify the distribution of service provision with a given and largely exogenously determined fixed total municipal budget. Accordingly, the activities of interest groups will focus heavily 'on the distribution of incremental expenditures and much attention is paid to annual budget changes which are small in relation to the overall budget' (Bailey 1999, p. 97). No distributional coalition will be willing to accept a fall in the services it receives because no corresponding change in its tax liability could occur, given the structure of municipal finances. Since opposing interest groups may tend to neutralize each other's influence, existing expenditure regimes would tend to remain fixed. This means *inter alia* that local governments experience great difficulties in meeting 'changed socioeconomic conditions', with the result that allocative inefficiencies would inevitably intensify.

Boyne (1998) believes that the degree of 'fragmentation' or decentralization of local government might affect the demand for 'spatially divisible' public goods as opposed to 'spatially indivisible' public goods. Spatially divisible goods benefit particular localities rather than encompassing neighboring zones whereas spatially indivisible goods benefit much greater areas. Thus residents of given jurisdiction will prefer relatively more spatially divisible goods on grounds that the benefits of these goods will fall exclusively on them and adjacent jurisdictions will not be able to 'free ride' on the fruits of their rates and taxes. A similar argument can be advanced with respect to the power and enduring nature of iron triangles. We would expect that the greater the degree of fragmentation, the more significant would be the impact of iron triangles on policy making. After all, small local governments will attract less voter interest, enjoy minimal oversight by elected politicians, and draw little media attention in comparison to larger municipal entities where the 'stakes are higher'. Accordingly, iron triangles are probably easier to form in fragmented systems.

Fiscal Illusion

In advanced modern economies governments undertake a bewildering array of expenditure and regulatory functions and finance these activities through a myriad of taxes and charges on their citizens. Measuring the size and cost of government has thus proved both conceptually and empirically difficult even for professional economists (see, for example, Dollery and Singh 1998), let alone for participants in the political process, especially voters. One consequence of the size and complexity of contemporary government in industrialized societies resides in the phenomenon of fiscal illusion. In essence, the concept of fiscal illusion revolves around the proposition that the actual costs and benefits of government may be consistently misconstrued by the citizenry of a given fiscal jurisdiction. Five specific forms of fiscal illusion can be identified (Dollery and Worthington 1996a). Firstly, the revenue complexity hypothesis holds that the more complex the public revenue-raising system, the higher will be the level of public sector expenditure *ceteris paribus*, since voters will be unaware of how much taxes they pay. Buchanan (1967, p. 135) has argued that 'to the extent that the total tax load on an individual can be fragmented so that he confronts numerous small levies rather than a few significant ones, illusionary effects may be created'. While empirical investigation of the revenue complexity hypothesis has found substantial support for this model at the local government level (see Dollery and Worthington 1996a, Table 1), it would nevertheless seem intuitively plausible that since higher tiers of government typically have much wider taxing powers, its effects would be more pronounced in state and national governments.

A second form of fiscal illusion springs from the income elasticity of the revenue system. The revenue elasticity approach holds that when increases in national or jurisdictional income 'automatically' translate into even greater proportionate increases in tax revenues, then these additional funds will tend to boost public expenditure rather than decrease tax rates, as in the well-known case of 'fiscal drag' and income taxes. Local governments would appear to be particular beneficiaries of revenue elasticity in respect of property taxes under inflationary conditions, since the appreciation of property values converts into higher tax yields with given tax rates and a given number of rateable properties. But because *ad valorem* or proportionate taxation is much more frequent in federal and state governments the phenomenon is likely to be much more widespread at these levels of government. Nonetheless, municipalities may benefit more in relative terms since property taxes often represent their major source of revenue.

A third kind of fiscal illusion has been identified as 'debt illusion'. Debt illusion refers to the proposition that voters are more aware of the costs of public sector programs if they are financed through current taxation rather than public sector borrowing. It is argued that this results from the imperfect information available to individuals on the time path of the future benefits and costs of government activity. From the perspective of local government, the significance of debt illusion is problematic. In general, since assets and not individuals are taxed at the local level, the empirical question thus becomes one of the degree to which community debt is capitalized into individual asset values. Oates (1988, p. 77) has observed that 'other things being equal, we should find, that if there is debt illusion, that the future tax liabilities associated with the debt are not fully capitalized into local property values'. Actual empirical evidence on the issue of debt capitalization is both limited and mixed (see Dollery and Worthington 1996a, Table 5).

A fourth dimension of fiscal illusion, known as the 'flypaper effect', has a much greater direct relevance to local government. The flypaper effect, so-called since 'money sticks where it hits', refers to the hypothesized tendency for categorical lump-sum grants from federal to state and local governments to increase public expenditure by more than an equivalent increase in income from other sources. This proposition contravenes the 'equivalence theorem', a central proposition of the traditional theory of intergovernmental grants (Oates, 1972), which holds that a lump-sum grant to a fiscal jurisdiction will stimulate the same increase in expenditure that would flow from an equivalent increase in the private incomes of people who comprise the population of the jurisdiction. It would seem that voters misperceive grants as 'gifts' to their jurisdictions and overlook the fact that their tax liability rises at higher levels of government. Despite some reservations about the methodologies employed to investigate the real-world prevalence of the flypaper effect in local government, it appears that empirical evidence exists in support of the model, although this conclusion should be qualified by noting that institutional structures underlying the grants process in any country (or the problem of 'endogeneity') obviously play a major role in determining the strength of the flypaper effect (Worthington and Dollery 1999).

Notwithstanding theoretical difficulties in explaining the flypaper effect (Bailey 1999), it seems clear that the stimulatory effects of intergovernmental grants on local government expenditure might prove to be a major source of government failure at this level of government. After all, around 35 per cent of American and 30 per cent of Australian local government revenues derive from grants from higher levels of government (Worthington and Dollery 1999, pp. 4–5), whereas in the United Kingdom the corresponding figure is almost 80 per cent (Bailey 1999, p. 87). Gramlich (1977) has estimated that in the United States, lump-sum grants from the federal government appeared to generate a fourfold increase in public expenditure in comparison to an equivalent increase in the income of local residents. Although the framework within which the intergovernmental grants process occurs differs in other advanced countries, and will obviously influence the expansionary effects of these grants accordingly, the resulting allocative inefficiencies are also likely to be substantial.

Finally, 'renter illusion' has quintessential significance in the local government milieu. This form of fiscal illusion holds that an increase in the proportion of property renters in a given municipal jurisdiction will increase the level of public expenditures *ceteris paribus*. The presumption is that since the primary revenue of local government derives from property taxes, only those voters who own property and are thus directly levied will correctly estimate the tax price of local public goods. Although we could expect that higher property taxes will be passed on to renters through higher rents, the renters illusion hypothesis contends that a disjunction exists between a rental voter's perception of the level of municipal services and the value of rents paid. Accordingly, renters will vote for higher levels of local public good expenditure than property owners.

A considerable body of empirical evidence has been amassed on the renters illusion hypothesis and the weight of this evidence appears to support the hypothesis (see, for example, Dollery and Worthington 1996a, Table 4). However, several scholars have argued that 'renter rationality' might better explain the ostensible propensity of renters to support higher levels of local expenditure. According to this view, in the short run property rentals are not affected by property taxes and so increases in taxes will not be passed on to renters (Barr and Davis 1996). From the perspective of local government policy makers, whether or not renter rationality explains some or all of renter illusion seems less important than the putative fact that a greater proportion of renters in a jurisdiction will tend to bias expenditure upwards.

Renter illusion makes local government especially susceptible to government failure for the obvious reason that higher levels of government are much less reliant on property taxes as a source of revenue. Moreover, rate-capping, rent controls and other factors which influence the nexus between rentals, property taxes and municipal income are typically exogenously imposed on local jurisdictions by state and federal governments. This means that allocative inefficiencies stemming from this source cannot easily be remedied by municipal policies themselves without the assistance of higher tiers of government.

3.5   CONCLUDING REMARKS

We have presented a taxonomic view of government failure in local government which draws strongly on the generic typologies which have been developed by theorists operating in the broad public choice tradition. Moreover, we have sought to argue that cogent reasons exist which suggest that government failure in general, and agency failure in particular, are likely to be more acute in municipal government than its counterparts at higher tiers in a federalism. This conclusion is in stark contrast to views of both Bailey (1999) and Boyne (1998) who contend that since intergovernmental competition is greater at the local government level it may be less susceptible to government failure.

Our argument has at least two broad ramifications. Firstly, does available empirical evidence support the notion that local governments are in fact comparatively inefficient in their operations? This theme is taken up in Chapter 4 where we explore the measurement of local government performance and examine the relevant empirical research on local government efficiency. And secondly, if local government is indeed more prone to government failure than state and federal governments, then this raises interesting questions about the design of appropriate governance mechanisms for municipalities.

These questions are investigated in Chapter 5.

4. The Empirical Measurement of Local Government Efficiency

With Andrew Worthington

4.1 INTRODUCTION

The economic theory of fiscal federalism and the market failure paradigm, which we examined in Chapter 2, provide theoretical guidance to policy makers in local government on how to assign the various functions of government between the tiers of government and, once these powers have been assigned, on the appropriate role of municipal government in carrying out its designated functions. Moreover, the market failure model prescribed government intervention only when private markets could not achieve economic efficiency unaided or, in its broader form, when these markets could not yield desired equity outcomes. In other words, the market failure paradigm provides intellectual arguments for more expansive government on the untenable assumption that state intervention always succeeds in meeting its objectives; that is, the market failure model emphasizes the benefits which can accrue from government intervention. By contrast, the literature on government failure, which we discussed in Chapter 3, also focuses on the appropriate role for government but instead stresses the costs attached to activist government policy. By imputing the *homo economicus* postulate to the behavior of the various participants involved in the process of policy formulation and implementation, the government failure model provides systematic grounds for believing that public policies seldom achieve their stated aims.

  Both the market failure paradigm and the literature on government failure thus hold firm *a priori* expectations of the probable efficiency consequences of government intervention. But the issue of how efficient local governments actually are in the real world is clearly an empirical question which can only be resolved by resorting to available empirical evidence. However, the measurement of the economic efficiency of local government service delivery is beset with a number of conceptual and methodological difficulties. This chapter seeks to investigate the nature of local government performance measurement and assess existing published empirical evidence on the efficiency of local government operations in advanced countries. Emphasis falls on so-called 'frontier measurement techniques' since this approach represents the current state of the art in the empirical analysis of public sector activities. The latter part of the chapter draws on Worthington and Dollery (2000b).

The chapter itself is divided into six main areas. Section 4.2 outlines the nature of local government performance measurement. The theoretical basis for frontier measurement techniques is examined in section 4.3. Section 4.4 provides a synoptic review of the different techniques for the measurement of public sector efficiency and section 4.5 deals with the literature on the empirical measurement of inefficiency in local public services. Section 4.6 discusses the determinants of local government efficiency. The chapter ends with some brief concluding remarks in section 4.7.

4.2 THE NATURE OF LOCAL GOVERNMENT PERFORMANCE MEASUREMENT

Local government service delivery has come under increased scrutiny in many countries. In the absence of contestable markets, and the information and incentives provided by these markets, performance information, particularly measures of comparative performance, have been seen as a means by which interested parties can gauge the effectiveness of the provision of local government services. The potential users of this information are threefold. First, the recipients (i.e. clients, users, customers or consumers) of these services can use this publicly available information to exercise client choice more effectively, and ensure the transparency and accountability of service providers for taxpayer funds.

Second, the providers and purchasers of services, governments, public agencies and service providers, can also make use of performance measures. Possible uses include the stimulation of policy development by highlighting influences on the operating environment, facilitating the monitoring of public sector managerial performance, and the promotion of 'yardstick' or benchmark competition for improving performance in areas where there is little competition in markets for inputs and/or outputs. These measures can also be used as an analytical tool in examining relationships between alternative agencies and programs and as a means of assisting resource allocation by way of linking allocated funding with agency and/or program objectives.

Finally, performance measurement can be used as a managerial decision-making tool. Attention can thereby be focused on practices in similar organizations that may assist the attainment of agency/program objectives, and thus facilitate programs of performance improvement.

The problem of measuring the performance of private or public sector organizations is fundamental to any economy concerned with the accountability, transparency, efficiency and effectiveness of these institutions. In the private sector it has long been assumed that, in the long run, the discipline imposed by the marketplace motivates corporations to strive for cost efficiency and profit maximization, enhanced by feedback from the markets for capital, corporate control and managerial labor. These include measures derived from profits, rates of return on assets, investment and invested capital, market shares and market power.

In contrast, the local public sector is generally seen to lack both an analogue for profit-seeking behavior and an adequate feedback system to assess the quality of decisions. It is argued that there are five main aspects of government services that may make it difficult to develop accurate performance indicators. First, the outputs of a service provider may be complex and/or multiple (Mark 1986; Hatry and Fisk 1992). Furthermore, there may be difficulty in establishing cause and effect between the activities of a service and the final outcomes it seeks to influence, and these may be evident only after considerable time (Steering Committee for the Review of Commonwealth/State Service Provision (SCRCSSP) 1998, p. 7). Second, government organizations may encounter problems in identifying the cost of producing and delivering services (Ammons 1986, 1992; Ganley and Cubbin 1992). For example, there may be difficulty apportioning costs across different services or the costs of a given program over long periods of time. Certainly, this problem has been mitigated by the introduction of systems of management accounting and accrual accounting (SCRCSSP 1998, p. 7).

Third, complexity in government services may exist due to the interplay of related services and programs (Epstein 1992; Carter et al. 1995). For instance, performance indicators may need to capture the positive and negative externality effects of service provision (SCRCSSP 1998, p. 16). Fourth, there are potentially many users of governmental performance information. Different lines of accountability and the disparate informational requirements of government, taxpayers, employers, staff, consumers and contractors create additional complications in performance measurement (SCRCSSP 1998, p. 16). For example, in Australia the Industry Commission's (1997, p. 58) report on Australian local government performance indicators received a number of submissions suggesting that the 'most relevant measure for the Commonwealth and state governments may be a financial measure, but for local government and its community stakeholders it is (the focus) on outcome measurements and the effectiveness

of resource inputs'.   Finally, a number of restrictions placed by these
stakeholders may impinge upon the theoretical ability of government entities
to improve performance, and therefore bring the orientation of performance
information into question. For example, Ammons (1986, p. 191) argued that
the intergovernmental mandating of expenditures and intergovernmental
grant provisions may restrict the ability of government bodies to modify
behavior, whereas Miller (1992) maintains that the budget process itself has
an important contribution to make to the notion of performance.

Many of these characteristics are closely aligned with Wolf's (1989) four
basic attributes of non market or public sector supply, which we examined in
Chapter 3. First, he argues that 'nonmarket outputs are often hard to define
in principle, ill-defined in practice, and extremely difficult to measure as to
quantity or to evaluate as quality' (Wolf, 1989, p. 51). Accordingly, inputs
generally become a proxy measure for output (Dollery and Worthington
1996b, p. 29). Secondly, non market outputs are usually produced by a
single public agency, often operating as a legally constituted monopoly. The
resultant lack of competition makes meaningful estimates of economic
efficiency difficult, and consequently obscures allocative and productive
efficiencies. Third, Wolf (1989, p. 52) argues that the 'technology of
producing nonmarket outputs is frequently unknown, or if known, is
associated with considerable uncertainty and ambiguity'. This may serve to
further obscure notions of performance in the local public sector. Finally, he
proposes that non market production activity is also usually characterized by
the lack of any 'bottom-line' evaluation mechanism equivalent to appraising
success. Moreover, there is often no specified procedure for terminating
unsuccessful production (Dollery and Worthington 1996b, p. 29).

One generic assessment framework that has been widely used in public
sector services is detailed in Figure 4.1 (Industry Commission 1997;
SCRCSSP 1998). The approach is largely based upon the premise that in
order to analyze performance a suite of outcome indicators should be
considered collectively.   Overall performance is divided into two
components: (i) efficiency, which describes how well an organization uses
resources in producing services; that is, the relationship between the actual
and optimal combination of inputs used to produce a given bundle of outputs;
and (ii) effectiveness, or the degree to which a system achieves its program
and policy objectives. In turn, effectiveness encompasses a number of
different desired aspects of service linked to program outcome objectives.
These are: (i) appropriateness (matching service to client needs); (ii)
accessibility (aspects such as affordability, representation amongst priority
groups and physical accessibility); and (iii) quality (the process of meeting
required standards or incidence of service failures).

However, this framework, whilst comprehensive, is claimed to suffer from a number of limitations. First, some authors have argued that the traditional public sector performance framework is too narrowly focused. For example, Carter et al. (1995, p. 37) support an additional category in the form of 'economy' with an exclusive focus on 'the purchase and provision of services at the lowest possible cost consistent with a specified objective'. Some authors have proposed restricting effectiveness to measuring the achievement of targets or objectives, and introducing 'efficacy' so as to measure the impact of services on the community. Still others have supported a similar argument for 'equity', in order to highlight the distinction between administrative and policy effectiveness. However, Carter et al. (1995) argue that doing so may increase the focus of effectiveness on administrative effectiveness and reduce the incentive to produce 'efficacy' and 'equity' or policy-related outcomes.

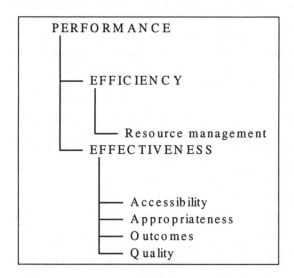

Figure 4.1   Framework for performance assessment

A second problem is that this generic performance framework makes no specific allowance for identifying additional variables relating to efficiency and the still largely unmeasured concept of effectiveness (Mann 1986). These 'contextual' variables include environmental characteristics relating to the input/output set and the task environment, individual characteristics such as motivation and incentive, and structural characteristics focusing on the degree of centralization, hierarchy and leadership style (Johnson and Lewin 1984, p. 230). For example, in Australia the Industry Commission (1997, p. 53) has argued that contextual information serves two main purposes.

First, it clarifies the environmental constraints on performance, aiding interpretation of the indicators. Second, it helps ensure that what is being reported as an indicator of performance is not merely an indicator of activity. For example, expenditure per capita on a particular service is not an indicator of performance unless the nature of the service is tightly defined.

Alternatively, Ammons (1992, p. 119) has argued that contextual information forms 'barriers' to performance analysis. That is, 'environmental barriers', such as political factors and intergovernmental relations, 'organizational barriers', including inadequate information systems and bureaucratic structures, and 'personal barriers' like managerial risk avoidance, imply that the concept of public sector 'performance' will always be compromised by largely unmeasured sets of contextual information.

In practical terms, the lack of treatment of contextual information is likely to affect interpretation in three ways. Firstly, 'organizations may pursue different objectives and this may be important when assessing services designed to local preferences' (SCRCSSP 1998, p. 18). Ignoring these differences could stifle local initiative and encourage uniformity, even when this is clearly inefficient. Secondly, the clients of services may differ across jurisdictions. For example, an increase in the aged proportion of the population in a local government area can affect the measured efficiency of aged community services. Finally, organizations may face different input prices (even when these can be accurately measured) or operate at different scales of operation. For instance, it is to a service provider's advantage to ensure its operations are of optimal size: that is, neither too small if there are increasing returns to scale, nor too large, if there are decreasing returns to scale. Clearly, an appropriate performance framework should take account of factors which affect a local government's measured efficiency.

The final problem is that the framework defined above effectively serves to 'disaggregate' performance. This makes the job of selecting and calculating partial performance measures more tractable. For example, it is possible to incorporate both qualitative and quantitative aspects of service quality, and incorporate partial measures of efficiency, such as outputs per unit of input. Yet it is also obvious that local governments are multi-dimensional entities: a single measure is unlikely to reflect the complexity of decision making or the scope of a council's entire activities. Furthermore, even when individual measures are combined using some weighting system, the resultant composite measure is ultimately arbitrary, and unlikely to be replicated in any systematic manner. A related issue is that the process of 'disaggregation' of performance often serves to introduce some difficulties into the process of performance assessment. For example, the division between efficiency, an essentially inward looking form of measurement of the council's own operations, and effectiveness, an outward perspective to the impact of services upon the community, has caused some confusion (Epstein 1992, p. 167). However, on this point the Industry Commission (1997, p. 103) maintained that:

> There can be debate about whether various indicators measure effectiveness or efficiency, but the classification adopted is not crucial to the value of having an overall framework which serves to ensure that all aspects of performance are assessed in an integrated way. The same types of indicators will always be relevant.

Notwithstanding the complexities of performance measurement in the local government context, as we have seen numerous pressures exist (and are likely to continue) which oblige the local government sector to provide transparent assessments of the efficiency of its operations. The use of frontier efficiency measurement techniques represents a theoretically well developed and statistically advanced method of determining both the absolute and relative economic efficiencies of particular local government jurisdictions. We now examine this methodology in some detail.

4.3 THE THEORY OF MICROECONOMIC EFFICIENCY MEASUREMENT

As we have seen in Chapter 1, economists have developed three main measures of efficiency. First, technical or productive efficiency refers to the use of productive resources in the most technologically efficient manner. Put differently, technical efficiency implies the maximum possible output from a given set of inputs. In cost terms, this means that an organization should produce a specified level of output in the cheapest possible manner. Second, allocative efficiency refers to the distribution of productive resources amongst alternative uses so as to produce the optimal mix of output. In other words, allocative efficiency is concerned with choosing between the different technically efficient combinations of outputs. Taken together, allocative efficiency and technical efficiency determine the degree of economic efficiency. Thus, if an agency uses its resources completely allocatively and technically efficiently, then it can be said to have achieved total economic efficiency. Alternatively, to the extent that either allocative or technical inefficiency is present, then the organization will be operating at less than total economic efficiency.

Third, and in contrast to both allocative efficiency and technical efficiency, dynamic efficiency is a much less precise concept. In general, dynamic efficiency refers to the economically efficient usage of scarce resources through time and thus embraces allocative and technical efficiency in an intertemporal dimension.

The empirical measurement of economic efficiency centers on determining the extent of either allocative efficiency or technical efficiency or both in a given organization or a given industry. Economists have employed production possibility frontiers, production functions and cost functions in their attempts to measure efficiency in actual organizations and industries. Production possibility frontiers map a locus of potentially technically efficient output combinations that an organization is capable of producing at any point in time. To the extent that an organization fails to achieve an output combination on its production possibility frontier, and falls beneath this frontier, it can be said to be technically inefficient. Similarly, to the extent to which it produces some combination of goods and services on its production frontier, but which do not coincide with the wants of its clients (usually expressed in terms of the prices they are willing to pay), it can be said to be allocatively inefficient. Production functions provide an analogous means of relating inputs to outputs in a production process by including input prices. Cost functions transform the quantitative physical information in production frontiers into monetary values. Cost functions can thus convey information about the allocative and technical efficiencies of organizations in pecuniary terms.

Accordingly, if we can determine production frontiers, production functions, or cost functions that represent total economic efficiency using the best currently known production techniques, then we can use this idealized yardstick to evaluate the economic performance of actual organizations and industries. By comparing the actual behavior of organizations against the idealized benchmark of economic efficiency we can determine the degree of economic efficiency exhibited by some real-world agency. One approach to establishing this benchmark is the use of least squares econometric techniques (LS) whereby a line of best fit establishes an average level of performance. Another is to use only organizations that are operating at the frontier as the standard of performance. This general approach to efficiency measurement has been termed the 'deterministic frontier approach' (DFA). However, it may well be that deviation away from a given efficiency frontier may be due not to inefficiency by the organization in question but rather to external factors beyond its control. This has led to the development of the 'stochastic frontier approach' (SFA) which seeks to take these external factors into account when estimating the efficiency of a given real-world organization.

In contrast to both the DFA and SFA techniques, which attempt to determine the *absolute* economic efficiency of organizations against some given benchmark of efficiency, the 'data envelopment analysis' (DEA) approach seeks to evaluate the efficiency of an organization *relative* to other organizations in the same industry. DEA thus calculates the economic efficiency of a given organization relative to the performance of other organizations producing the same good or service rather than against an idealized standard of performance. An important variant of the DEA methodology sometimes employed in the analysis of economic efficiency in the public sector is known as the 'free-disposal hull' (FDH) approach. This technique has the advantage of being able to determine existing best practice in an industry on the basis of fewer observations and it does not assume the existence of many different ways of producing some good or service. We will return to these five different methods of measuring efficiency in our discussion of the empirical measurement of inefficiency in local public services.

In essence, the literature on frontier production and cost functions and the calculation of efficiency measures begins with Farrell (1957). Whilst the empirical estimation of production functions had begun long before Farrell's (1957) paper, this made the first tentative steps in adapting these to rigorous microeconomic analysis.

In parenthesis for technically inclined readers, Farrell's (1957) argument is contained in Figure 4.2.

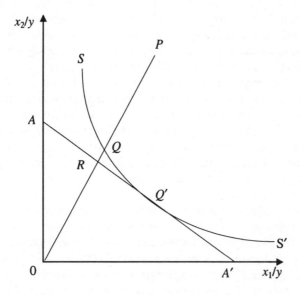

Figure 4.2   Technical, allocative and productive efficiency

Here two inputs, x_1 and x_2, are utilized to produce a single output y, so that the production frontier is $y = f(x_1, x_2)$. If we assume constant returns to scale (where the relationship between output y and inputs x_1 and x_2 does not change as the inputs increase), then $1 = f(x_1/y, x_2/y)$. The isoquant of the fully efficient firm SS' permits the measurement of technical efficiency. An isoquant is a locus of points representing a given level of output (say, 100 units of y) using different combinations of the two inputs x_1 and x_2.

Now, for a given firm using quantities of inputs (x_1^*, x_2^*) defined by point P $(x_1^*/y, x_1^*/y)$ to produce a unit of output y^*, the level of technical efficiency, or the ability of a firm to maximize output from a given set of inputs, may be defined as the ratio OQ/OP which measures the proportion of (x_1, x_2) actually necessary to produce y^*. Thus 1 minus OQ/OP, the technical inefficiency of the firm, measures the proportion by which (x_1^*, x_2^*) could be reduced (holding the input ratio x_1/x_2 constant) without reducing output. It also measures the possible reduction in the cost of producing y^*. Finally, given constant returns to scale, it roughly estimates the proportion by which output could be increased, holding (x_1^*, x_2^*) constant. Point Q, on the other hand, is technically efficient since it already lies on the efficient isoquant.

If the input price ratio AA' (which computes the prices of inputs x_1 and x_2) is known, then allocative efficiency (referred to by Farrell (1957) as price efficiency), or the ability of a firm to use these inputs in optimal proportions, given the respective prices at point P, is the ratio OR/OQ, and correspondingly the allocative inefficiency is 1 minus OR/OQ, where the distance RQ is the reduction in production costs which would occur if production occurred at Q' – the allocatively and technically efficient point, rather than Q – the technically efficient, but allocatively inefficient point. Hence, total economic efficiency (referred to by Farrell (1957) as overall efficiency) is the ratio OR/OP, and total inefficiency is 1 minus OR/OP which is the possible reduction in cost from moving from P (the observed point) to Q' (the cost minimizing point); the cost reduction achievable is the distance RP. As we have seen, technical efficiency can be decomposed as the product of technical and allocative efficiency; and total (or productive) inefficiency can be decomposed roughly as the sum of technical and allocative inefficiency.

Of course, these measures of efficiency have been defined on the assumption that the standard of efficient production is known. Farrell (1957) suggested the use of several known and observable production techniques to estimate this isoquant. It is this suggestion that efficiency could be measured against an idealized frontier isoquant that then forms the basis of subsequent empirical analysis. More detailed analyses of the theoretical foundations of microeconomic efficiency measurement may be found in Färe et al. (1994) and Coelli et al. (1997).

4.4   REVIEW OF EFFICIENCY MEASUREMENT TECHNIQUES

As discussed earlier, five principal methods have been used to measure efficiency in local government. These are: (i) least squares (LS) econometric production models; (ii) the deterministic frontier approach (DFA); (iii) the stochastic frontier approach (SFA); (iv) the data envelopment analysis or DEA approach; and (v) free-disposal hull or FDH approach. Summary properties of these five methods are provided in Table 4.1 following Coelli et al. (1997).

To start with, for much of the history of production analysis, at least since Cobb and Douglas first ran ordinary regressions, one focus of analysis has been on traditional least squares (LS) econometric production models by which estimated functions of interest pass through the data. For example, in a cost function, costs are specified as the dependent variable in a regression against output quantities and input prices, while for a profit function approach profits are regressed against input and output prices. While no strict behavioral assumptions are made in regard to production functions, the behavioral assumption underlying the specification of a cost function is cost minimization, while an assumption of profit maximization is made for profit functions.

Irrespective of the model actually specified, the line of best fit always defines the standard of performance against which all organizations within a sample are compared. For example, most studies use a simple Cobb Douglas or translog cost function to estimate the efficiency of local authorities. The efficiency measures themselves are calculated from the residuals of the regression equations, with positive and negative residuals indicating authorities with costs that were higher or lower than the predictions associated with the cost function.

Unfortunately, while least squares econometric production models (LS) are well within the computational abilities of most researchers and all statistical programs, for the purposes of efficiency measurement the resulting *average* function can be a misleading indicator of efficient production possibilities in both theory and practice. In practice, the emphasis on average performance serves to institutionalize inefficiency: that is, the average standard acts as a disincentive to improvements in performance. And in theory the concept of an average production function is largely inconsistent with the notion of any form of maximizing behavior that may be expected to hold within most, if not all, production processes.

Table 4.1 Summary of the properties of the five methods

	LS	DFA	SFA	DEA and FDH
Is the method parametric or non-parametric?	Parametric	Parametric	Parametric	Non-parametric
Is the method stochastic or non-stochastic?	Stochastic	Non-stochastic	Stochastic	Non-stochastic
What behavioral assumptions are made?	Production function - none, cost function - cost minimization, profit function - profit maximization	Production function - none, cost function - cost minimization, profit function - profit maximization	Production function - none, cost function - cost minimization, profit function - profit maximization	None

What data is required variables?	Production function – input and output quantities, cost function – costs, output quantities and input prices, profit function – profit and input and output prices.	Production function – input and output quantities, cost function – costs, output quantities and input prices, profit function – profit and input and output prices.	Production function – input and output quantities, cost function – costs, output quantities and input prices, profit function – profit and input and output prices.	Standard – input and output quantities, cost efficiency – input and output quantities and input prices, profit efficiency – input and output quantities and prices.
What types of data can be examined?	Time-series, cross-section and panel data.	Cross-section and panel data.	Cross-section and panel data.	Cross-section and panel data.
What types of efficiency can be measured?	Scale and scope efficiency.	Technical and allocative efficiency.	Technical and allocative efficiency.	Technical, allocative and scale efficiency.

As a result of this fundamental limitation, the focus of the more recent development of efficiency measurement has been on the evocative term frontier. That is, interest is now placed upon extreme values and bounding functions, rather than those of central tendency and best fit. Thus, production may take place below or on the frontier, but at no points beyond it. This is the primary departure point from the LS approach to efficiency measurement and has been manifested in both the statistical (DFA and SFA) and non-statistical (DEA and FDH) approaches to efficiency measurement. It is also a logical extension since frontier performance comparison flows directly from the definition of a production function itself. Put simply, if production is a process of physical transformation whereby inputs are translated into outputs, then the production function should be interpreted as a purely technical relationship which defines efficient transformation possibilities, given the feasible set of technology. Specified rates of output thereby correspond to given factor inputs and they may be said to represent solutions to a technical maximization problem.

In the process of econometric analysis being brought to bear on the investigation of the structure of economic frontiers, a number of broad distinctions or approaches have also been made. The first fundamental distinction is between statistical and non-statistical approaches to production frontiers. Following Schmidt (1985, p. 295), 'a statistical approach depends on assumptions about the stochastic properties of the data, while a non-statistical approach does not'. Within this distinction, Schmidt (1985, p. 295) argues that differences may be reflected as 'Ways that are trivial (e.g. econometrician speaks of "estimating" inefficiency while a management scientist speaks of "measuring" it) and in some ways that are not (e.g. a statistical analysis should yield standard errors for its estimates, while a non-statistical analysis cannot).'

The second fundamental distinction is between the econometric approach to the construction of frontiers (DFA and SFA) and what may be termed the mathematical programming approach (DEA and FDH). As a general rule, the econometric approach represents a significant modification to conventional econometrics, whilst the mathematical programming approach as an inherently bounding technique requires little or no modification in the analysis of production frontiers. The two approaches also use different techniques to envelop data, and therefore make different accommodations for random noise and for flexibility in the structure of the production technology. And all other things being equal, the econometric approach is stochastic, attempting to distinguish the effects of random noise from the effect of inefficiency, and parametric, combining the effects of a unspecified functional form with inefficiency, whilst the mathematical approach is non-stochastic and non-parametric. These differences between the two approaches serve as a suitable framework for future discussion, although, and as we shall see, attempts have been made to make the econometric approach more flexible in its parametric structure, and the programming approach more stochastic.

First, the econometric approach is stochastic and thus noise can be separated from the inefficiency measure while the mathematical approach is non-stochastic (or deterministic) and it is impossible to clearly distinguish between noise and inefficiency. The exception to the stochastic properties of the econometric approach (as epitomized in the SFA) is the earlier work encompassed in the deterministic frontier approach (DFA). In that instance, all deviation from the estimated frontier is interpreted as inefficiency, and no allowance is made for either measurement or misspecification error. However, apart from this distinction the DFA and SFA are remarkably similar since as econometric techniques both can be employed to conduct conventional tests of hypotheses.

Second, the econometric approach is parametric, thus suggesting that a functional form is required and thereby risks the problem of specification error. This holds for both the DFA and SFA methods. This is an important consideration because in many contexts the normal axioms of productive activity (cost minimization, profit maximization, and so on.) may break down. Contrary to this the mathematical approaches (namely DEA and FDH) are non-parametric, and thus largely avoid the problem of misspecification (FDH differs from DEA only in that has even less-restrictive assumptions). This has widened their appeal in public sector applications. However, in order to compute this, a large amount of data is required to ensure that the majority of efficiency points are considered, and as nonstochastic techniques both of these methods are particularly susceptible to measurement error and the presence of outliers.

With the exception of the largely obsolete least squares (LS) and deterministic frontier (DFA) econometric methods, the present section has addressed two separate, though conceptually similar, theoretical approaches to the assessment of efficiency. These are the stochastic frontier approach (SFA) and the mathematical programming DEA approach (including FDH). Whilst the selection of any particular approach is likely to be subject to both theoretical and empirical considerations, it may be useful to summarize the strengths and weaknesses of each technique. The emphasis here is not on selecting a superior theoretical approach, rather it should be emphasized that the SFA and DEA approaches address different questions, serve different purposes and have different informational requirements.

The most commonly used approach, namely DEA, differs from the econometric approaches to efficiency measurement in ways that are both non-parametric and non-stochastic. Thus, no accommodation is made for the types of bias resulting from environmental heterogeneity, external shocks, measurement error, omitted variables, and so on. Consequently, the entire deviation from the frontier is assessed as being the result of inefficiency. This may lead to either, under or over statement of the level of inefficiency, and since it is a non-stochastic technique there is no possible way in which probability statements of the shape and placement of this frontier can be made. In view of erroneous or misleading data, some critics of DEA have questioned the validity and stability of measures of DEA efficiency.

However, there are a number of benefits implicit in the mathematical programming approach that makes it attractive on a theoretical level. Given its non-parametric basis, it is possible to vary considerably the specification of inputs and outputs, the formulation of the production correspondence relating inputs to outputs, and so on. Thus, in cases where the usual axioms of production activity break-down (that is, profit maximization) the programming approach may offer useful insights into the efficiency of these types of industries. This is especially the case with local public sector activities. Similarly, it is entirely possible that the types of data necessary for the statistical approaches are neither available nor desirable, and therefore the imposition of as few restrictions as possible on the data is likely to be most attractive.

The second approach examined, namely the stochastic frontier (SFA), removes some of the limitations of DEA. Its biggest advantage lies in the fact that it introduces a disturbance term representing noise, measurement error, and exogenous shocks beyond the control of the production unit. This in turn permits the decomposition of deviations from the efficient frontier into two components, inefficiency and noise. However, in common with other econometric approaches, an assumption regarding the distribution (usually normal) of this noise must be made along with those required for the inefficiency term and the production technology. The main effect here is that when using the stochastic frontier approach, considerable structure is imposed upon the data from stringent parametric form and distributional assumptions.

Notwithstanding these comments, stochastic frontiers and DEA should be thought of as complementary tools in the analysis of local public sector efficiency. In both cases it is possible to think of the calculated and estimated production frontiers as being the maximal output that can be obtained given a set of input quantities and prices. But it is also possible to think of the maximum as being taken with respect to either those local governments in the sample (as with DEA), or with respect to all local governments that could conceivably exist and still embody the current technology (as with the stochastic frontier). In the first instance, the frontier adheres closely to the notion of best practice efficiency, whereas in the second it refers to an absolute measure of efficiency. Clear advantages thereby accrue to DEA in identifying benchmark local governments and peer groups for comparison, while the stochastic frontier permits the opportunity for direct comparison with other institutional milieus.

4.5 MEASURING EFFICIENCY IN LOCAL SERVICES

As we have seen within the theoretical framework discussed earlier, at least five different approaches have been employed in the analysis of local public sector efficiency. These are: (i) least squares econometric production models (LS); (ii) the deterministic frontier approach (DFA); (iii) the stochastic frontier approach (SFA); (iv) the data envelopment analysis or DEA approach; and (v) the free-disposal hull or FDH approach. Table 4.2 includes details of the various empirical studies using these approaches.

First, as observed earlier some of the earliest work undertaken concerning local government efficiency measurement is within the context of the long-established least squares econometric techniques. In this approach, negative deviations from the line of best fit are interpreted as representing entities that are less efficient than average, while positive deviations represent entities that are more efficient than average. Examples of work in this area include Domberger et al. (1986), Deller et al. (1988) and Deller and Rudnicki (1992). Second, the deterministic frontier approach is an econometric technique which assumes that all deviations from the frontier are the result of inefficiency: that is, inefficiencies are embedded in a strictly one-sided disturbance term. Studies by Bjurek et al. (1990) and De Borger and Kerstens (1996a) have used this approach.

Third, as we have seen the stochastic frontier approach is also an econometric technique, though it assumes a two-component error structure so that the inefficiencies usually follow an asymmetric half-normal distribution and the random errors are normally distributed. Examples of work in this area include Viton (1992), Deller and Halstead (1994) and Vitaliano (1997). Fourth, in line with our earlier comments the DEA approach is a mathematical programming technique which assumes that all deviations from the estimated frontier represent inefficiency. This approach has been applied to local governments by Cook et al. (1990), Rouse et al. (1995), and Worthington (1999). Finally, as we have noted earlier the FDH approach is a variant of DEA that allows the assumptions concerning the production technology to be kept to a minimum. Examples of work using this approach include Tulkens (1993), De Borger et al. (1994), and De Borger and Kerstens (1996b).

Table 4.2 Applications in the local public sector

Author(s)	Methodology[a]	Sample[b]	Inputs, outputs, explanatory variables[c]	Analytical technique	Main findings
Domberger et al. (1986)	LS	305 UK local authorities, 1983–85.	Total costs of refuse collection. Frequency of collection, method of pickup, density of units, distance to disposal points, percentage of household units, amount of waste paper reclaimed, number of abandoned vehicles collected and bottle-banks operated, average earnings of manual workers, dummy variable for tendered contract or 'in-house' services.	Interpretation of parameter estimates, distributional analysis.	Costs significantly lower for tendered collection services. Tendering results in a significant improvement in efficiency.
Deller, Chicoine and Walzer (1988)	LS	1,799 Illinois, Minnesota, Ohio and Wisconsin municipalities, 1982.	Total costs, hourly wage rates, input prices for materials and operations, regional cost-of-living index, replacement prices for earth graders and trucks, index of utilization and intergovernmental road aid. Miles of paved, aggregated surface, and low and high bituminous surface roads.	Interpretation of parameter estimates.	Joint use of inputs produces lower overall costs, emphasis on local government consolidation or contract tendering to capture scale economies.

| Charnes, Cooper and Li (1989) | DEA | 28 Chinese cities, 1983–84. | Number of industrial staff and workers, amount of 'circulating' capital and total annual wage bill, investment on capital construction of state-owned units and acquisition of machinery and fixed assets for collective units. Gross industrial output value, profits and taxes generated by state-owned enterprises, retail sales. | Descriptive analysis across time and interpretation of scale economies. | DEA as a tool to identify technical inefficiencies in centrally-planned cities. |
| Bjurek, Hjalmarsson and Førsund (1990) | DEA and DFA | 392–462 Swedish local social insurance offices, 1974–84. | Number of working days, capital (proxied by office space and computer terminals). Income evaluation assessments, sickness reports and control minor reimbursements of personal outlays, evaluation of pension and social insurance payments. | Descriptive and diagrammatic analysis. | Differences in efficiency due to different scale and transformation properties. |

Table 4.2 continued

Author(s)	Methodology[a]	Sample[b]	Inputs, outputs, explanatory variables[c]	Analytical technique	Main findings
Cook, Roll and Kazakov (1990)	DEA	244 Ontario highway maintenance patrols, 1990.	Maintenance and capital expenditures, climatic factor. Area served factor (including length of road section, shoulder width, road service type, winter operations and number of lanes), average traffic served, pavement rating change factor and accident prevention factor (number of road accidents).	Descriptive analysis, comparison of efficiency across privatized/non-privatized patrols.	Use of DEA for peer group comparisons.
Grosskopf and Yaisawarng (1990)	DEA	49 Californian municipalities, 1982,	Aggregate total and variable costs. Capital outlays, police and fire employment.	Interpretation of parameter estimates and efficiency indexes.	Economies of scope, and therefore case for specialization or diversification.

90

Hayes and Chang (1990)	SFA	191 U.S. municipalities, 1982.	Total costs (fire, police and refuse collection), cost of capital (municipal bond rating), cost of labor (average salary), percentage of owner-occupied housing, minority households, population aged over 25 tears, and fir rating. Number of police, fire and refuse collection employees.	Descriptive analysis, ANOVA, Median and Kruskal-Wallis tests of efficiency between mayor–council and city manager-type municipalities.	No difference in the efficiency of different municipal government structures.
Cook, Kazakov, Roll and Seiford (1991)	DEA	244 Ontario highway maintenance patrols, 1990.	Maintenance and capital expenditures, climatic factor. Area served factor (including length of road section, shoulder width, road service type, winter operations and number of lanes), average traffic served, pavement rating change factor and accident prevention factor (number of road accidents).	Descriptive analysis and comparison of efficiency scores across privatized/non-privatized patrols and traffic level.	Use of DEA in not-for-profit setting.

91

Table 4.2 continued

Author(s)	Methodology[a]	Sample[b]	Inputs, outputs, explanatory variables[c]	Analytical technique	Main findings
Deller and Nelson (1991)	DEA	446 Illinois, Minnesota and Wisconsin municipalities, 1990.	Number of full-time equivalent labor, road graders, single-axle trucks, amount of purchased surface material, price of labor (average annual salary), price of capital (fixed proportion of depreciated capital values), price of surfacing material (estimates of material requirements for re-surfacing projects), regional cost-of-living indexes. Miles of gravel, and low and high bituminous roads.	Descriptive analysis on sample disaggregated by mileage range, Anova, Wilcoxon, van der Waerden and Savage tests of efficiency equality across mileage ranges.	Increases in jurisdictional size associated with improvements in efficiency.

Study	Method	Data	Inputs and outputs	Analysis	Comments
Bjurek, Kjulin and Gustafsson (1992)	DEA	194 Swedish public day-care centers, 1988–89.	Number of hours worked by pre-school teachers, nursery nurses and cooking and cleaning personnel, size of center in square meters. Full-time equivalent capacity, 0–2 years and 3–6 years. Days worked by substitute teachers and nurses; mean parental income, years of experience of center director, index of director cooperation.	Second-stage tobit regression.	DEA assessment of efficiency in bureaucratically-controlled units. Role of administrative staff in efficiency.
Chang and Kao (1992)	DEA	5 Taipei municipal bus firms, 1956–88.	Capital (number of buses in operation), number of full-time equivalent labor, amount of diesel fuel used. Vehicle kilometers, revenue, number of bus traffic trips on routes.	Descriptive analysis and Wilcoxon, Mann-Whitney tests of efficiency differences over time and private/public firms.	Publicly owned bus firms increased efficiency after liberalization of bus routes.

Table 4.2 continued

Author(s)	Methodology[a]	Sample[b]	Inputs, outputs, explanatory variables[c]	Analytical technique	Main findings
Deller (1992)	SFA	1,319 Illinois, Minnesota and Wisconsin municipal areas, 1982.	Number of full-time equivalent labor, road graders, single-axle trucks, amount of purchased surface material, price of labor (average annual salary), price of capital (fixed proportion of depreciated capital values), price of surfacing material (estimates of material requirements for re-surfacing projects), regional cost-of-living indexes. Miles of gravel, and low and high bituminous roads.	Descriptive analysis on sample disaggregated by mileage range, Anova, Wilcoxon, van der Waerden and Savage tests of efficiency equality across mileage ranges.	Need for productive efficiency of local government due to federal policy and fiscal pressures.
Deller and Rudnicki (1992)	LS and SFA	147 Maine public elementary schools, 1985–89.	Average total school expenditure costs, average daily attendance, male and female teacher salaries, administration expenses per pupil, operations and maintenance expenditures per pupil. Cumulative test achievement scores.	Interpretation of parameter estimates, second-stage OLS regression on school size.	Managerial inefficiencies may be incorrectly attributed to size economies. Consolidation may be inappropriate.

Deller, Nelson and Walzer (1992)	SFA	435 Illinois, Minnesota and Wisconsin municipal areas, 1982.	Number of full-time equivalent labor, road graders, single-axle trucks, amount of purchased surface material, price of labor (average annual salary), price of capital (fixed proportion of depreciated capital values), price of surfacing material (estimates of material requirements for re-surfacing projects), regional cost-of-living indexes. Miles of gravel, and low and high bituminous roads.	Disaggregation of efficiency index across township road size.	High cost inefficiencies, gains in efficiency largely possible through input consolidation.
Hjalmarsson and Veiderpass (1992)	DEA	285 Swedish retail electricity distributors, 1985.	Hours worked by all employees, kilometers of low-voltage and high-voltage electricity power lines, total transformer capacity. Consumption of low-voltage and high-voltage electricity, numbers of low-voltage and high-voltage electricity customers.	Descriptive analysis.	Impact of not-for-profit constraints on efficiency of municipal distributors, modest difference between public and private firms.

Table 4.2 continued

Author(s)	Methodology[a]	Sample[b]	Inputs, outputs, explanatory variables[c]	Analytical technique	Main findings
Viton (1992)	SFA	289 U.S. multi-modal transit firms, 1984–1986.	Total operating expenses. Motorbus, rail, streetcar, trolleybus vehicle miles, hourly wage rates, ratio of peak operating fleet to base operating period, speed of transport (ratio of vehicle-miles to vehicle-hours), dummy variable for transport-type.	Interpretation of parameter estimates, implied impact of single-firm municipal consolidation.	Economies of scope exhausted before scale economies are attained. Consolidation will reduce cost only in limited circumstances.
Tulkens (1993)	FDH	Brussels buses, streetcars and subway, 1977–89.	Total hours of labor worked, energy (in kWh), number of seat-vehicles. Number of monthly seat-kilometers.	Descriptive analysis over time.	Application of efficiency concepts to transportation efficiency.

Vanden Eeckaut, Tulkens and Jamar (1993)	FDH and DEA	235 Belgian municipalities, 1986.	Total costs, Total population, length of roads in municipality, numbers of persons aged over 65 years, beneficiaries of minimal subsistence grants, crimes reported, students enrolled in local primary schools. Dummy variables for socialist, liberal, anti-socialist, local, and coalition dominated municipalities.	Disaggregation of efficiency scores across political majorities.	Multi-party, local coalition-led municipalities less efficient than single-party, national led ones.
Cook, Kazakov and Roll (1993)	DEA	62 Ontario highway maintenance patrols, 1990.	Maintenance and capital expenditures, climatic factor. Area served factor (including length of road section, shoulder width, road service type, winter operations and number of lanes), average traffic served, pavement rating change factor and accident prevention factor (number of road accidents).	Descriptive analysis and comparison of efficiency scores across privatized/non-privatized patrols and traffic level.	Unbounded DEA will not satisfactorily account for real-life situations.

Table 4.2 continued

Author(s)	Methodology[a]	Sample[b]	Inputs, outputs, explanatory variables[c]	Analytical technique	Main findings
De Borger, Kerstens, Moesen and Vanneste (1994)	FDH	589 Belgian municipalities, 1985.	Number of white-collar and blue-collar municipal employees, capital stock (proxied by surface area of municipal owned buildings). Municipal road surface, numbers of beneficiaries of minimal subsistence grants, students enrolled in local primary schools, surface of area of public recreational facilities, ratio of non-residents to residents in municipality. Dummy variable for liberal or socialist party as ruling coalition, average personal income, block grants, proportion of population with higher education, total population.	Descriptive analysis, second-stage tobit regression.	Scale and fiscal revenue capacity are important determinants of efficiency.

Study	Method	Sample	Inputs/Outputs	Analysis	Findings
Deller and Halstead (1994)	SFA	104 Maine, New Hampshire and Vermont municipalities, 1987.	Total road costs, labor wages, price of grader and single-axle-dump truck, cost of capital (weighted average of new capital items by municipal bond interest rate). Miles of roads under town jurisdiction. Chief engineers formal training, educational level, years of experience and age.	Interpretation of parameter estimates, Anova, Wilcoxon, van der Waerden and Savage tests of efficiency equality across characteristics of chief engineer.	Placing of rural road maintenance in municipalities highly-inefficient. Positive outcomes from higher levels of training.
Rouse, Putterill and Ryan (1995)	DEA	62 New Zealand territorial local authorities, 1993–94.	Total expenditure on reseals, rehabilitation, and general maintenance, index of environmental factors. Kilometers of road resealed and rehabilitated, general maintenance expenditure, annual vehicle kilometers, roughness index for urban and rural roads, index of road surface defects.	Interpretation of efficiency scores across a number of input-output specifications.	Insights into local authority efficiency by partitioning measures across efficiency, effectiveness and economy.

Table 4.2 continued

Author(s)	Methodology[a]	Sample[b]	Inputs, outputs, explanatory variables[c]	Analytical technique	Main findings
De Borger and Kerstens (1996a)	FDH, DEA, DFA and SFA.	589 Belgian local governments, 1985.	Total expenditure. Number of beneficiaries of minimal subsistence grants and students enlisted in local primary schools, surface area of public recreational facilities, total population and proportion of population over 65 years. Per capita personal income, municipal property tax rate, per capita block grants, number of coalition parties in government, dummy variable for liberal or socialist ruling party, proportion of adults with primary education as highest qualification, population density.	Descriptive analysis, Spearman and Pearson correlation coefficients between efficiency measures, second-stage tobit regression.	Rank correlation between parametric and nonparametric measures low. Local tax rates and education influence efficiency positively, per capita grants and income negatively.

Study	Method	Data	Variables	Analysis	Findings
De Borger and Kerstens (1996b)	FDH	589 Belgian local governments, 1985.	Total municipal expenditures. Surface of municipal roads, number of beneficiaries of minimal subsistence grants, students enrolled in local primary schools, surface area of public recreational facilities, total population and proportion of population aged over 65 years. Municipal property tax rate, per capita block grants, number of coalition parties in government, dummy variable for liberal or socialist ruling party, proportion of adults with higher education as highest qualification.	Descriptive analysis, second-stage tobit regression.	Substantial differences in inefficiency measures possible. Fiscal revenue capacity and grants an important determinant of efficiency.
Vitaliano (1997)	SFA	235 U.S. public libraries, 1992.	Total costs (excluding capital equipment), librarian starting salary wage rate, director's salary wage rate. Total circulation of books and serials, weekly hours of operation, number of books added to collection each year. Dummy variable for municipal or private not-for-profit library, percentage of local funding, gifts and investments, population served.	Second-stage tobit regression.	Government-run libraries are more inefficient than private not-for-profits. Donated resources and reliance on local taxation linked to less inefficiency.

Table 4.2 continued

Author(s)	Methodology[a]	Sample[b]	Inputs, outputs, explanatory variables[c]	Analytical technique	Main findings
Vitaliano (1998)	DEA	184 New York state public libraries, 1992.	Total holdings (books, audio-visual, maps, etc.), hours of operation, new books purchased, total serial subscriptions. Total circulation, reference questions answered. Manager and director salaries, public or association control (city, town, village, other), population.	Second-stage tobit regression.	Association libraries relatively more efficient. Dominant determinant of inefficiency are excessive opening hours.
Worthington (1999)	DEA	168 NSW local government libraries, 1993.	Population, area, proportion of population NESB, aged, or student, proportion of non-residential borrowers, socio-economic index, gross library expenditure. Library issues. Library expenditure and issues per capita, geographic catgories.	Spearman rank correlation amongst efficiency indexes. Second-stage logistic regression.	Case for exogenous factors and scale effects to be incorporated into DEA.

| Worthington (2000) | SFA and DEA | 177 NSW local governments, 1993. | Full-time equivalent employees, other physical (materials and plant) and financial (excluding depreciation) expenses. Population, properties receiving domestic waste management, sewerage and water services, length of urban, sealed rural and unsealed rural roads. Grants dependence, debt service ratio, current assets, current ratio, staff per 1,000 capita, average residential rate. | Second-stage tobit regression, non-parametric tests of efficiency differences. | Identification of empirical differences between SFA and DEA techniques. |

Table 4.2 continued

Author(s)	Methodology[a]	Sample[b]	Inputs, outputs, explanatory variables[c]	Analytical technique	Main findings
Worthington and Dollery (2000)	DEA	166 NSW local governments, 1993	Library services (library expenditure), waste management services (collection expenditure) and planning and regulatory services (planning and legal expenditure, staff). Library services (library issues), waste management services (garbage and recyclables collected) and planning and regulatory services (building and development approvals determined).	Second-stage tobit regression.	Linkage between grant mechanism and local government efficiency.

Notes:
(a) DEA – data envelopment analysis; FDH – free-disposal hull; SFA – stochastic frontier approach; DFA – deterministic frontier approach; LS – least squares econometric method.

(b) Singular dates represent calendar or financial year cross-sections, intervals represent time-series.

(c) Ranked in order by paragraph.

A number of studies have used stochastic frontiers (either cost or production) to analyze the efficiency of the local public sector. For example, Hayes and Chang (1990) used a sample of 191 US municipalities to test efficiency differences between 'city manager' and 'mayor–council' forms of government. Formulating a cost frontier, they obtained total costs for three categories of local public sector output (fire, police and refuse collection) and specified outputs in terms of the number of respective employees. The price of capital was proxied by the municipalities' bond rating and the price of labor by the average municipal employee's salary. They found that the mean cost efficiency of mayor–council municipalities (84.78 per cent) was higher than that of city manager type councils (81.21 per cent). Put differently, mayor–council municipalities could reduce costs by 15.22 per cent and produce the same level of output, while city manager councils would need to reduce total costs by 18.79 per cent to become purely cost efficient.

Subsequent to Hayes and Chang (1990), a number of studies also examined municipal service efficiency employing stochastic frontiers. Using this approach, Steven Deller made an extended inquiry into the efficiency of municipal road services in Illinois, Minnesota and Wisconsin (Deller and Nelson 1991; Deller 1992; Deller et al. 1992) and Maine, New Hampshire and Vermont (Deller and Halstead 1994). In the latter study a cost frontier was used, with the cost of capital proxied by the weighted average of new capital items, the price of labor by wages, and output by the length of roads under municipal jurisdiction. In the former studies, standard production frontiers were employed. In these cases there was an attempt to incorporate quality considerations into municipal output, with roads defined as being gravel, or low -or high-volume bituminous roads. Regional cost-of-living indexes were also included. The resultant empirical evidence indicated *mutatis mutandis* that current expenditures on rural low-volume road service were unnecessarily high because of managerial inefficiencies: in particular, 'efficiency measurements suggested that costs could be reduced, on average, to 45 percent of current levels' (Deller et al. 1992, p. 364).

An increasing number of studies have employed the non-parametric technique of data envelopment analysis to investigate local public sector efficiency. Cook et al. (1990) used DEA to measure the relative efficiency of Ontario's highway maintenance patrols. The inputs in this case were patrol maintenance and capital expenditures (along with an allowance for environmental factors) and the outputs were stipulated in terms of the characteristics of the roads serviced and an accident prevention factor. The resulting efficiency scores were then used to classify maintenance patrols into a number of classes for analytical purposes. One finding was that the technical efficiency of patrols where the proportion of 'privatized' work was 20 per cent or more was higher than those patrols with less than 20 per cent of privatized work.

An identical theoretical framework and sample was subsequently employed in Cook et al. (1991) and Cook et al. (1993). Bjurek et al. (1992) examined the technical and scale efficiency of Swedish public day-care centers. Inputs were defined in terms of the number of hours worked by pre-school teachers, nurses and cooking and cleaning staff, and outputs denominated by the capacity of children, aged up to two years, and from three to six years. Hjalmarsson and Veiderpass (1992) examined the efficiency of 285 Swedish retail electricity distributors. Inputs included the discretionary levels of labor, and the non-discretionary length of transmission lines and transformer capacity, and the outputs were specified in terms of both volume of kilowatts and the number of customers. Hjalmarsson and Veiderpass (1992) found only modest efficiency differences between public and private electricity distributors.

DEA has also been used in a study of New Zealand local authority road maintenance by Rouse et al. (1995). Conceptually very similar to the earlier stochastic frontier work of Deller (1992) and the non-parametric approaches of Cook et al. (1990) and Cook et al. (1991), the study incorporated environmental factors as major cost and process drivers. The empirical analysis contained an index of road surface defects and a measure of 'roughness' for both urban and rural roads. For the measures obtained under the assumption of variable returns to scale, 39 of a possible 62 transport local authorities were judged to be 100 per cent technically efficient, with 12 below 70 per cent, and the remainder between 70 and 100 per cent efficiency.

More recent work has employed the FDH approach to efficiency measurement, and has been based largely on studies of Belgian municipalities, with a focus on cost efficiency. De Borger and Kerstens (1996, p. 149) argue that this approach is closely related to the nature of the data:

> A consequence of the Belgian institutional framework is that the sample does not contain input price variability. There is no wage flexibility as salary scales of municipal personnel are completely fixed. Moreover, all municipalities have access to the same capital market, and in fact obtain most of their funds from one and the same specialized financial institution. Therefore, the assumption of identical input prices across municipalities may not be too unreasonable. Consequently, throughout the analysis we focus on the measurement of cost efficiency.

Within this approach, and those followed by Vanden Eeckaut et al. (1993) and De Borger and Kerstens (1996a, 1996b), the inputs into the FDH model are total municipal expenditures. The outputs are denoted in terms of variables intended to reflect the responsibilities of Belgian municipal governments. These include total population, length of roads, number of persons aged over 65 years, those living on subsistence grants, the number of students enrolled in local public schools, and the maintenance of recreational facilities. The results indicate that mean relative cost efficiency scores range from 0.57 to 0.94. Put simply, inputs (and therefore costs) could be reduced anywhere from 6 per cent to 43 per cent across Belgian councils. Moreover, by using FDH the measure of performance is drawn from the actual sample so that cost efficient councils can easily be identified for benchmarking. In addition, productive efficiency frameworks have also been used to test the relative efficiency of the same sample of Belgian municipalities. De Borger et al. (1994) employed an analogous conceptualization of outputs, although inputs were measured in terms of white -and blue-collar employee and capital stock (proxied by the surface area of municipal-owned buildings). Significantly, De Borger and Kerstens (1996a), amongst others, attempt to incorporate the multiple-outputs produced by Belgian municipal governments into a single measure of efficiency. This stands in stark contrast to the other work on public sector efficiency which focused on specific aspects of service provision, such as roads, schools, welfare services and transportation (see, for example, Bjurek et al. 1992; Tulkens 1993; and Rouse et al. 1995).

At least three aspects of the efficiency measurement of local public services deserve further attention. These are: (i) the appropriateness and sensitivity of efficiency measures to the postulated reference technology, (ii) the appropriate treatment of non-discretionary inputs/outputs in local public services, and (iii) the choice of input or output orientation in efficiency measures. First, several studies have analyzed the efficiency of local governments using a broad variety of reference technologies (see, for instance, Bjurek et al. 1990; Vanden Eeckaut et al. 1993 and De Borger and Kerstens 1996a). In a study of Belgian municipalities, De Borger and Kerstens (1996a) used both parametric (deterministic and stochastic frontiers) and non-parametric (FDH and DEA) methods to evaluate the sensitivity of the rankings of municipalities with respect to the underlying reference technology. They observed that not only may the shape of the efficiency distribution be affected by the use of different approaches, but that they can also alter the implied rankings of individual observations. Using Spearman rank correlation and Pearson product moment correlation coefficients, they demonstrated that statistically significant differences existed between FDH and DEA, whilst 'DEA has a slightly higher similarity in ranking relative to the (parametric approaches)' (De Borger and Kerstens 1996a, p. 159). The estimated range of mean efficiency scores also was quite large, with cost efficiency measures between 0.59 and 0.83. Using these observations, De Borger and Kerstens (1996a, p. 167) concluded, 'it would seem prudent to analyze efficiency questions using a broad variety of methods to check the robustness of the results'.

Vanden Eeckaut et al. (1993) undertook a similar comparison. However, their results were disaggregated on the basis of expenditure classifications, and thereby indicate how consistency between rankings may vary over the sample. Comparing FDH and DEA under variable returns to scale, constant returns to scale and non-increasing returns to scale assumptions, they found that all three DEA methods yielded similar results for large expenditure class municipalities. Some 15 to 22 per cent were found to be cost efficient. For the second expenditure class some divergence between the methods was found, and accordingly, concordant rankings and mean efficiency scores were once again established.

Second, the standard Charnes et al. (1978) and Banker et al (1984) model formulations implicitly assumed that all inputs and outputs are discretionary (that is, controlled by the management of each municipality and varied at its discretion). In most circumstances we would expect that this assumption would not hold for the local public sector. For example, in a technical efficiency formulation the geographic, environmental and demographic characteristics of a given municipal area are important inputs into the process of providing local public services, yet they are also exogenously fixed and thereby non-discretionary. Alternatively, in a cost efficiency model (such as those employed by De Borger and Kerstens 1996a) the outputs of the local public sector relate directly to the demographic and socioeconomic characteristics of the municipality. The usual case is that these outputs, both quantitatively and qualitatively, are largely imposed by some minimum state or national legislation.

Two approaches are available to purge efficiency measures of these exogenously fixed non-discretionary inputs and/or outputs. The first method is to incorporate these assumptions into a single-stage procedure following Banker and Morey (1986) and Golany and Roll (1993). Efficiency measures thus obtained are based on the premise that for an input (output)-oriented model, it is not relevant to maximize the proportional decrease (increase) in the entire input (output) vector. Rather maximizations should only be determined with reference to the sub-vector that is composed of discretionary inputs (outputs). Examples of this approach include Worthington's (1999) analysis of New South Wales local government libraries, where the non-discretionary inputs include socioeconomic, demographic and geographic characteristics.

The second method uses a 'two-stage approach'. In the first stage, a frontier model is used in which only factors under a municipality's control are included as inputs in computing efficiency scores. In the second stage, those efficiency scores obtained are regressed on factors beyond a municipality's control. The difference between the computed efficiency score from the first stage and its predicted value form the second stage. The residual is used as an index for measuring 'pure' technical efficiency, which could be attributable to management. Examples of this kind of work include De Borger and Kerstens (1996a).

The final issue revolves around the selection of an input or output orientation in efficiency models. For instance, in an input orientation focus falls on the proportional reduction of inputs to achieve efficiency, whereas in an output orientation emphasis is placed on the proportional augmentation of outputs. Although many contributions to the performance literature on the local public sector have focused on input efficiency measures (see Hayes and Chang 1990 and Vanden Eeckaut et al. 1993), the use of the output orientation is not unknown (see, for example, Deller 1992). Whilst the exact formulation will depend on a particular empirical context, De Borger and Kerstens (1996b, p. 11) reason as follows:

> In principle, the choice of orientation should be inspired by the postulated underlying behavioral mode. If one assumes that local governments take outputs as exogenous (for example, determined by citizen's demand) and have substantial control over inputs, then an input orientated measure seems appropriate. Input measures can then detect failures to minimize costs resulting from discretionary power and incomplete monitoring, and provide an indication of possible cost reductions. If on the other hand municipalities have limited control over inputs and face fixed budgets, then an output oriented approach may be quite informative. Output measurement can then identify municipalities that fail to maximize the quantity of the local public services subject to the budget they face, and provide indications of the increase in outputs that could potentially be realized.

4.6   DETERMINANTS OF LOCAL PUBLIC SECTOR EFFICIENCY

In contrast to other areas where frontier efficiency measurement techniques have been employed, hypotheses to explain variation in local public sector efficiency are relatively underdeveloped. However, three exceptions should be noted. These include empirical research relating to the impact of political factors, community characteristics and the impact of financial structure on local public sector efficiency.

First, a number of studies have postulated a relationship between the political composition of the municipal council and the level of efficiency. For example, Vanden Eeckaut et al. (1993) generate evidence for the case that political majorities are an explanatory factor for observed inefficiencies. Using municipalities in the (French-speaking) Région Wallone area of

Belgium, they obtained data on the three major national political parties (Parti Socialiste, Parti Social Chrétian, and Parti Réformateur Liberal) and local parties, and categorized municipalities in terms of coalition composition, party majority and strength and mayoral affiliation. Their results indicate that the proportion of inefficient municipalities is lowest for liberals and socialists, followed by anti-socialist (majorities obviously formed to exclude socialists), local parties, and finally tripartite coalitions. However, municipalities with liberals and socialists in the majority also have the highest proportion of efficient municipalities 'by default': that is, whilst they do constitute the frontier, they do not dominate any interior municipality. Vanden Eeckaut et al. (1993, p. 317) note that 'this finding qualifies somewhat the superiority of their performance relative to other parties'.

De Borger et al. (1994) further emphasized the contention that a politician's emphasis on political rather than economic rationality is likely to contribute to inefficiency. They postulate that the influence of political agents on bureaucratic selection and the use of explicit and implicit log-rolling may be an important factor in this process, which in turn is construed to be a function of the size of political coalitions. Expounding no compelling *a priori* argument for party-related inefficiency, they incorporate a qualitative variable for liberal and socialist party coalitions, and a quantitative variable for the number of coalition partners in a tobit censored regression model. The results indicate that the number of coalition partners does not exert an influence on municipal efficiency, although the presence of liberals tends to decrease technical efficiency, while the presence of a socialist party does not seem to have any statistically significant effect.

Second, several studies have incorporated community characteristics in two-stage efficiency models. For example, De Borger and Kerstens (1996a) incorporate the use of per capita income on the grounds that 'bureaucratic slack' increases with organizational income. In other studies they also include the proportion of the population with a primary (De Borger et al. 1993) or higher (De Borger and Kerstens 1996b) education qualification to quantify political participation. Only in the case of the latter is their hypothesis (that is, that education increases efficiency) confirmed. In the analysis of a specific local government function, namely library services, Worthington (1999) specified municipal population and area, the proportion of the population from various groups (non-English speaking background, aged and students) and an index of socioeconomic disadvantage as relevant community characteristics. Worthington (1999, p. 41) concluded, 'the study reinforces the importance of taking into account the imposed conditions that impinge upon a given local government's ability to perform efficiently'.

Vitaliano (1997) used a stochastic cost frontier to analyze the technical efficiency of US public libraries with an expanded set of public choice type determinants. These included the percentages of total funding derived from local sources, gifts and investments. His study concluded that 'government-run libraries are 2.7% more inefficient than private not-for-profits. And donated resources and greater reliance on local taxation are linked to less inefficiency' (Vitaliano, 1997 p. 640). A number of studies use a broad demographic indicator, either total population (De Borger et al. 1994) or population density (De Borger and Kerstens 1996a). The basic argument is that a low population level may inhibit exploiting economies of scale in some or all of the production processes. Equivalently, the cost of provision will rise with lower population density. Both of these studies concluded that increases in actual population and population density are associated with improvements in efficiency.

The final set of explanatory variables employed relates to the fiscal parameters of the local public sector. For example, high tax prices may enhance the monitoring process of constituents. Likewise, the well-established and extensively surveyed fiscal illusion literature indicates that misperceived fiscal parameters, like total per capita tax burdens or total expenditure outlay, may increase local expenditure, and accordingly be associated with inefficiency (see Dollery and Worthington 1996a). De Borger et al. (1994) and De Borger and Kerstens (1996a) use the size of intergovernmental grants to present a case for the influence of the flypaper effect in particular. The results in both cases are generally similar: 'grants may not only encourage local service provision, but that they also lead to some additional technical inefficiency...the local tax rates that we experimented with failed to produce significant estimates' (De Borger et al. 1994).

Worthington and Dollery (2000) provide evidence concerning the interplay between the productive performance of local governments and the revenue-raising system under which they operate. While this paper only addressed the issue of intergovernmental grants, it suggested that it was possible that other revenue-raising devices may also exert an influence on local government efficiency. For example, while rate revenue is subject to rate-pegging and other controls, fewer restrictions are placed on local governments' use of user charges and fees and contributions. Ease of access and the growing importance of these alternative sources of revenue means that local governments may be able to prop up inefficient operations from sources other than grants. Alternatively, the use of user-pays systems such as these may actively promote efficient outcomes in local government services. Whether the level and composition of own-source non-rate revenue has a systematic influence on productive efficiency is an empirical question that needs to be addressed.

4.7 CONCLUDING REMARKS

Whilst relatively underdeveloped, especially when compared to the extensive financial services literature, a good foundation for frontier efficiency measurement of local public sector efficiency has nevertheless been laid. Problems do remain. For example, the appropriate behavioral specifications to employ, problems with unmeasured inputs and outputs, and the choice between alternative computational techniques. However, these are no more insurmountable than related issues that have arisen in the adjacent fields of financial services, health and education, amongst others. To some extent, the lessons learned from these related areas serve as useful pointers to solutions in the analysis of local public sector efficiency. That said, empirical analysis of local public sector efficiency suggests that it is a unique product of complex non-discretionary inputs and outputs and constraints, multiple inputs and outputs, and inherently complicated political, institutional and cultural factors.

What implication can then be drawn from the preceding discussion of frontier efficiency measurement for practitioners in local government? In the first place, despite significant technical advances in the application of frontier efficiency measurement techniques to the local public sector, as we have seen there are important caveats in the manner in which their results should be treated. For example, most efficient measurement methodologies embody both discretionary variables (i.e. those variables which can be controlled by management) and non-discretionary variables (i.e. those variables which are exogenously determined and cannot be influenced by management). Obviously the spatial distribution of local government (with attendant differences in climatic conditions, socioeconomic characteristics of the jurisdictional population, regional input price variations, etc.) and structural constraints imposed by higher levels of government (competitive tendering procedures, accounting methodologies, rate-capping, etc.) can greatly influence the efficiency of local government operations. Likewise, the idiosyncrasies arising from elected municipal councils (political interference with operational matters, special interest considerations, etc.) imply that local government managers are once again constrained by a host of non-discretionary factors in arriving at efficient outcomes. Accordingly, frontier efficiency measurement techniques that do not explicitly acknowledge the significance of these factors should be treated with caution.

Second, the complex politicized milieu of local government implies that the effectiveness of services is at least as important as economic efficiency in gauging the success of specific municipalities facing different demands. Frontier efficiency measurement is concerned only with the dimensions of economic efficiency and takes no account of the effectiveness of service provision. It is thus, at best, only a partial view of the operations of councils.

Notwithstanding these caveats, frontier efficiency measurement techniques are increasingly applied to local governments throughout the developed world. The results of these statistical exercises will surely continue to show differences in efficiency within and between local authorities. Moreover, critics of local government will doubtless seize on results of this kind as a means of attacking existing service provision and its management. Clearly, familiarity with frontier efficiency measurement techniques and their drawbacks will assist local government practitioners in dealing with this kind of criticism.

5. New Institutional Economics and Alternative Mechanisms of Local Governance

5.1 INTRODUCTION

The book so far has treated the problem of defining an appropriate economic role for local government as a 'second order' variant of the more general problem of ascertaining an appropriate role for government in a mixed market economy. The broad consensus that appears to have emerged in the field of public economics that the potential welfare gains from state intervention to correct market failure should be balanced against the scope such intervention allows for various types of government failure can be reformulated in a way that relates to the central concerns of local government economics. It would then hold that the incremental welfare gains associated with devolving to local government the responsibility for correcting local instances of market failure should be balanced against the greater potential for government failure attributable to local rather than central government involvement.

From the point of view of policy analysis, this 'second order' proposition reflects the same 'top-down' perspective that characterizes the contribution public sector economics makes to this field. In general, the theories of market failure and government failure seem implicitly to share the agency theoretic view that the public sector in a representative democracy can be seen as a vertical interlocking series of principal-agent relationships, from citizen to politician to bureaucratic managers to bureaucratic subordinates down the hierarchy of government to the actual service deliverers. From this top-down perspective, the policy implementation capacity of governments can be inhibited both by factors that tend to (i) generate 'incoherence' at the top an inability to articulate clear, stable policy goals and limit the access of different pressure groups to formulation of policies to achieve these goals; and (ii) create the scope for agency failure as responsibilities for implementation are delegated down the hierarchy of government. If local authorities are simply seen as agents of identifiable principals in central government, then they can clearly contribute to both types of implementation problem. To the extent that there is jurisdictional overlap and a lack of coordination between central and local agencies, it will be that much harder to sustain the coherence of overall policy development. Moreover, as local governments strive to forge for themselves an autonomous role in their local communities, the scope for agent discretion and agency failure will become that much greater from the point of view of their central principals.

This agency theoretic approach can therefore be subjected to the same lines of criticism that 'bottom-uppers', such as Hjern and Hull (1982), have, more generally, directed toward the top-down approach to policy implementation. These include (i) its focus on central objectives and central actors and failure to emphasize the activities of street level bureaucrats (Lipsky 1973) who generate 'control deficits' as they develop coping mechanisms to deal with the pressures on them; and (ii) its implicit distinction between policy formulation and implementation which cannot be sustained in practice since the objectives of policy makers often evolve as policies are made and remade in the process of implementation.

The bottom-up approach they advocate is primarily concerned with the capacity of the state to address problems in those policy areas such as training, employment creation, crime prevention, local community development and so on, in which there is no dominant policy or agency but rather a multiplicity of governmental directives and organizations involved from both the public and private sector. In contrast to the top-down approach, which starts from a policy decision and examines the extent to which its objectives are realized over time, the method of implementation analysis deployed by bottom-uppers like Hjern and Hull (1982) is to: (i) identify the network of actors involved in service delivery in one or more local areas; (ii) ask them about their goals, strategies, activities and contacts; and (iii) construct from this information an understanding of the network that links local, regional and national actors involved in the planning, financing and execution of the relevant government and non-government programs.

We will argue that local authorities are increasingly moving into non-traditional activities where their officials find themselves functioning as key actors in such implementation networks. A bottom-up approach would therefore seem to have considerable relevance to understanding the role local bodies can play in the public policy process. Sabatier (1986, p. 34) does point out, though, that while the chief strength of the 'bottom-up' approach is its focus on the strategies pursued by a wide range of actors, its 'fundamental' limitation is 'its failure to start from an explicit theory of the factors affecting its subject of interest'.

This chapter draws from a number of recent theoretical developments to address this limitation. Section 5.2 examines some contributions to 'new institutional economics' that treat networks as an institutional alternative to markets and hierarchies as mechanisms of social coordination. This provides a useful framework to underpin the analysis of the comparative institutional advantage local authorities might have in the supply of 'community governance' considered in section 5.3. Local governments will, of course, have a variable capacity to exploit this advantage. This section also attempts to generalize the implications of this analysis by suggesting a framework in terms of which the role of local governments can be matched to their capacity. The chapter concludes by proposing the outlines of a 'possibilist' approach that will be applied along with the more conventional economic approach to evaluate specific cases of local government reform in subsequent chapters. The relationship between local government capacity and 'social capital' is explored in the appendix to this chapter. It will be argued that many of the findings of the recent outpouring of research into the relationship between social capital and regional variations in economic performance and the effectiveness of public administration have a striking relevance to local government policy.

5.2 NEW INSTITUTIONAL ECONOMICS AND ALTERNATIVE FORMS OF GOVERNANCE

The study of networks has been very much in vogue in recent years. According to Kenis and Schneider (1991), the network concept seems to have become 'the new paradigm for the architecture of complexity'. The widespread use of network concepts across a variety of disciplines is reflected in the following comments by Borzel (1998, p. 252):

> Microbiologists describe cells as information networks, ecologists conceptualize the living environment as network systems, computer scientists develop neuronal networks with self-organizing and self-learning capacities. In contemporary social sciences, networks are studied as new forms of social organization in the sociology of science and technology, in the economics of network industries and network technologies, in business administration and in public policy.

This writer is particularly concerned with the 'Babylonian' variety of different understandings and applications of the policy network concept in policy studies. She proposes bringing order by delineating two schools of analysis. The first one is the 'interest intermediation school' that analyzes the interrelationship between state and societal actors (mainly interest groups) in the formulation, implementation and evaluation of public policy. We will draw from theories associated with this school in later chapters that analyze the political economy of local government reform. However, this chapter focuses on the core concern of the second policy network school identified by Borzel. This is the 'governance school' that views policy networks as an alternative form of governance to hierarchy and market and analyses network mechanisms for mobilizing resources that are widely dispersed between public and private actors.

Within economics, the comparative institutional approach that characterizes the governance school is most commonly associated with the 'New Institutional Economics' (NIE). The main features of this tradition must be considered before a transactions cost analysis can be made of markets, hierarchies and networks as solutions to the horizontal coordination problems that arise when the relationship between local authorities and both central government agencies and non-government organizations are characterized by what Rhodes (1988) has termed 'structures of resource dependency'.

The New Institutional Economics

In common with the major earlier institutionalist tradition associated with Thorstein Veblen, Wesley Mitchell, John R. Commons and Clarence Ayres, new institutional economics (NIE) represents a loose collection of ideas, including the economics of property rights (Alchian and Demsetz 1973), law and economics (Posner 1977), rent-seeking and distributional coalitions (Olson 1982), agency theory (Jensen and Meckling 1976), transaction costs economics (Williamson 1975), game theory in institutional situations (Shubik 1975), and the new economic history of Douglas North (1984), aimed at bringing institutional characteristics back to the core of economic analysis (Rutherford 1996). However, unlike the older tradition, NIE scholars have few problems with *a priori* deductive theorizing. For example, Furubotn and Richter (1992, p. 1) have observed that:

> The change in analytic approach adopted by the new institutionalists has not resulted from any deliberate attempt to set up a new and distinct type of doctrine in conflict with conventional theory. Rather, the tendency to introduce greater institutional detail into economic models has come about gradually over time because of the recognition that standard neoclassical analysis is overly abstract and incapable of dealing effectively with many current problems of interest to theorists and policy makers.

Although NIE does not contest the methodology of contemporary neoclassical economics, it does make several crucial changes to it.

Firstly, following Simon (1975), NIE recognizes that in the real world, individuals possess an inherently limited capacity to process information and accordingly are 'boundedly rational' in the sense that their calculations include only immediate and readily assimilated information. Bounded rationality necessarily implies that the complexities of actual economic exchange cannot be fully captured by hierarchical contracts or market mechanisms.

This leads to a second difference between NIE and conventional economic analysis. Since bounded rationality prevents the construction of complete contracts between agents and principals, scope exists for opportunistic behavior by economic agents, who can conceal their preferences and actions from contractual partners (Williamson 1975). Indeed, it is precisely because of real-world phenomena, like bounded rationality and incomplete contracts, that economic activities have to be conducted in an environment characterized by asymmetric information and costly transactions, and it is these features which lend crucial importance to institutions.

Perhaps even more significant than these methodological issues are the differences between NIE and orthodox neoclassical analysis on the question of what should constitute the appropriate measure(s) to gauge economic efficiency. In common with the conventional approach, normative problems are usually framed in individualistic terms and focus on the efficiency of alternative conceivable institutional arrangements. But many theorists working in the NIE tradition have expressed strong reservations about using the Pareto efficiency criterion to justify government intervention. For instance, Demsetz's (1969) 'nirvana fallacy' argument holds that by comparing real-world arrangements against the ideal of allocative efficiency rather than feasible institutional alternatives, policy makers have become far too inclined to prescribe government intervention. Similarly, De Alessi (1983) has argued that many of the supposed inefficiencies identified in practical institutional situations by neoclassical economics are actually due to the existence of transaction costs.

Arguments along these lines have led many in the NIE tradition to favor a comparative institutions approach to the question of economic efficiency. In general, it seems clear that theorists in the NIE tradition advocate a concept of efficiency that embodies organizational costs, like transactions costs, which can be used to evaluate various feasible reorganizations of economic activity that could yield social gains net of the costs of reorganization (see, for example, Coase 1960; Demsetz 1969; Dahlman 1979; and Bromley 1989).

Despite the fact that Coase (1937, p. 390) originally specified transaction costs as the 'cost of using the price mechanism' more than 60 years ago, a satisfactory definition of this concept remains problematic. As Allen (1991, p. 2) has observed 'the literature on transactions costs is replete with papers which use the term and provide examples, but which never pause to define the phrase'.

In general terms, a transaction can be defined as an agreed exchange or transfer of goods and services across technologically separable boundaries. The costs involved in such an agreement and which facilitate such a transfer are collectively known as transactions costs (Williamson 1985). In other words, transaction costs are the costs of facilitating economic exchange or, in the language of Kenneth Arrow (1970, p. 48), the costs incurred in 'running the economic system'. Transaction costs are contrasted with transformation costs (sometimes also called production costs) which are the costs involved in transforming inputs into outputs.

Theorists have adopted two generic ways of specifying transactions costs. First, it has been common to adopt somewhat narrow definitions of transactions costs closely bound up with the notion of property rights. For example, Eggertsson (1990, p. 14) delineated transaction costs as 'the costs that arise when individuals exchange property rights to economic assets and enforce their exclusive rights'. Similarly, Barzel (1982) and McManus (1972) emphasize the costs of enforcement and negotiation of property rights. A second and more contemporary view of the nature of transaction costs focuses on the costs of creating and maintaining the institutions characteristic of modern market economies. Furubotn and Richter (1992, p. 8) have described this approach as 'most easily understood as embracing all those costs that are connected with (i) the creation or change of an institution or organization, and (ii) the use of the institution or organization'. In the present context we follow this latter approach.

The theory of transaction costs arose from Coase's (1937) question of why it is that two institutions, the market and the firm, perform the same basic functions and yet continue to coexist. He argued that these two alternative methods of coordinating economic activities exist because there are transaction costs associated with using the price mechanism. Accordingly, rational economic agents will seek to minimize transaction costs and will use either markets or hierarchies, whichever is cheapest. Thus, for example, whether a firm decides to own or lease a particular machine will depend on the transaction costs involved.

The modern theory of transaction costs has extended Coase's market hierarchy dichotomy to include the third institutional alternative of a network and has sought to characterize the properties of transactions in order to determine which institution is optimal in any specific case. Williamson (1979) has argued that the critical features of transactions are their uncertainty, the frequency with which they recur, and the extent to which parties to these transactions are obliged to make investments in transaction-specific assets. All features underlie the characteristics of bounded rationality and opportunism that can shape agent behavior and institutional choice. For example, once parties in an initial competitive market commit themselves to a specialized transaction (involving, say, substantial investments in specific assets, or high 'asset specificity') this leads to an ongoing 'small number' bargaining situation between the two parties, often termed bilateral bargaining. Williamson (1985, p. 47) has hypothesized that these kinds of arrangements encourage opportunistic behavior or 'self-interest seeking with guile', and he has called them 'idiosyncratic' transactions, since the benefits of the transaction are dependent on the absence of opportunistic behavior in its execution. Obviously specialized institutional arrangements will be required to govern idiosyncratic transactions.

A consideration of the degree of bounded rationality, opportunism and asset specificity can influence local government policy with respect to whether or not they 'contract out' a particular service or provide it 'in-house'. A rating of these sources of transaction costs by Stewart and Stoker (1989) in respect of UK local government services is reproduced in Table 5.1.

Table 5.1   Transactions costs for local government services

Service	Bounded rationality	Opportunism	Asset specificity
Refuse collection	Low	Medium	Medium
Street cleaning	Low	Medium	Low
Building cleaning	Low	Medium	Low
Catering	Medium	High	Medium
Vehicle maintenance	Medium	High	Medium
Grounds maintenance	Low	Medium	Low
Leisure services	High	Medium	High

Taken together, these factors appear to have the highest rating with regard to the provision of leisure services. Bounded rationality is high in this case since goal specification and performance measurement are problematic. For example, should the provision of leisure services be directed toward improving physical and mental health or reducing crime and vandalism (Bailey 1999, p. 291)? Asset specificity is also high since sports and leisure facilities tend to be highly specific in their uses and cannot be readily re-deployed. Moreover, these writers would argue that the scope for opportunism may be at least at a medium level if the managers of these facilities have the discretion to pursue revenue-raising strategies that effectively reduce their accessibility to low-income groups.

The relevance of transactions cost analysis to local governance does, however, go significantly beyond the issue of the appropriateness of contracting-out as a service delivery option. The way that it can penetrate to the heart of the coordination issues that constitute a core concern of governance theory must now be considered.

Local Government Involvement in Multi-organizational Partnerships

Although the bottom-up approach to implementation research, discussed at the start of the chapter, would be concerned with the role local government actors have in 'implementation networks', a number of writers have sought to distinguish between multi-organizational partnerships as implementation structures and networks, along with markets and hierarchies, as alternative governance mechanisms that can be deployed by these structures (Lowndes and Skelcher 1998; Rhodes 1997). We will follow this distinction in the remainder of this chapter.

There would seem to be two main ways in which local authorities can be involved in multi-organizational partnerships. Firstly, central government may co-opt local bodies, along with other organizations, into policy initiatives that are targeted at local communities. Secondly, local authorities may exercise their own initiative in establishing collaborative partnership arrangements with other organizations. Typical examples of this would be where local governments join with local business leaders and tertiary institutions to facilitate small business development or develop a strategy to make the local area more attractive for new investment. In many countries, local authorities have been active in establishing collaborative relationships with businesses, voluntary organizations and community associations in the fields of urban and rural regeneration as well as in social care, education, environmental and other policy sectors (Lowndes and Skelcher 1998, p. 314).

These tendencies appear to have gained momentum in the last two decades as 'decrementalist' fiscal policies have placed resource-constrained local bodies under more pressure to develop new sources of finance. In this regard multi-organizational partnerships can enable local bodies to gain access to grant regimes that require financial and in-kind contributions from the private and voluntary/community sectors. They can also use their private sector partners to overcome public sector constraints on access to capital markets (Mackintosh 1992).

Over the same period, the organizational and management changes that have been undertaken at all levels of government have also expanded the scope for multi-organizational partnerships. In particular, the restructuring of large bureaucratic structures into single goal agencies (Hood 1991) that, in some cases, have been sold off to the private sector, and, in other cases, been kept at arm's length from each other through quasi-market arrangements, such as the 'purchaser-provider split', has tended to increase the fragmentation of the public sector. As the range of different agencies responsible for shaping and delivering policy has increased dramatically, the problems of horizontal coordination that arise in this 'polycentric terrain' (Rhodes 1997, p. xii) have often been addressed at the local level where partnerships provide a means of developing strategic direction and sustaining coordination. The possible benefits of partnership arrangements have been summed up by Lowndes and Skelcher: 'Partnerships have the potential to increase resource efficiency, making better use of existing resources by reducing duplication and sharing overheads. They can add value by bringing together complementary services and fostering innovation and synergy' (1998, p. 315).

Problems of Horizontal Coordination

The central feature of multi-organizational partnerships is their underlying 'structures of resource dependency' (Rhodes 1988). This arises because the groups and organizations that could potentially belong to them control different amounts and types of resources authority, legitimacy, money, information and so on. They could therefore benefit from engaging in processes of deliberation, compromise and negotiation that produce a system of horizontal coordination through which dispersed resources can be mobilized and pooled so that 'collective (or parallel) action can be orchestrated towards the solution of a common policy' (Kenis and Schneider 1991, p. 36).

Two major problems would appear to stand in the way of the emergence of this system of horizontal coordination. The first is the 'prisoner's' or bargaining dilemma that arises in situations where defection from cooperation is more rewarding for opportunistically rational actors than compliance due to the risk of being cheated (Scharpf 1992). Some actors may withhold the resources they have agreed to contribute to partnerships and attempt to 'free-ride' on the contributions other parties make to the advancement of common goals. Secondly, there is what Borzel (1998) terms the 'structural dilemma' that arises because the actors that engage in partnership decisions are often agents of the groups they claim to represent. As Borzel (1998, p.261) puts it:

> Horizontal coordination between organizations is based on bargaining between the representatives of the organizations. These representatives are not completely autonomous in the bargaining process. They are subject to the control of the members of their organization. These intra-organizational 'constraints' have major consequences for the representatives' orientations of action and the reliability of their commitments made in interorganizational bargaining, rendering the finding of consensus in interorganizational bargaining processes more difficult for two reasons: first due to the self-interest of the organizational representatives, and second, because of the insecurity caused by intra-organizational control and the need for intra-organizational implementation of interorganizational compromises.

This agency problem is likely to become particularly acute when the issue of whether collaborative arrangements should be extended to include the purported 'leaders' of community groups. A number of doubts are likely to be expressed by the representatives of more formal organizations. 'Do they really speak for the groups or organizations they claim to lead?' 'Can they bind these groups or organizations to the agreements or understandings we reach together?' These attitudes can, in turn, be a source of frustration to the community leaders concerned. Lowndes and Skelcher (1998, p.325) cite the following comment made by a community worker during an interview:

> I think a lot of time is wasted...in saying Well, exactly who do you represent?" For the voluntary and community sector it's one of the biggest time-wasters, trying to pin down people and make them responsible for a certain section of society rather than just recognizing that they are entitled to their own particular opinion and that it's how you build a network that's important.

Attempts by economists to differentiate alternative modes of governance often take as their point of departure the emphasis seminal thinkers in the NIE tradition (Coase 1937; Williamson 1985) gave to markets and hierarchies as distinct governance structures associated with specific types of transaction costs. Subsequent developments in this tradition have added a third category to this scheme. Different triads of terms have thus emerged: markets, hierarchies and networks (Thompson et. al. 1991); community, market and state (Streek and Schmitter 1985); markets, bureaucracies and clans (Ouchi 1991); price, authority and trust (Bradrach and Eccles 1991); and markets, politics and solidarity (Mayntz 1993). All these hark back, in a sense, to Boulding's (1978) distinction between exchange, threat and integrative relationships. Although there are different emphases in these schemes, three ideal types can be delineated as shown in Table 5.2. It should be borne in mind, though, that no feasible system of governance is likely to conform exactly with a pure ideal type. As Bradrach and Eccles (1991, p. 289) point out, 'price, authority and trust are combined with each other in assorted ways in the empirical world'.

The Market Mechanism of Governance

Table 5.2 indicates that one possible solution to horizontal coordination problems in multi-organizational partnerships may be through a market system of governance in terms of which the resource contributions of the various partners would be specified through a series of legally binding contracts. At least some measure of hierarchy may be required to operate this contractualist mode of governance. This could take the form of an organizational structure, such as a contract management agency with the authority to enter into and manage contracts with the various partners. The property rights implications and key features of this predominantly market mode of governance have been succinctly summarized by Lowndes and Skelcher (1998, p. 318):

> Price mechanisms are the means by which the relationships are mediated and where conflicts emerge there may be haggling or recourse to law in order to determine the liabilities of the parties involved. Markets provide a high degree of flexibility to actors in determining their willingness to form alliances, although the competitive nature of the environment and the parties' underlying suspicion may limit the degree of commitment to any collaborative venture.

This mode of governance may give rise to particular transaction costs that render it incomplete in the case of multi-organizational partnerships. Hindmoor (1998, p. 30) has identified four different sources of transactions costs that could have this effect: 'complexity'; 'power asymmetries'; 'information asymmetries'; and 'thinness'.

With respect to complexity he argues that 'a proposed exchange is more complex the larger the number of contingencies that have to be considered *ex ante* by both parties before being able to specify what will *ex post* constitute satisfactory performance of an agreement' (p. 30). The number of contingencies that arise in multi-organizational partnerships may simply be too large to be governed by a complete system of contracts. Moreover, the qualities of 'consummate cooperation' the use of judgment, enthusiasm and initiative- that may be expected of the parties involved in these collaborative arrangements may simply be too difficult to define in contractual terms.

Table 5.2 Modes of governance: market, hierarchy and network

	Market	Hierarchy	Network
Normative basis	Contract property rights	Employment relationship	Complementary strengths
Means of communication	Prices	Routines	Relational
Methods of conflict resolution	Haggling resort to courts	Administrative fiat supervision	Norm of reciprocity reputational concerns
Degree of flexibility	High	Low	Medium
Amount of commitment	Low	Medium	High
Tone or climate	Precision and/or suspicion	Formal, bureaucratic	'Open-ended' mutual benefits
Actor preferences or choices	Independent	Dependent	Interdependent

Source: Adapted from Powell (1991)

Apart from these complexities, the potential effect of power asymmetries may discourage some groups and organizations from participating in these arrangements. In this regard, Hindmoor (1998) suggests that some parties may be reluctant to engage in contractual arrangements with central government agencies since they may fear that they will be unable to enforce compliance or achieve compensation through the courts because of the unique capacity the government has to 'overturn or ignore judgments against it' (p. 31). Lowndes and Skelcher (1998) have found that where contractualist arrangements are used to govern program delivery by multiorganizational partnerships, power asymmetries may work to the detriment of voluntary and community organizations. Despite 'official insistence' on community involvement in the urban regeneration projects they studied in the UK, these organizations were often excluded. As one of their interviewees commented:

> Unless you're cute and big, the voluntary sector could get squeezed out. Small and specialized voluntary organizations haven't got the clout or understanding required by the process. These organizations are valuable because they bring enormous energy and commitment, but you need political clout and strategic nouse to get into partnerships. (p. 327)

A third, and very familiar, source of transactions costs in contractualist arrangements are information asymmetries. These 'occur and complicate exchange when the underlying circumstances relevant to a trade are known by one or more but not all parties to that exchange' (Hindmoor, 1998, p. 31). The tendency by actors in market modes to treat information as a type of property to be used to gain an advantage over their collaborators as well as their competitors may inhibit the free flow of information and cause information asymmetries to persist to a degree greater than that observed with network modes of governance.

The fourth source of transaction costs mentioned by Hindmoor (1998) arises when transactions are 'thin' since 'the smaller the number of trading partners an actor can deal with to achieve their desired objectives', the more likely it is that 'the very consummation of an exchange can leave one or both actors more reliant upon the other' (p. 32). This appears to be a general formulation of the problem of asset specificity analyzed by Williamson (1985). In the context of multi-organizational partnerships, Hindmoor (1998) essentially argues that the more complex the system of contracts becomes in terms of the contingencies it covers, and the more specific tasks are contractually allocated to different partners, the greater the dependence these partners will have on one another and therefore the greater the risk they face of being opportunistically exploited by each other.

When these factors cause the transactions costs associated with market modes of governance to be high, other modes such as hierarchies or networks may be more efficient. Consideration does need to be given, though, to the types of transaction cost they generate. We will first do this in regard to the hierarchical mode of governance.

The Hierarchical Mechanism of Governance

A hierarchical solution to the problems of horizontal coordination in multi-organizational partnerships could involve the establishment of a bureaucratic structure with clear roles, responsibilities and reporting lines to coordinate the inputs of the different organizations. This could be overseen by a partnership board in which the number of votes held by the representatives of the different organizations could be clearly established. This may overcome some of the problems of coordination and collaboration found with market modes. As Lowndes and Skelcher (1998, p.318) put it 'The imposition of an authoritative, integrating and supervisory structure enables bureaucratic routines to be established. Coordination can be undertaken by administrative fiat, and the employment relationships pertaining within the organization encourage at least a certain level of commitment by staff'.

Significant transaction costs could, however, be involved in establishing such a hierarchical structure and maintaining its authority over time. Lowndes and Skelcher (1998, p.325) refer to the potentially high negotiation costs that could be involved in establishing a partnership board:

> Partnership creation involved negotiation and contest over who's in and who's out, a significant shift to hierarchical structures compared with the relatively fluid memberships and indistinct boundaries in pre-partnership collaborations. This was sometimes focused on a particular issue like the allocation of seats to a board or management committee; at other points it was played out in terms of debates about leadership, remit and priorities. We observed the tensions that arose in the context of a lack of 'common currency' among agencies and interests of different types. Different representatives within a partnership drew their legitimacy from different sources – from election, appointment, common experience, professional expertise, leadership skills – but these various mandates were not mutually recognized and there was a lack of clarity about their relative value.

The transactions costs associated with establishing a hierarchy would thus appear to be related to the degree to which a contest for authority arises between the potential partners. This may explain why hierarchical structures can emerge with relative ease in cases where the vertical line of authority is largely uncontested. Hindmoor (1998, pp. 33–4) thus observes that 'in the case of the employee-employer relationship, hierarchy is attractive to both parties because it is assumed that the employee has no particular preference over the nature of the tasks they are called upon to perform'.

Unfortunately this is unlikely to be the case with a multi-organizational partnership since the potential partners 'cannot remain indifferent to the direction in which authority is exercised as it is precisely this that they seek to influence' (Hindmoor 1998, p. 34). Indeed, it is possible that the contest for authority between these actors may be unresolved and a hierarchical structure may fail to form. Alternatively it may only be possible to form a partnership board by deliberately excluding groups or organizations that cannot accept its authority. The multi-organizational partnership may thus have to function without their cooperation. However, even if a reasonably inclusive structure can emerge from this contest for authority it is likely to have a tendency toward formalization and routinization that may result in further transactions costs in terms of reduced flexibility and innovation.

It would seem, then, that both market and hierarchical modes of governance may be incomplete or subject to high transactions costs. Questions must then be raised about the relative desirability of networks as a mode of governance for multi-organizational partnerships. Can they form and function with lower transaction costs than markets or hierarchies? Are they more flexible or inclusive? Can they elicit greater commitment from potential partners? It is to these questions that we now turn.

The Network Mechanism of Governance

Networks cannot simply be distinguished from other governance mechanisms by the presence of trust and absence of rules in network-like relationships. Although most writers on networks would agree with Hindmoor (1998, p. 25) that to understand how these governance mechanisms develop, 'it is necessary to understand how and why trust emerges', this does not imply that trust is not also an important factor in reducing the transactions costs of markets and hierarchies. The essential difference is that while 'markets and hierarchies generate trust by providing institutional safeguards...the defining characteristic of a network is a trust that does not depend on the presence of formal and exogenous safeguards' (Hindmoor 1998, p. 34).

Moreover, this trust is based on a confidence that the actors in a network will not break the rules that circumscribe the boundaries of their cooperative behavior. These rules have been conceived in a variety of ways. Rhodes (1988, pp. 42–43) finds the differences between various types of 'policy networks' residing in the 'operating codes', 'underlying philosophies' and 'rules of the game' that govern relations within them. Wilks and Wright (1987, p. 305) refer in a similar vein to how the avoidance of disputes within such networks is tantamount to 'an unwritten constitution' governing relationships.

In a corresponding manner Jordan and Richardson (1979, pp. 100–101) have sought to identify the 'operation understandings' that influence 'the process by which and the atmosphere within which...policy-making is resolved'. They highlight the importance of rules which allow actors to achieve 'understandings which benefit all participants' (p. 472). According to this view, such rules are constitutive of policy networks since they give each actor information about how others can be expected to act and thereby enable collaborative activity to be undertaken 'in a context where participants already have mutual needs, expectations and experiences' (Jordan 1990, p. 326).

The main difference between the rules and understanding that govern network relationships and those that characterize markets and hierarchies would thus seem to lie in the informality. As Hindmoor (1998, p. 35) has pointed out:

> Because they are informal and unwritten, such rules cannot be enforced in the way that a legally recognized contract can. Neither is compliance ensured by giving one actor hierarchical authority over the actions of another. Clearly the actors in a (network) must trust each other not to exploit their positions and trust each other in the absence of any external safeguards. It is trust that makes the emergence and survival of such rules possible.

The main problem facing network theorists would therefore seem to be to explain how the collaborative activities within the context of 'interdependent relationships based on trust, loyalty and reciprocity' that they typically associate with networks can be developed and sustained. Most of the solutions to this problem can be grouped into two categories. The first is derived from the type of strategic game theory that has become very familiar to economists. It seeks to explain the formation of networks based on complementary interests. The second is derived from the (less familiar) concept of 'expression games' formulated by Goffmann (1959). We will seek to compare and contrast two types of network – one interests-based and the other 'hope-based' – that can be explained in terms of these two types of game. Although the expression games that give rise to hope-based networks (HBNs) may seem to lie more within the domain of social psychology than economics, we will try and suggest how rational choice theory can be modified to help it explain better this type of interaction.

Interest-Based Networks (IBNs)

Over the last two decades game theorists have made considerable progress in developing their understanding of the conditions under which it is rational for agents to trust and cooperate with one another (Axelrod 1984; Coleman 1990; Kreps 1990). The following factors differentiate the games modeled by these theorists from the Prisoner's Dilemma situations that render socially sub-optimal non-cooperative strategies rational from an individual perspective:

1. the number of actors is relatively small;
2. contact with those outside the network is limited;
3. interaction between actors is expected to be frequent; and
4. cooperation in one area can be made contingent upon cooperation in other areas.

Under these conditions actors will calculate the impact their non-compliance with network rules will have on their reputation within, and future access to, the network. Where each member holds a mutual expectation that the costs of non-compliance will exceed the benefits, trust and cooperation can develop since, as Gambetta (1988, p. 10) puts it, 'actors will trust since they have reason to trust'. The resulting interest-based network (IBN) can thus be expected to function as a stable governance mechanism despite the absence of formal sanctions against non-compliance with its 'rules'.

Hindmoor (1998) has suggested that the IBNs that emerge from these repeated games are likely to take the form of 'policy communities' rather than 'issue networks'. A distinction between these two types of 'policy network' has been made by Marsh and Rhodes (1992, p. 25) along the lines shown in Table 5.3. For governance within a multi-organizational partnership to take the IBN form of a policy community it would seem that the complementarity of interests between partners should arise from a relatively balanced structure of resource dependencies. Access to the multi-organizational partnership must therefore be limited to those partners who can make significant resource contributions. Moreover, these contributions would not be limited to a particular project but would occur in the context of an ongoing policy issue, or series of interconnected issues, in respect of which the actors share the same tacit or paradigmatic understanding. Their need to engage in 'frequent, high-quality interaction' with respect to this issue or issues would have the effect of transforming a 'one-off' game into an iterated relationship. As negotiations become embedded within other negotiations, trust and cooperation can develop since actors will realize that defection in any one area can lead to the unraveling of cooperation in other areas. This characteristic of what Granovetter (1985) termed 'embeddedness' would seem to save the transactions costs of setting in place more formal safeguards against non-compliance with network rules.

Table 5.3 Policy communities vs. issue networks

	Dimension	Policy community	Issue network
			Large
Membership	Number of participants	Very limited, some groups consciously excluded	Encompasses range of interests
	Types of interests	Economic and/or professional interests dominate	
Integration	Frequency of interaction	Frequent, high quality interaction of all groups on all matters related to policy issues	Contacts fluctuate in frequency and intensity
	Continuity	Membership, values and outcomes persist over time	Access fluctuates significantly
	Consensus	All participants share basic values and accept the legitimacy of the outcomes	Some agreement exists but conflict is ever present
	Distribution of resources	All participants have resources, basic relationship is an exchange relationship	Some participants may have resources, but they are limited. The basic relationship is consultative.
Resources	Internal	Hierarchical; leaders can deliver members	Varied, variable distribution and capacity to regulate members
	Power	There is a balance of power among members. Although one group may dominate, it must be a positive sum game if the community is to persist	Unequal powers, reflecting unequal resources and unequal access– zero-sum games

The institutional disadvantages of IBNs do, however, become clearer the more they conform to the ideal type of a policy community. In the first place, these governance mechanisms can become as elitist and exclusive in their own way as hierarchies. Moreover, their informality can make it difficult to hold them publicly accountable in the same way as hierarchical structures that function under the aegis of elected public bodies such as local authorities. In their survey of the urban regeneration activities of multi-organizational partnerships, Lowndes and Skelcher (1998, p. 328) found that 'The importance of informality, personal relationships and trust ... was regarded negatively by some of our informants. Network-style relationships were viewed by those who felt excluded or marginalized as "cozy", "cliquey" or "sewn-up".' The reliance on social contact, friendship and personal trust made it hard for new actors to 'break in' to networks. Information was seen as passing between those 'in the know' with little consideration for new groups, those outside established relationships (often women's and minority ethnic groups), or for small or poorly resourced organizations with little opportunity to 'play the networks.'

These observations have recently been echoed by writers such as Krugman (1998) in the critical reappraisals they have made of those features of 'croney capitalism' in East Asian developmental states that lay behind the recent outbreak of 'Asian contagion'. Not only were the financial initiatives of elite policy communities in these countries lacking in the transparency that characterized arm's length financial transactions in Western countries but, in many cases, they involved an implicit government guarantee of business solvency that encouraged the kind of risky investment decisions that contributed to the speculative 'bubbles' that preceded the eventual 'crash' in asset values in these countries.

Policy communities have also been portrayed as sources of resistance to change. In Britain, case studies based on the 'Rhodes model' have been made of policy networks in agriculture, civil nuclear power, youth employment, smoking, heart disease and health services, information technology and exchange rate policy (Marsh and Rhodes 1992). Most of these networks were found to exhibit, to a varying degree, the properties of policy communities so that 'in each area a limited number of groups enjoyed privileged access to policy making shaping both the policy agenda and policy outcomes' (Rhodes and Marsh 1992, p. 199). Significantly, Rhodes and Marsh (1992) conclude that such policy networks can act as a major constraint on policy change. These writers point out that such networks 'do not necessarily seek to frustrate any and all change but to contain, redirect and ride-out such change, thereby materially affecting its speed and direction' (pp. 196–7).

There are also opportunity costs associated with the time and effort involved in networking activities. In this regard Lowndes and Skelcher (1998, pp. 322–3) make the following comment:

> Getting to know key individuals and building relationships took time and could distract organizations from their 'core business'. As one informant noted: 'You could pack your week with inter-agency meetings, but what would you drop then?' Networking was seen as having costs as well as benefits: agencies sought to balance the possible costs of involvement against uncertain long term gain, and their own organization's interests against wider service or policy concerns.

Less obviously, from a perspective that focuses narrowly on transactions costs, there may be what Borzel (1998, p.262) terms 'redundant possibilities' in such apparently wasteful networking activities.

> Networks can provide additional, informal linkage between the inter- and intra-organizational decision-making arena ... (that) help to overcome the structural dilemma of bargaining systems ... Networks do not directly serve for decision-making but for the information, communication and exercise of influence in the preparation of decisions.

We will revisit this 'possibilist' theme later in the chapter. Borzel does, however, broaden her critique of the NIE approach to analyzing the comparative institutional advantage of networks by referring to the way it neglects 'the role of consensual knowledge, ideas, beliefs and values' (p. 264). She goes on to suggest that alternative, more cognitive, approaches to the studies of policy networks may be emerging in theories of learning and communicative action. These theories appear to conceive of a fundamentally different type of network to the IBN type associated with strategic game theory. With reference to this alternative type of a network Borzel (1998, p. 264) proposes that:

> Members...share consensual knowledge and collective ideas and values, a specific belief system ... Such 'advocacy coalitions' or 'discourse coalitions' are formed to influence policy outcomes according to the collectively shared belief systems of their members. Pursuing their goals, advocacy and discourse coalitions do not resort to strategic bargaining but rather rely on processes of communicative action such as policy deliberation (Majone 1993) or policy change through policy learning, i.e. a change in the belief system of advocacy coalitions.

At first sight such theories may seem to be suggesting a mode of network interaction that lies outside the explanatory domain of conventional economic analysis. However, in a previous book (Wallis and Dollery 1999), we commended the 'economic theory of the emotions' developed by Jon Elster (1998) as providing a modified rational choice approach that can make sense of the way shared emotions and their associated 'action tendencies' are developed and sustained in 'hope-based networks'. The distinctive features of this type of network must now be considered.

Hope-based Networks (HBNs)

In an important survey article on 'The Emotions and Economic Theory', Jon Elster (1998) has suggested a number of ways in which rational choice theories could be modified to better explain the effect the emotions have on behavior. According to this writer, emotions such as hope can be distinguished from non-emotional mental states by six features, namely 'cognitive antecedents, intentional objects, physiological arousal, physiological expressions, valence, and action tendencies' (p. 49). This scheme may be simplified and made applicable to HBNs by distinguishing three components of the emotion their members come to share in common.

In the first place their shared hope will be triggered by the 'core beliefs' they have about the possibility of advancing their common goals through engagement in the policy process. In essence a belief that it is 'neither inevitable nor impossible' (Sutherland 1989, p. 193) that certain goals can be advanced through participation in the policy process must be combined with a belief that these goals are 'worthy of pursuit in a special way incommensurable with other goals we might have' (Taylor 1985, p. 135) to elicit a hope that is expressed through an investment or commitment of self to the realization of these goals.

Emotions such as hope, nevertheless, involve more than a set of beliefs. These beliefs must be expressed with a degree of 'emotional energy' that is reflected in the characteristics of physiological arousal, physiological expression and valence described by Elster (1998). Collins (1993) has formulated a theory in which emotional energy is 'the common denominator in rational social action'. According to this writer, only people with very high or very low levels of emotional energy will pass the attention threshold at which their degree of emotional intensity becomes 'empirically visible, both in behavior (especially nonverbal expressions and postures) and in physiology' (Collins 1993, p. 211). We have suggested that the beliefs underlying hope will be expressed with a high and observable *passion* to advance the goals in which it is placed. This passion can 'either draw people toward, or repel them away from, interactions in which it is generated by participants' (Wallis and Dollery 1999, p. 144). In his survey of emotion theory, Elster (1998, p. 47) has pointed out that:

> by and large, psychological studies of the emotions have not focused on how emotions generate behavior. Instead, they have tried to identify the proximate or ultimate causes of the emotions. To the extent that psychologists are concerned with behavior, it is usually with *action tendencies* rather than with observable actions.

These 'action tendencies' have been defined by Frijda (1986, p. 70) as 'states of readiness to execute a given type of action'. Three distinctive action tendencies would appear to be produced by the shared emotion that is developed within HBNs. In the first place, the shared hope of members will give rise to an entrepreneurial alertness to opportunities to advance their common goals. Erich Fromm (1968, p. 9) has highlighted this characteristic of hope: 'Hope is paradoxical. It is neither passive waiting nor is it unrealistic forcing of circumstances that cannot occur. It is like the crouched tiger, which will jump only when the moment for jumping has come.'

A second (and related) action tendency is a readiness to keep striving to advance their goals in the face of cumulative disappointment. Snyder (1994, p. 5) defined hope as 'the sum of the willpower and waypower that you have for your goals'. He proposes that, in the course of striving to achieve the goals they place their hopes in, people need to exercise (i) 'willpower' as they draw on their reserves of emotional energy or 'determination and commitment', and (ii) 'waypower' as they generate one or more effective paths to their realization. They will particularly need to exercise willpower and waypower in the face of opposition or resistance or when the path they are pursuing toward a goal comes to be blocked.

From this perspective, hope primarily generates an action tendency toward perseverance. It can thus be seen as an important source of the in-process benefits that reward people for their participation in that type of activity where, according to Hirschman (1985), a 'fusion of striving and attaining' may occur as individuals 'savor in advance' the realization of what they are striving for. This not only compensates them for 'the uncertainty about the outcome, and for the strenuousness or dangerousness of the activity' but can act as a disincentive to free-riding in team situations (pp. 14–15).

The action tendencies of alertness and perseverance appear to characterize the ideal type of a 'policy entrepreneur' that Kingdon (1984) depicted as 'lying in wait' for an opportunity to advance their pet proposals or concerns. HBNs can therefore be conceived as bringing together policy entrepreneurs who seek to engage in the policy process in pursuit of goals that are the object of their shared hopes.

The third action tendency produced by hope is a tendency to be drawn to interact with actors who share the same hope. To explain this action tendency Elster (1998, p. 64) rejects a cost benefit model of the emotions that treats them 'as psychic costs and benefits that enter into the utility function on a par with satisfactions derived from material rewards' in favor of an approach that views them both as sources of dissonance and as mechanisms of dissonance reduction. He thus seeks to apply to a study of the emotions the theory of 'cognitive dissonance' popularized by Leon Festinger (1957) which suggests that to reduce the unpleasant feeling of tension they experience when they act on their tendencies, individuals will look for cognitions that support their actions and reduce the feelings of tension or dissonance that arise when they engage in them. This approach can explain why individuals who hold the beliefs associated with hope will be drawn to interact in HBNs that share their beliefs. There would appear to be two ways in which network interaction can strengthen the emotions shared by members: through the rhetoric that strengthens the beliefs that underlie shared emotions; and through the production and reproduction of emotional energy through interaction with other members of the group.

Interaction within HBNs is likely to involve a mutual sharing of reasons for the beliefs that trigger these emotions. Each member is likely to have his or her own reasons for participating in the network but these will always, to a degree, be implicit, inchoate and partially articulated. They will therefore look to others to provide a clearer, more explicit articulation that reinforces the beliefs they share in common. This will not only strengthen the cohesion of the network but may also serve an 'evangelistic' function, persuading outsiders to commit themselves to these groups as an expression of how much these beliefs mean to them.

An HBN can come to be identifiable by its rhetoric. It can be seen as being engaged in what Goffman (1959) called 'expression games'. These are typically a form of social interaction that involve 'senders' who express themselves in particular ways, and 'receivers' who take in and react to such expressions, forming an impression of the 'senders'. Loury (1994, pp. 432–3) has argued that this concept is particularly pertinent to policy studies since the interpretation of political expression generally involves 'making inferences from the expressive act about the sender's motives, values and commitments'. He suggests that acceptance by a particular may require the use of 'code words' and the resort to 'groupspeak'. These expressive acts will induce a dissonance that impacts on group members according to the degree that they compromise their autonomy by engaging in them. They may therefore function as a selection mechanism, screening out those members for whom this dissonance is most intense so that the internal cohesion of the HBN increases with time as it comes to comprise a membership who genuinely share the beliefs that are expressed through this rhetoric.

Another type of selection mechanism has been identified by Collins (1993). This writer emphasizes what he calls the 'interaction ritual' (IR) aspect of expression games. He proposes that an IR can only be successful in the sense that it augments the reserves of 'emotional energy' that the members of a group need to draw on if they are to maintain the action tendencies associated with the emotions they share in common, if it passes two important thresholds. The first is a 'threshold of boundedness'. This is likely to be passed in interactions within HBNs since their members will hold the set of beliefs that give rise to their shared emotion with a level of emotional energy that is high enough to be observable. A person who does not have the passion of other members will find it more difficult to interact within these networks than Kuran's (1990) theory of preference falsification seems to suggest. It will be hard to 'keep up an act', continuously 'fooling' other members about their lack of emotional intensity and, even if they succeed in this falsifying strategy, they will derive no satisfaction from a sense of belonging to these groups. A culture of passion can therefore function as a selection mechanism, screening out those participants who do not genuinely share the HBNs beliefs. The boundedness of these networks may thus be enhanced over time by the selective effect of this culture.

The second threshold that must be passed for a successful IR to occur is what Collins terms a 'threshold of density'. This threshold is passed when at least two persons are close enough for a sufficient period of time to ensure that they can be moved by one another's passion or rage. Frequent, face-to-face interactions could be regarded as having a high density in this sense.

Collins argues that once the thresholds of boundedness and density are passed in a particular IR, the participating group's focus of attention and common emotional mood will go through a short-term cycle of increase and mutual stimulation until a point of emotional satiation is reached. The interaction will leave each participant with an 'energetic afterglow' that 'gradually decreases over time' so that individuals have an incentive to reinvest their emotional energy in subsequent interactions. It may therefore accumulate across IRs so that individual members may build up 'a long-term fund' (Collins 1993, p. 212) of passion or rage by repeated participation in successful IRs. It is this fund or reserve of 'willpower and waypower' that can be drawn on by the members of an HBN to counter the emotional component of the dissonance they experience as a result of accumulated disappointments and to sustain their 'action tendencies' to 'lie in wait' 'like crouched tigers' for opportunities to advance their common goals. A comparison between IBNs and HBNs is made in Table 5.4.

From a comparative institutional perspective, there would seem to be a number of advantages an HBN has compared to an IBN as a governance mechanism within a multi-organizational partnership. The action tendencies toward entrepreneurial alertness and perseverance that are produced within an HBN are likely to make their members both more flexible and more committed than the members of an IBN. These action tendencies can be regarded as a type of 'value-added' to the expression games played within HBNs since these are just as likely to solve 'prisoner's' and 'structural' dilemmas as the repeated strategic games played within IBNs. In addition, the members of an HBN are likely to have a strong 'change orientation' compared to the members of an IBN. Rather than simply seeking to 'contain and ride-out' changes imposed from the top-down, they will 'lie in wait', preparing themselves to take advantage of opportunities either to initiate changes that advance their common goals or advance one another into positions from which they can launch such initiatives.

The recognition that HBNs are effective 'change agents' may provoke strong opposition from those groups that are excluded from the multi-organizational partnerships the HBNs manage to take over. While IBNs may be just as elitist, exclusion from, say, a typical policy community may be viewed as less threatening to the groups concerned. They will view it as constituting the 'local establishment' that needs to be accommodated or circumvented if they are to advance their own goals. The emergence of an HBN that not only holds the levers of local power but is committed to using them to overcome all resistance to the changes it is seeking to implement does, however, present a more serious institutional threat to groups with rival goals. To counter this 'imminent danger' they may mobilize 'reactionary' HBNs that are committed to impede the forward momentum of 'progressive' HBNs. In a study of the trajectory of the neo-liberal reform process that was implemented in New Zealand after 1984, Wallis (1999, p. 51) observed that both the internal cohesion and external resistance to the 'policy quest' of a reformist HBN are likely to strengthen over time:

> Political parties may come to be factionalized between committed reformers and pragmatists who become increasingly concerned that the reform process is being pushed too far and too fast in a particular direction. Rival advocacy coalitions may form within the policy networks the (members of the HBN) are attempting to penetrate and lead. These groups will advocate values and represent interests that they consider to have been neglected by the reformist network. These sources of resistance will not be directed toward a reversal of the reform process but (as the New Zealand experience suggests) they can gather strength and cohesion to a degree that stalls its forward momentum.

This corresponds, of course, with Sabatier's (1988) finding that in policy sub-systems where participants are divided on a narrow set of core beliefs, a stable alignment of rival advocacy coalitions can emerge over time. The balance of power between these groupings is only likely to be disturbed by exogenous factors such as an election or economic crisis. This structure may therefore produce a 'policy paralysis' no matter how strongly orientated any one advocacy coalition or HBN is to paradigmatic change.

The potential for HBNs to provoke the mobilization of resistance sufficient to produce such policy paralysis may mean that they may be less long-lived than IBNs. The 'long march' strategies of IBNs with their characteristic emphasis on 'incremental change through partisan mutual

Table 5.4 Interest-based vs. hope-based networks

	Interest-Based Network	Hope-Based Network
Type of game	Repeated strategic game	Expression game with repeated IRs
Motive for cooperation	Resource dependence	Shared belief in the worth and possibility of goals
Explanation of actor behavior	Cost-benefit analysis of cooperation vs. defection	Search for cognitions to reduce dissonance
Tone or climate	Open-ended mutual benefits	Passion
Flexibility	Medium	High
Commitment	Medium	High
Orientation to change	Contain and 'ride it out'	Overcome resistance to it
Potential opposition from excluded groups	Low/medium	Eventually high
Continuity	Long term	Medium term
Deliberative rationality	Encouraged	Discouraged by 'political correctness'
Leadership dependence	Medium	High

adjustment' (Lindblom 1959) may thus ensure a longer continuity of these governance mechanisms than is the case with HBNs whose 'blitzkrieg' strategies eventually produce strong resistance and the accumulation of disappointments that can eventually 'douse the fire' produced by their early success in advancing their goals.

In addition to the degree that an HBN seeks to strengthen its internal cohesion through a 'politically correct' language involving 'code words' and 'groupspeak' they may become more prone to policy errors (Loury 1994) and less likely to deliberate about the scope for compromise between competing goals than are IBNS that often require a high degree of deliberative rationality to forge a reconciliation of interests.

Finally, HBNs are likely to be more dependent on actor-specific leadership skills than IBNS. At least one actor in an IBN is required to initiate and facilitate the informal pre-partnership collaborative activities out of which a multi-organizational partnership may be formed. However, for an HBN to emerge from these networking activities the members may have to look to one actor as the 'leader'. In an earlier book we examined how leaders could play a focal role in HBNs, facilitating the development of a 'culture of passion' and the convergence of follower hopes on a shared vision:

> Leaders may ensure that (the) thresholds of density and boundedness are passed by structuring group interaction into a number of levels descending in status from the 'inner circle' of followers who the leader chooses to interact directly with. Access to this level of interaction will be limited to those followers in whom the leader has placed the highest level of trust. This trust will be based not just on the skills and resources which these followers can deploy in performing the tasks allocated to them, but also on the passion which they express in seeking ways to advance the leader's quest ... Leaders can thus shape the development of their follower culture by setting the terms according to which followers compete for access to their inner circle. Moreover, they can influence the passion that is generated in this circle and which filters down the different levels of followership by enhancing the commonality of focus and emotional mood that is stimulated by IRs. Bennis and Nanus's (1985) conception of leaders as 'managers of meaning' would seem to be pertinent in this regard. Leaders direct followers' attention to the point and significance of their actions and interactions and they narrow their evaluation of this point and significance to a simple consideration of whether these activities are moving the quest in the direction intended by the leader. (Wallis and Dollery1999, p. 151)

The comparative institutional analysis we have undertaken of markets, hierarchies and both interest- and hope-based networks would suggest that no mechanism can *a priori* be argued to be a superior mode of governance for multi-organizational partnerships. The importance of the role local author-ities can play in these structures needs, however, to be explored in more detail. Are they uniquely placed to bring potential partners together? Do they have the capacity to select which governance mechanism is the most efficient and effective in a particular situation and the flexibility to adapt the mix of modes to changing circumstances? And, in particular, can they deploy the facilitation and leadership skills required to take full advantage of the possibilities for networking within a local governance system?

5.3 THE CAPACITY OF LOCAL AUTHORITIES TO SUPPLY LOCAL GOVERNANCE

The comparative analysis of markets, hierarchies and networks in the previous section seemed to suggest a potentially important role for local government in the implementation structures that deploy these governance mechanisms at the local level. This section will focus on the special resources local governments can contribute to these structures and will then turn its attention to factors that can determine whether they play a 'minimalist' or 'activist' role in the supply of local governance.

The Potential Catalytic Functions of Local Government

In many countries local governments can make use of unique institutional resources that can enable them to play a catalytic role in the formation and development of multi-organizational partnerships. Their multi-purpose structure and the discretion they typically have over the range of community services they seek to provide and the delivery mechanisms they use in providing them has been a concern to government failure theorists since these characteristics of local authorities make it difficult to subject them to vertical lines of authority within which they can be made accountable for clearly specified outputs. However, it is these same characteristics that make local authorities particularly suited to their role as suppliers of community governance. As they seek to develop this role they are also likely to expand their institutional memory as a result of having to learn how to cope with, and adapt to, the range of pressures that can be traced to the drive by both central government and citizen ratepayers to make local governments deliver more for less.

To cope with these pressures, local authorities have had to restructure themselves to both retain an in-house capacity to supply strategic direction to the range of organizations and groups they collaborate with and to develop a capacity to manage the mix of governance mechanisms they deploy in serving their communities of interest. An intra-organizational structure that separates advice from implementation, regulation from service delivery and commercial from non-commercial functions can enable a local authorities to contract-out those services and functions in respect of which the transactions costs of market governance are lower than those associated with hierarchical in-house provision. At the same time the pressure on local authorities to deliver more for less may induce them to engage in the type of networking activities that Lowndes and Skelcher (1998) suggest can constitute necessary preparation for the formation of multi-organizational partnerships.

Local authorities can position themselves at the center of these networks whether they take the IBN or HBN form discussed in the previous section. Within an IBN they can bring key resources of democratic legitimacy and the informational advantages they may have developed where they have a history of working with local groups and agencies to solve problems that cross organizational boundaries. As Painter et.al. (1997, p. 242) have pointed out:

> At issue is a catalytic role in facilitating liaison where problems are not susceptible to single-agency solutions. Given the perspective that only a local authority as a multi-purpose body can bring, in some respects the onus is on it to make linkages, strategically intervening to draw agencies together. As a senior officer in a London borough observed of the changing environment: 'The local authority world will just die away if they don't, not just respond to it, but manage the new world'.

With regard to HBNs, local authorities may be well placed to prevent, or break through, the type of policy paralysis that can emerge when a reactionary HBN is able to mobilize sufficient resistance to stall the forward momentum of the advance of a progressive HBN's policy quest. To do this they must be able to deploy officials who have a tolerance for what Barber (1984) terms 'autonomous politics'.

According to this writer there can only be scope for the emergence of 'autonomous politics' on those occasions when 'some *action* of *public* consequence becomes *necessary* and when men must thus make a *public choice* that is *reasonable* in the face of *conflict* despite *the absence of an independent ground'* (Barber 1984, p. 122, original emphasis). For autonomous politics to occur, each value, belief, interest or obligation affected by a particular choice opportunity must have an 'equal starting place' and then be required to earn legitimacy by running the 'gauntlet of public deliberation and judgment' (Barber 1984, p. 137). Where conflict emerges, each side is given an adequate opportunity to make their case so that where one prevails, the other is left with the impression that they have been the subjects of a reasonable process. As Barber (1984, p. 127) points out:

> The word reasonable bespeaks practicality. It suggests that persons in conflict have consented to resolve their differences in the absence of mediating common standards, to reformulate their problems in a way that encompasses their interests

(newly and more broadly conceived) even while it represents the community at large in a new way. 'Well, I guess that's reasonable', admits an adversary who has not gotten his way but has been neither coerced nor cajoled into the agreement he has consented to. He is neither victor nor loser; rather he has reformulated his view of what constitutes his interests and can now 'see' things in a new manner.

When local officials bring together HBNs the very fact that the local authority has multiple goals and is therefore less committed to the advancement of any of the particular goals these different groups place their hope in, may allow them to play a mediating role as they strive to preserve these norms of reasonableness in inter-group interaction. Moreover, the local authority is likely to be uniquely concerned with the possibilities this type of interaction holds for the forging of a common vision of community development that can engage the support of divergent HBNs. To the degree that its representatives have a propensity to internalize politics, to encourage debate, to relax the norms of political correctness (Loury 1994), to allow the expression of dissent and to strive to forge from conflicting views some common and yet creative conception of how the local public interest is affected by the issues at hand, they may be able to exercise what Burns (1978) termed 'transformational leadership'. This is the force that though 'closely influenced by particular local, parochial, regional, and cultural forces' is able to 'find a broadening and deepening base' from which 'to reach out to widening social collectivities to establish and embrace "higher" principles and values'(Burns 1978, p. 429).

The potential for local authorities to exploit the integrative possibilities of their facilitative role in IBNs or transformational leadership role with HBNs will depend on their political and administrative capacity. The relationship between the relative 'activism' of the role local authorities can play in their communities of interest and the various dimensions of governmental capacity must now be considered.

Matching the Role of Local Government to its Capacity

Two opposing principles are commonly proposed to guide the devolution of government functions to the local level. The first is the *residuality principle* which holds that local government should be selected only where the benefits of such an option exceed all other institutional arrangements. One rationale for the application of this principle is the view that local authorities are even more prone to the types of government failure discussed in Chapter 3 than other forms of public organization. As a result local governments should play a minimalist role in the local economy that restricts them to the provision of those local public goods in respects of which the benefits from decentralization significantly exceed the costs associated with potential government failure.

A second principle that is the logical antithesis of the residuality principle in that it implies a presumption for, rather than against, the devolution of responsibilities to local government is the subsidiarity principle which holds that no organization should be bigger than necessary and nothing should be done by a larger and higher unit than can be done a lower and smaller unit. The most notable international application of this principle is by the European Union in its relations with individual nation states. It appears to legitimize a highly activist role for local government in the local economy since it would not only appear to be based on an optimistic assessment of the benefits of decentralization relative to the costs of local government failure, but also an appreciation of the comparative institutional advantage local bodies can play in the partnership-forming and networking activities described in this chapter.

Reid (1999) argues that the subsidiarity principle can be used to formulate a checklist of the key criteria for determining the location of accountability – not only between different spheres of government but also between governments and communities. Specifically he contends that any such checklist 'needs to address the distribution of benefit; information needs and complexity; the relative importance of local knowledge and national consistency; the degree of national significance; the importance of critical mass and value of local discretion' (Reid 1999, p. 180). In practice, the application of this principle would seem to require an empirical assessment of the capability of different levels of government to undertake particular activities.

This pragmatic approach is reflected in a recent contribution by the World Bank to the problem of defining an appropriate role for government in a way that takes account of the significant variations in 'state capacity' that were highlighted as 'considerable evidence accumulated during the 1980s to suggest that states varied widely in their ability to set the terms for economic and political interactions and to carry out the functions assigned to them' (Grindle 1996, p. 4). These contributions express a growing awareness that although governments cannot create wealth per se they nevertheless can play a key role in the process of economic development. Indeed, the World Bank now tends to refer to the 'enabling state' as a crucial ingredient in achieving higher rates of economic growth (World Bank Development Report 1997). At the very least the state must provide various fundamentally important functions, including the creation and maintenance of law and order, the provision of basic social services and physical infrastructure, and the establishment of a stable and coherent policy environment. But apart from these minimalist functions, the state can enhance economic activity in other ways too. Chhibber (1997, p. 17) has put the argument thus:

Although the importance of these fundamentals for development has long been widely accepted, new insights are emerging as to the appropriate mix of market and government activities in achieving them. We now see that markets and governments are complementary: the state is essential for putting in place the appropriate institutional foundations for markets.

A useful way of conceptualizing the problem of matching the role of the state to its capabilities is provided in Table 5.5, which illustrates the potential functions that can be undertaken by local government provided it has the capacity efficiently and effectively to engage in them.

Table 5.5   Minimalist, intermediate and activist functions of local governments

Minimal Functions	Intermediate Functions	Activist Functions
Providing local public goods	Addressing externalities Regulating monopoly Overcoming imperfect information	Coordinating private-public partnerships Developing social capital

Source: Adapted from World Bank Development Report (1997, Table 1.1, p. 27)

The table outlines three basic levels at which local governments can intervene, depending on their institutional capacity. To undertake even minimal functions, local governments must have both the revenue-raising and institutional capacity to administer necessary local regulations and provide genuinely local public goods, such as library services and rubbish collection, whose benefits do not extend significantly beyond a particular community. The demands on local government capacity will be much greater where they seek to provide intermediate functions. The World Bank Development Report (1997, p. 27) has described the role of government in the provision of intermediate functions as follows: 'Here, too, the government cannot choose whether, but only how best to intervene, and government can work in partnership with markets and civil society to ensure that these public goods are provided.'

While these remarks are directed toward an assessment of the capacity of national states, they are also clearly relevant to local government as the discussion of different governance mechanisms in this chapter has made clear. Finally, it would appear that activist functions, like intervention to generate increased coordination and develop social capital (see the appendix to this chapter), should only be undertaken by local authorities with a highly sophisticated capacity for governance and even then only with great care.

A number of writers have sought to differentiate the various dimensions of this governance capacity. For example, Polidano (2000, p. 810) has distinguished between 'policy capacity' ('the ability to structure the decision making process, coordinate it throughout government, and feed analysis into it'), 'implementation authority' ('the ability to carry out decisions and enforce rules, within the public sector itself and the wider society') and 'operational efficiency' ('the ability to deliver services ... efficiently and at a reasonable level of quality'). Similarly, Grindle (1996) has proposed a somewhat broader fourfold typology of state capacity, which incorporates institutional capacity, technical capacity, administrative capacity, and political capacity. Both taxonomies would seem to be relevant to local governance although we will only elaborate on this with reference to Grindle's scheme.

Grindle (1996, p. 8) relates the 'institutional capacity' of government bodies to their ability to uphold authoritative and effective 'rules of the game', to regulate economic and political interactions and to assert the primacy of their policies, legal conventions and norms of sociological and political behavior over those of other groupings. Local authorities will mainly derive this capacity from their relationship with central government to the degree that this relationship is based on a mutual trust. Central government will only have the confidence to devolve functions to local authorities if they expect their officials to behave in a 'responsible' way that is governed by the same rules that ensure proper behavior by their own officials. A focus by central control agencies on the potential for agent opportunism and government failure at lower levels of government may actually undermine this confidence. At the same time, local authorities may only have confidence in such devolution if it is based on:

> clear and shared understandings of what is being transferred and who will be expected to bear the costs. ... (This) means assuring the parties who may receive the allocation that they will not be exposed to the political risk which can arise, for example if government reduces its financial commitment once a program has become well established in new hands'. (McKinlay 1998, p. 31)

According to Grindle (1996, p. 8) the technical capacity of governments is related to their capacity to set and manage coherent economic strategies based on the advice of a cadre of well-trained analysts and managers who operate out of appropriately placed units for policy analysis. While Grindle relates this capacity to the ability of a central government to sustain coherent macroeconomic stabilization policies, it can also be related to the capacity of 'enabling authorities' to supply effective leadership and strategic direction to the range of agencies and organizations that can potentially be brought together to advance local community and economic development. The potentially catalytic functions of local government referred to in the previous section would thus seem to be based on this capacity.

Local authorities are, however, unlikely to be trusted to perform this role unless they have demonstrated what Grindle (1996) calls an 'administrative capacity' through their track record of effectively administering local infrastructure and supplying local public goods. Indeed any attempt by local authorities to take on more activist functions may not secure the external resources and support they depend on, if there is a widely held belief that this more activist role could undermine the capacity of these authorities to give proper attention to their core business.

Grindle's (1996, p. 44) fourth category is political capacity, which refers to 'the ability to mediate conflict, respond to citizen demands, allow for representation of interests, and provide opportunities for effective political participation'. As the previous section made clear, in situations where conflict arises between IBNs and HBNs, this capacity is a precondition for local government officials exercising a transformational leadership that forges a common vision from these divergent views and interests.

The issue of how to address the gap between the functions that local authorities can be called upon to perform, either by central government or by their local electors, and their capacity to perform them must now be considered by way of conclusion to this chapter.

5.4 CONCLUSION

The 1997 World Bank Development Report identifies two generic approaches to the problem of closing the gaps that exist between the functions and capacity of government bodies. First, policy makers can attempt to match the agency's role 'to its existing capability, to improve the effectiveness and efficiency of public resource use' (World Bank Development Report 1997, p. 25). In the case of local government reform this may involve a recognition of the high propensity for government failure at this level that leads to a 'minimalist' approach to downsize local government so that it can focus on maintaining its administrative capacity to engage in the core business of supplying local public goods.

Second, policy makers can seek ways of enhancing government 'capacity by reinvigorating public institutions' (p. 3). This quest may involve both a comprehensive reform of the structure and management of local authorities to reduce the scope for government failure and an exploration by the management of these authorities of the range of mechanisms discussed in this chapter that can enhance their capacity to play a more activist, catalytic role in local governance.

This quest may therefore have to embrace elements of the 'possibilism' that Hirschman (1971) argued could counter and balance the 'fracasmania' an exclusive focus on the potential for government failure that could blind development analysts to the possibilities of forming 'linkages' or networks to address the unexpected problems that arise during the course of implementing development programs. Hirschman famously favored an 'unbalanced' growth strategy that encouraged governments to set up disequilibria that would stimulate effort and mobilize hidden and under utilized resources. It is an approach to development problems which embodies respect for complexity and an openness to the possibility of genuine novelty what Hirschman (1971, p. 27) once called 'the discovery of an entirely new way of turning a historical corner'.

We would submit that the comparative institutional approach discussed in this chapter can be applied in a way that embodies a similar openness to the possibilities of alternative governance mechanisms in general, and networking in particular. Moreover, it can augment the analysis of market and government failure in earlier chapters in a way that provides a conceptual background to the minimalist and activist approaches to local government reform that will be discussed in the next chapter.

APPENDIX: SOCIAL CAPITAL AND LOCAL GOVERNMENT

The dimensions of institutional, technical, administrative and political capacity that constrain the ability of local governments to take on more active functions would all appear to be affected by a type of community resource that is not the property of any institution but can be drawn upon to facilitate the achievement of collaborative action. The contribution various social capital theorists have made to the contemporary understanding that political scientists and economists have of this resource will be considered in this appendix.

The concept of social capital has been popularized by Putnam (1993), although he gives primary credit to Coleman (1988) for developing it. Putnam (1993) defines social capital as those features of social life that enable participants to act together more effectively to pursue shared objectives. Unlike physical or human capital, it is not the property of individuals or institutions. Rather it is produced 'in the spaces between people' and affects their ability to associate with one another, particularly outside immediate and intimate relationships. Like other forms of capital, it is productive but differs 'in that it is self re-inforcing and cumulative' (Putnam 1993, p. 38). Its depletion is more likely to occur through under rather than over use. In his study of regional governments in Italy, Putnam identifies the key components of social capital and argues that their establishment is 'a precondition for economic development as well as for effective government' (p. 36). This finding has attracted considerable interest in the economics profession. For instance, it has both been cited with approval by Fukuyama (1995) and been subject to rigorous empirical analysis by Knack and Keefer (1997).

The key components of social capital identified by all these writers are 'networks of civic engagement', 'norms of generalized reciprocity' and 'relations of social trust'. Like the IBN theorists discussed in Chapter 5, they draw from game theory, arguing that through repeated interaction in networks that 'are primarily "horizontal" bringing together agents of equivalent status and power', norms are 'inculcated and sustained by modeling and socialization (including civic education) and by sanctions' (Putnam 1993, pp. 171–2). The most important of these norms is a generalized reciprocity which 'refers to a continuing relationship of exchange that is at any time unrequited or imbalanced, but that involves mutual expectations that a benefit granted now should be repaid in the future'. The establishment of this norm will allow 'dense networks of social exchange' to form in which 'people can be confident that trusting will be requited, not exploited' (p. 172). It is important to emphasize that the stock of social capital is not specific to any network. It is an area-specific resource that may be drawn on by the networks in a particular locality such that it is augmented rather than depleted by these networking activities. The stock of social capital in a particular area may thus be the product of a long tradition of civic engagement. Thus although Putnam (1993) found that in northern Italy this tradition had its modern expression in the form of high levels of participation in sports clubs, voluntary associations and choral societies, he pointed out that these patterns of social cooperation go back to the thirteenth century.

Various mechanisms have been proposed whereby the elements of social capital can contribute to better outcomes by facilitating greater cooperation. Most significantly from the perspective taken in this chapter, Putnam (1993) posits a direct relationship between the administrative capacity of public institutions and social capital. He attributes regional variations in public sector efficacy in Italy to the density of associational life, finding, for example, that the more likely a region's citizens are to join football clubs and choral societies, the faster the regional government is in reimbursing health care claims. One explanation for this result is that monitoring the performance of bureaucrats is facilitated by greater social capital. This can occur, directly, because these agents themselves are more concerned with their reputation amongst people with whom they horizontally interact on a regular basis. It can also occur, indirectly, because monitoring officials is itself a public good and the norms formed within networks of civic engagement help citizens overcome the collective action problems involved in providing this good. In addition, Putnam suggests that citizen-initiated contacts with public officials in the less trusting, less civic-minded regions of southern Italy tend to involve issues of narrowly personal concerns, while contacts in the more trusting, more civic minded northern regions tend to involve larger issues with implications for the welfare of the region as a whole.

Knack and Keefer (1997) have found evidence that social capital is a determinant of measurable economic performance. They used Barro-type cross-country tests to estimate the impact of trust, civic norms and associational activity on growth rates using indicators of these social capital variables taken from the World Values Surveys (WVS) (Inglehart 1994) for a sample of 29 market economies. While they found a significant positive relationship between the first two variables and growth rates they also established that 'group membership is not significant in either growth or investment equations' (Knack and Keefer 1997, p. 1272). They explained the apparent insignificance of associational activity as a predictor of growth by suggesting that the positive effect Putnam (1993) accorded this variable in inducing greater cooperation and solidarity that can be invoked in resolving collective action problems would be offset by the negative effects groups have on growth when they act as rent-seeking organizations (Olson 1982), lobbying for preferential policies that impose disproportionate costs on the rest of society. In investigating the determinants of the significant social capital variables, Knack and Keefer (1997, p. 1283) found that they are stronger in countries where 'low social polarization, and formal institutional rules that constrain the government from acting arbitrarily, are associated with the development of cooperative norms and trust'.

This finding is crucially important since it suggests that social capital can only enhance the capacity of governmental institutions and economic growth where it promotes social cohesion, a goal that is realized in a 'society in which people work toward common goals and in which diversity is recognized but does not lapse into conflict' (Robinson 1997, p. 2). However, communities where social ties between members are strong do not always enhance social cohesion. They may be so hostile to outsiders that they may instigate civil, racial or sectarian conflict or, as tends to be the case with gangs, they may promote illegal or morally reprehensible behaviors.

In general, the social capital that is formed in the context of a cohesive society, can lower the transactions costs associated with all three types of governance mechanism that were referred to in the previous section. It is, however, its effect on the density of network interaction between local authorities and voluntary organizations that has engaged the attention of local government policy analysts. Of particular interest has been Putnam's (1993) 'Bowling Alone' thesis that urban governance in the United States has been adversely affected by a decline in civic organization.

To test the applicability of this thesis to the United Kingdom, Maloney et al. (2000) replicated an earlier study by Newton (1976) of the number of voluntary associations in Birmingham in 1970 and their perceptions of their relationships with one another and the city council. They found evidence to support the view expressed by other writers (Hall 1998; Lowndes et al. 1998; Young 1999) that the 1990s had seen a continuation of the trend in this country toward 'a general opening out of local authorities and a strengthening of the diversity and capacity of local group politics ... with increased support for local voluntary associations and more avenues for engagement with local authorities' (Maloney et al. 2000, p. 804). Not only had there been an 'increase of at least a third in the number of voluntary organizations in Birmingham' (p. 805) between 1970 and 1998, but 'they are more politically active, better connected and generally positive about associational life' with many associations being 'involved in extensive networks of organizations both inside and outside the geographical boundaries of Birmingham' and placing 'a high premium on contact with other associations and public authorities, arguing that these contacts are important for networking and information exchange' (p. 807). The significant role the local authority plays in these networks also emerges from this study:

'Nearly 70 per cent of groups describe the City Council as an important source of information...Moreover the overwhelming majority of the sample (86 per cent) recognize that trust between the Birmingham City Council and voluntary and community groups is essential' (p. 808).

From this study these writers conclude that 'if Robert Putnam was to visit Birmingham in the late 1990s, we suspect that he would be impressed by the vibrant voluntary and community sector and would in all probability declare that the civic community was alive and well, and that Birmingham had high "stocks" of social capital' (p. 817).

They, nevertheless, caution against an approach based on the assumption that it is possible to 'read off' the implications for governance from knowledge about the quantity and quality of associational activity in a particular area. They point out that:

Knowledge of civic organizations and a generic understanding of their civic vibrancy expressed through their numbers, their access to information and networks does not enable us to make immediate comment on the quality of governance in a given locality. Nor does the identification of a certain set of

values and attitudes held by individuals in a community provide a sufficient basis
for ascertaining the performance of governance arrangements. It is behavior that
matters. As Coleman emphasizes, social capital is a relational concept. It is
specific to and is made manifest in particular relations ... Moreover it is important
to recognize that there is an uneven distribution of social capital and that different
actors have differential access to social capital resources. (Maloney et al. 2000, pp.
803–4)

A link between social capital and the networking capacity of local
governments would have to be based on an analysis of the ways in which the
'political opportunity structure' (Kriesi 1995; Tarrow 1994) affects the
access to, and formation of, social capital in a particular locality. Moreover,
to the extent that the political opportunity structure (POS) is modifiable
through local government policy, there would have to be a reappraisal of the
laissez-faire implications of Putnam (1993) and Fukuyama's (1995) claim
that government policies can do little to influence the accumulation of social
capital.

A number of contributors to the new social movement theory have sought
to refine the concept of the political opportunity structure. Eisinger (1973)
used this term to describe the 'openings, weak spots, barriers and resources
of the political system itself'. Tarrow (1994, pp. 85–6) defined the POS as
those 'dimensions of the political environment that provide incentives for
people to undertake collective action by affecting their expectations of
success or failure' and suggested that these dimensions would be subject to
significant change through 'the opening up of access to power, shifting
alignments, the availability of influential allies, and cleavages within and
among elites'.

Maloney et al. (2000) suggest that these concepts can be used to
understand how changes in the POS affect the ability of voluntary
associations to engage with local authorities if consideration is given to three
properties of the political system within which such relationships take place.
The first is the 'formal institutional structure' reflected in the degree of
decentralization, the degree of coherence in public administration and the
capacity of local authorities to impose conditions or requirements for
collaboration with voluntary or community associations. The second is the
'informal manner in which these arrangements are applied'. Quite clearly
different authorities can 'develop different cultures towards the voluntary
sector' (pp. 810–11). These can range from full exclusion through limited
engagement with only those groups who share the ideological outlook or
professional background of council officials to an actively 'integrative'
approach (Kriesi 1995, p. 174) that seeks to make contact and build
relationships with previously marginalized groups. Thirdly, associational
engagement is affected by the political context within local authorities since

'the nature of political alignments and conflict amongst political elites and the presence and absence of allies' (Maloney et al. 2000, p. 811) can create openings for voluntary associations to link up with factions seeking support from this sector.

The usefulness of this concept can be illustrated with reference to the likely impact on these three elements of the POS of the implementation at the local level of the doctrines of the 'New Public Management' (NPM). At the very least, this will increase the coherence in local government administration, as management authority is concentrated in the hands of a new-style 'chief executive'. Moreover, since this official will have the discretion to consider institutional alternatives to bureaucratic provision, more opportunities for engagement with voluntary and community groups may arise. Critics of the NPM have, however, tended to emphasize the potentially damaging effect it can have on the social capital that is formed through collaboration between local government and the voluntary sector. Riddell (1997, p. 27) has argued that the most disturbing feature of the drive to specify more tightly the terms and conditions under which voluntary organizations can function as service suppliers 'is the pressure to change the nature and purpose of the voluntary sector'. This view is echoed by Nowland-Foreman (1995, p. 46) who points out that if voluntary organiz-ations 'allow their vision to be narrowed to merely agents providing government-defined services in response to specific contracts, then they will become indistinguishable from sub-contractors or "little fingers of the state"'. The comparative advantage of such organizations lies not just in their capacity to mobilize volunteer support, but also in integrating people into the community through preventive, developmental and advocacy activities that are unlikely to attract funding since they generate outputs that are difficult to measure. At the informal level, those voluntary organizations that assert their autonomy by seeking to maintain these distinctive activities may find their culture clashing with that of a managerialist local organization to a degree that excludes them from opportunities for engagement. They may, however, be able to establish links with councilors and officials who are seeking external sources of support for their resistance to managerialism.

A strategy through which local authorities can engage with voluntary organizations in a way that encourages social capital formation has been proposed by Reid (1997). This writer acknowledges that social capital is primarily constructed at the community level but suggests that local governments can contribute to its formation by providing opportunities for citizens and communities to influence the outcomes of local issues and decisions; providing facilities and types of infrastructure that allow voluntary associations to develop and flourish; providing assistance through grants, advice and training to people involved in developing local service delivery networks; undertaking monitoring, research and data collection on the strength of the local voluntary sector; coordinating the delivery of services and funding between agencies, voluntary associations and firms to ensure local needs are being addressed; and giving voice and legitimacy to community concerns about the level and range of local services, especially where they are provided by central government agencies.

A key dimension of this strategy is that the network relationships that local authorities seek to build with other agencies, voluntary organizations and community groups should be in the form of horizontal partnerships rather than vertical principal-agent or patron-client relationships. However, if the partnerships that local authorities forge with voluntary associations are to preserve and enhance social capital, then it is important that the local authority avoids treating them like any other service provider and recognizes the distinctiveness of the voluntary or membership nature of these organizations. Reid (1997, p. 114) argues that for this to occur there are at least two factors that need to be protected: the freedom of these associations to determine their priorities according to the preferences of their members; and the primary accountability they have back to their own members rather than to an external funding or sponsoring body. The local authority should therefore see itself as funding community-driven initiatives rather than purchasing contractually specified outputs from the voluntary organizations concerned.

Once consideration is given to the role that local authorities can play in social capital formation, a significantly different concept of the 'enabling authority' emerges from that which simply seeks to enable the private market to participate more fully in service provision. The examination of theories of social capital in this appendix thus provides a useful additional background to the discussion of two approaches to local government reform in Chapter 6.

6. The Political Economy of Local Government Reform

6.1 INTRODUCTION

Over the past two decades a global wave of local government reform has taken place against a background of far-reaching economic and political changes and a radical reconstruction of economic policy regimes. These changes have been most dramatic in the developing and transitional countries that have implemented comprehensive reform programs (CRPs) based on the 'Washington consensus' that recommends the abandonment of Keynesian demand management and import-substituting industrialization policies in favor of a strategy that focuses on 'macroeconomic stabilization' (of debt and inflation) and 'structural adjustment' through market-oriented reforms (Williamson 1994; Rodrik 1996).

While the reform processes undertaken in advanced industrial countries have often been less abrupt and comprehensive, they have tended to follow the same direction. This is most striking in the area of macroeconomic policy where the shift to a generalized system of floating exchange rates after 1975 has prompted a growing number of countries to reverse their priorities with monetary policy being aimed at inflation or exchange rate targets and fiscal policy being aimed at long-term targets for government debt and/or spending in relation to GDP. The incorporation of these goals into the 'Maastricht criteria' for membership in the European monetary union is the latest indication of a global convergence on a common approach to macroeconomic stabilization. However, it is in the English-speaking nations that the reconstruction of macroeconomic policies in the 1980s occasioned a reappraisal of the role of the state that can be viewed as a concerted attack on pervasive problems of government failure and a radical break from a Keynesian-interventionist policy paradigm that had become increasingly incoherent as it generated piecemeal, incrementalist solutions to problems of market failure (Castles 1993; Hall 1993).

It is against this background that reformist governments have had to decide whether to steer local government reform in the minimalist or activist

direction described in the previous chapter. In most cases these approaches
are not sufficiently compatible to allow reformers to deploy them as two
prongs of a balanced strategy designed to match the functions of local
government to its capacity by combining the minimalist approach of
relieving local governments of those functions in respect of which some
other institution has a comparative advantage with the activist approach of
enhancing their capacity. This incompatibility arises from the different
conclusions the theories underpinning these approaches reach with respect to
the scope of the discretion central governments should trust local
governments to exercise. A minimalist approach that is based on the line of
theoretical argument discussed in Chapter 3, which seeks to show that local
authorities are prone to varieties of government failure that go beyond those
found in other public bodies may thus give rise to a drive to increase central
control over the revenue-raising and service functions of local government.
This would, however, amount to a withdrawal of the trust on which many of
the social capital building and networking initiatives associated with a more
activist approach would appear to depend.

     This chapter will argue that the minimalism or activism with which
reformers seek to restructure the local public sector will be related to the style
of policy leadership that is being exercised at the different stages of a more
comprehensive reform process that seeks to reconstruct public policy
according to principles derived from a government failure paradigm. Despite
its relative neglect of leadership theory by economists, traditions of inquiry
into this phenomenon have been particularly prominent in philosophy,
politics, anthropology, psychology, sociology and history. Moreover,
insights from all these traditions have been integrated into studies of
management and organizational behavior that have been of both an academic
and popular nature (Bass 1990). Distinctions are repeatedly made in this
literature between styles of leadership that are 'democratic', 'participative',
'group-developing', 'relations-centered', 'supportive' and 'considerate', on
the one hand, and those which are 'autoritative', 'dominating', 'directive',
'autocratic', 'task-orientated' and persuasive on the other hand. Bass (1990,
p. 33) suggests that 'it is possible to encapsulate many of these typologies
into the autocratic versus democratic dichotomy'. We will, however, largely
follow a trichotomy proposed by Little (1988) since the three styles of
leadership he differentiates would all seem to be capable of contributing, at
some stage, to the advancement of the 'paradigmatic reform process' that
provides the context for the local government reforms we will be
considering.

     In the first place, there is the 'inspirational' style exhibited by leaders who
tend to be 'political Pandoras, liberating hopes ... unrealistic, inventive
imprudent, careless, enraptured with change and the future' (Little 1988,

p. 5). Little, suggests that at certain stages of their political careers John F. Kennedy in the United States, Harold Wilson in the United Kingdom, Pierre Trudeau in Canada, Gough Whitlam in Australia and David Lange in New Zealand may have exhibited some of these traits. Second, there is the 'strong' style exhibited by leaders who 'prefer to implement ideas rather than to debate them' (Little 1988, p. 45). Although they are 'deliberately unvisionary and unexciting' (p. 5) they have a reputation for decisive action based on 'simple, tangible goals, minimal entanglements and reluctance to compromise' (p. 15). Little devotes much of his book to examining the degree to which Margaret Thatcher in the United Kingdom, Ronald Reagan in the United States and Malcolm Fraser in Australia conformed to this type. Third, there are leaders who exercise what Little calls a 'group' style of leadership. They 'are reluctantly aggressive and tend to idealize solidarity, equality and consultative processes' (p. 6). Little tends to see them as more appealing but less effective than strong leaders. We would suggest that this conclusion is dependent on the context of 1980s politics that Little is studying and fails to appreciate the effectiveness of the style of leadership offered in the 1990s by leaders such as Clinton in the US and Blair in the UK. This style can be more helpfully characterized as 'empathetic' since while it encompasses the more inclusive style that Little associates with group leaders, it dispenses with the nostalgia that can make this style of leadership irrelevant in the aftermath of radical change and emphasizes the necessity of adjusting to the new realities.

In examining the conditions under which each of these leadership styles is likely to prevail and the influence they are likely to have on the direction of local government reform, the chapter is divided into four main sections. Section 6.2 examines the demand and supply side of the strong leadership style that is likely to be required to overcome the resistance to the redirection of policy that can arise during the implementation phase of a CRP. To the degree that the local public sector is seen as a source of such resistance, strong policy leaders are likely to have a minimalist orientation with regard to local government reform. Section 6.3 advances the view that although local government reforms often involve territorial amalgamation and organizational restructuring according to the principles of the New Public Management (NPM) these measures alone cannot ensure that local authorities internalize strong leaders' concerns with reducing the financial burden of local government. We will focus our attention in this section on a range of initiatives that the Thatcher government in the UK took to address this concern since this government appears to stand out in terms of the way it pursued a minimalist agenda of reducing local discretion over services and revenue-raising. Moreover, local government appears to have been the area of public policy in which this government was susceptible to the accumulation of disappointments that eventually catalyzed a shift away from its strong leadership style. Section 6.4 then examines how these disappointments may be countered by the emergence of the style of empathetic policy leadership undertaken by so-called 'Third Way' governments. The way in which the Blair government has taken a more activist approach to local government reform as an important element of its Third Way program is considered as well as the sources of incoherence in this approach that may, in the future, cause policy leaders to disengage from sub-systems such as those surrounding local government. We argue that such disengagement is likely to characterize the successful consolidation of a paradigmatic reform process and in section 6.5 go on to compare the linear concept of modernization with our more cyclical perspective of local government reform by way of conclusion to this chapter.

6.2 THE DEMAND AND SUPPLY OF STRONG LEADERSHIP

The impressive volume of case study literature on the reform experiences of countries that have sought to reconstruct their economic policy to bring it into line with the Washington consensus has tended to focus less on the rationale for this shift than on the reasons for the observed unevenness in its implementation. One factor that is often cited as contributing to this unevenness in implementation is the strength and effectiveness of the policy leadership exercised by the governments concerned (Krueger 1993; Williamson 1994; Dunham and Kelegama 1997; Wallis 1999). While economic theory has tended to neglect the supply side of leadership, there are a number of theories that highlight the factors that can give rise to a demand for strong leadership. We will focus, in particular, on the contribution New Classical macroeconomics (NCM), public choice and agency theory have made in this regard.

Economics and the Demand for Strong Leadership

Within the policy reform literature it is possible to discern an ideal type of 'strong', 'visionary' or 'autonomous' policy leaders who are characterized by their willingness to face the risks associated with implementing CRPs, to use their own authority and political skills to overcome and circumvent resistance to their reform initiatives, to bring bureaucrats into line, to lead public opinion by taking firm positions on contentious issues, and to 'stand before the bar of history' and be held to account for their persistence in striving to impose a new policy paradigm. A number of theoretical developments in the

1970s and 1980s provided explanations as to why such a style of leadership may be necessary.

In the first place, Keynesians and monetarists appear to have reached a consensus that governments are essentially to blame for inflation (Dornbusch and Fischer 1990, pp. 685–6). Both schools thus implicitly attributed the apparent intractability of the high inflation most countries experienced during the 1970s to the weakness of policy leadership reflected in the unwillingness of governments to use tight monetary policies to keep unemployment above its 'natural rate' until inflationary expectations had come down in line with their target inflation rates. Indeed some countries seemed to be prepared to continue accommodating 'cost-push' pressures through expansionary monetary and fiscal policies whenever they caused unemployment to rise above a politically unacceptable threshold even where this appeared to be below the natural rate. The short-term rise in unemployment that occurred in the UK and US in the early 1980s after the Thatcher and Reagan administrations abandoned this accommodating approach in favor of a tough medium-term 'monetarist' strategy designed to bring inflation under control appeared to confirm the view that this was a politically risky approach that required strong policy leaders to remain in power until the pressures to reverse direction had subsided and its long-term benefits were more tangible to the electorate.

Secondly, the NCM pioneered by Lucas (1972; 1973) and Sargent and Wallace (1976) related the social costs, and consequent political risks, of disinflation to the credibility of inflation targets. If these targets were credible, then these economists saw no reason why the announcement of a new low inflation target should not produce an immediate downward revision of inflationary expectations without there being any transition period during which unemployment would have to be above its natural rate. Although none of the countries undertaking disinflation during the 1980s appear to have gone through this kind of 'costless' transition, NCM did draw attention to credibility as a factor accounting for cross-country variations in the social costs of this strategy and focused the attention on factors that could influence the credibility of their anti-inflationary policies.

Two theoretical contributions by new classical macroeconomists were germane in this regard. Kydland and Prescott (1977) showed that credibility could only be achieved if the incentives for politicians to behave in a 'time inconsistent' way were overcome. For example, there may be a political payoff for the government to pressure the central bank to relax monetary policy before an election to move the economy up a short-run Philips curve. If inflation rises above its target rate, the credibility of the target will be damaged and the long-term trade-off between inflation and unemployment could worsen as the target ceases to provide an 'anchor' for inflationary expectations. According to Kydland and Prescott (1977), the problem of time-inconsistency can be overcome through a system that requires governments to provide 'hostages' against this form of 'cheating'. This could be done if the central bank is made accountable for the single objective of achieving and sustaining price stability and is technocratically insulated from political pressures to ease monetary policy.

Sargent (1981), however, demonstrated that even where this type of system of hostages against cheating could be set in place, the inflation targets of countries with high and rising government debt/GDP ratios would lack credibility unless they could make a credible commitment to 'fiscal consolidation'. A long-term fiscal policy designed progressively to reduce government debt in relation to GDP would complement and reinforce the credibility of an anti-inflationary monetary policy since it would remove fears that the country concerned may experience a future debt crisis. According to Sargent's 'unpleasant monetarist arithmetic' a debt crisis is inextricably linked with a loss of control over inflation since it is a situation in which government debt has to be monetized since no institution other than the central bank is prepared to buy newly issued government bonds.

To achieve and sustain prudent levels of debt, debt-ridden governments typically have to focus on cutting and controlling their spending since rising levels of debt are usually a reflection of their limited capacity to further raise taxes while there is also a limit on the extent to which they can use the proceeds of state asset sales to retire debt. Strong policy leadership will, however, be required to overcome the resistance to spending cuts and fiscal discipline that is likely to be generated by the providers and users of public services.

The public choice and agency theories discussed in Chapter 3 can complement NCM by giving some insight into the nature of this resistance. In particular, where providers are not made accountable by funders for the delivery of clearly specified outputs to users, they may respond to funding cuts by reducing the quality and quantity of output provided, rather than by striving to realize gains in productive efficiency. Their scope for pursuing this option will be greater where they are accountable to multiple principals for multiple outputs and where they can exercise professional discretion in setting quality standards and the level of provision of the 'invisible', and unspecified outputs. By reducing levels of service provision they may thus mobilize a public backlash to spending cuts and thereby place vote-seeking politicians under pressure subsequently to reverse them.

More generally, these theories of government failure can highlight the risks strong policy leaders must face when they seek to implement a coherent macroeconomic strategy designed to stabilize and control debt and inflation. In an earlier book (Wallis and Dollery 1999, p. 105) we attributed these risks to what Rodrik (1996) termed the *ex ante* uncertainty that typically surrounds the distributional consequences of these strategies as well as their tendency to depart from the centrist position associated with the Downsian consensus and to create an opportunity to win the next election for a coalition of minorities that is committed to reversing the change in macroeconomic policy direction.

This analysis should, however, be modified to take account of the external pressures governments face when they delay implementing these macroeconomic strategies. Most obviously, the World Bank and the International Monetary Fund can make their implementation a condition of lending to countries with a risk profile that precludes or significantly raises the cost of their access to international credit. In general, the globalization of international financial markets has increased the leverage of international financial institutions seeking to protect the interests of savers who usually stand to lose the most from inflation. In particular, they can apply the discipline of 'capital flight' to those countries that avoid making, or subsequently break, commitments to sustain a strategy that will eventually bring inflation and fiscal aggregates under control.

While economic theory highlights the achievement of policy credibility as an important concern of strong policy leaders, it does not have much to say about the conditions that create an opportunity for elected governments to exercise this style of leadership nor about the ways in which reformists inside and outside of government can most effectively mobilize to take advantage of this type of opportunity. We will briefly consider this issue before considering the approach to local government reform that is likely to be undertaken by governments seeking to exercise strong policy leadership.

The Window of Opportunity to Exercise Strong Policy Leadership

The literature on policy reform has largely focused on the factors that can influence the opportunity for newly elected governments to implement in one 'big bang' a CRP that packages a macroeconomic stabilization strategy with a wide range of microeconomic liberalization measures. Balcerowicz (1994, p.62) has argued that the opportunity to launch a 'big bang' is most likely to occur during periods of 'extraordinary politics' characterized by institutional meltdown and an 'exceptional level of public readiness to accept radical economic measures'. Williamson (1994) has sought to extend this approach by relating public receptivity to CRPs to four factors: the severity of the economic crisis; the size of the new government's winning majority; the length of its 'honeymoon' period during which the public will give it the benefit of the doubt and blame any sacrifices and difficulties on its predecessor; and the presence of a fragmented and demoralized opposition that is identified with past policy failures.

An approach to this issue that is more applicable to the conditions surrounding a shift in policy direction in well-established, stable democracies has been developed by Peter Hall (1993). This political scientist has pointed out that for long periods a reigning 'policy paradigm' can operate as 'a framework of ideas and standards that specifies not only the goals but also the very nature of the problems (policy makers) are meant to be addressing' so that policy changes may be limited to second order changes in policy instruments and first order adjustments in the settings of these instruments (p. 270). This concept of a paradigm as the common epistemological vision and value consensus of a knowledge-based community is, of course, derived from the seminal work of Kuhn (1962).

Hall argues though that during the, typically lengthy, periods of paradigm stability the authority of the reigning policy paradigm may be gradually eroded by the accumulation of anomalies and the resort by policy makers to ad hoc experimentation that stretches its coherence. The most striking anomaly with a paradigm that came to be associated with piecemeal, incremental interventions to correct instances of 'market failure' was that it neglected the potential for government failure created by these interventions. Moreover, the coherence of an interventionist paradigm can clearly be stretched in cases where new forms of state intervention are introduced to correct the problems and distortions associated with existing interventions. The erosion of authority of the old paradigm may be accompanied by an accumulation of disappointment with the pragmatic, risk-averse style of leadership that tends to prevail during the long period of paradigm stability. Both tendencies can combine eventually to produce a climate of frustration with the unwillingness of policy leaders to embrace the risks of what Hall (1993) calls third order policy change the replacement of one policy paradigm with another. This climate would seem to be most effectively countered by an inspirational leadership style that is sufficiently open to new ideas and autonomous from the constraints of the old paradigm to encourage policy actors to engage in a quest for alternative directions for policy development. This shift is likely to contribute to the fragmentation of authority and the emergence of rival paradigms that Hall (1993) considers to be characteristic of the first phase of a shift to a new paradigm.

The very openness of inspirational leaders to new ideas may, however, render them incapable of resolving the problem of incommensurability that comes to the fore during periods when a number of rival paradigms are being pushed forward for consideration. Hall (1993, p. 280) writes that

> Paradigms are by definition never fully commensurable in scientific or technical terms. Because each paradigm contains its own account of how the world facing policy makers operates and each account is different, it is often impossible for the advocates of different paradigms to agree on a common body of data against

which a technical judgment in favor of one paradigm over another might be made.

Inspirational leaders may thus contribute to the climate of confusion and puzzlement that develops during the fragmentation phase. The accumulation of disappointment with failure of this style of policy leadership to limit or resolve the generation of conflicting ideas about the 'way forward' for the policy process may give rise to a demand for 'strong leadership' to 'bring hardness in decision making and clear purpose where before there was irresolution and drift' (Little 1988, p. 5).

The Collective Supply of Strong Leadership

Although many of the case studies on policy reform identify the strong leadership traits exhibited by key players, it would seem that on closer inspection the strong policy leadership required to implement CRPs is, in most cases, collectively supplied. The study of the supply side of strong policy leadership should therefore follow those modern theories of leadership that tend to emphasize the collective dimension of this phenomenon (Bryson and Crosby 1992).

The collective supply of strong policy leadership can be conceived as being undertaken by a network of 'policy entrepreneurs' (Kingdon 1984) who strive to advance one another into positions of leverage over the agenda-setting, formulation, decision making, implementation and evaluation stages of the policy process. Once they have secured positions of authority so that they reconstruct public policy on the basis of the principles they share in common, the strength of their policy leadership would appear to depend on a number of factors.

In the first place their collective strength would be related to the coherence and authority of the new policy paradigm they are striving to impose. With reference to two Conservative governments that were elected on promises to lower inflation, cut taxes, and reduce the role of the state in the UK economy, Hall (1993, p. 290) argues that, between 1979 and 1983, the Thatcher government was more able to resist pressures to make a U-turn back toward reflation and interventionist policies than the 1970–74 Heath government. This was because 'the platform on which Heath was elected was a jerrybuilt structure with no underpinning in an alternative economic theory, while Thatcher's was based on a much more fully elaborated monetarist paradigm' that Thatcher could appeal to 'for authoritative arguments with which to resist mounting pressure for reflation'.

The strength of policy leadership would also be related to the internal cohesion of the reformist network that seeks to supply it. This would tend to exhibit the features of the hope-based networks discussed in Chapter 5.

Through interactive expression games' that reinforce the beliefs and emotional energy that underpin their shared hopes, the members of these networks could come to trust one another to sustain a first order commitment to take advantage of opportunities to advance the quest to impose and institutionalize their policy paradigm and a second order commitment to advance one another into key positions of leverage over the reform process.

Through such expression games the suppliers of strong policy leadership would also try and differentiate themselves from the suppliers of alternative styles of policy leadership. To present themselves as effective, decisive change agents, they may try to differentiate themselves from inspirational leaders through their commitment to implement reform according to a simple, narrow and coherent set of principles derived from the new policy paradigm. Theirs is an emphatic style of leadership that resists giving the impression of doubt. It also resists any empathy with potential losers.

The members of a reformist network seeking to supply strong leadership will also deliberately distinguish themselves from leaders with a more empathetic style by refusing to take seriously the arguments of groups whose interests may be harmed by the reforms they are striving to implement. They will tend to dismiss these arguments as rhetorical smokescreens designed to conceal the vested interests these groups have in preserving their privileges. By provoking these arguments, strong leaders will be able to identify the sources of resistance that need to be marginalized and overcome if they are to steer policy in the direction they intend. The typical ways in which an impression of strong leadership is created by expressing resistance to alternative ideas and opposing interests have been summarized by Little (1988, p. 17):

> The strong leader must steel himself against distraction, ignore alternative ideas, remove himself from the clamor of those excluded or getting hurt. This means that a critical boundary has to be established separating the strong from the weak. Strong leadership energetically resists empathy with opponents, competitors or strangers, but above all it resists identification with those who are defeated or doubtful.

The focus of strong policy leaders will thus be on identifying, marginalizing and overcoming potential sources of resistance so that their initiatives can proceed in a virtually unmodified form through the various stages of the policy process. The approach to local government reform that a governing coalition seeking to supply strong policy leadership is likely to take will thus vary according to the extent to which local government is seen as a potential source of resistance to its policy direction.

In developing or transitional countries where local government has tended to be undeveloped or suppressed under pre-reform regimes, local government reform may not be high on their reform agenda during the implementation phase of a paradigmatic policy change. Their focus will be on taking advantage of crisis conditions to drive through a CRP in one 'big bang'. They will typically not seek to develop local government capacity since at this stage they are unlikely to be willing to encourage alternatives to their policy leadership. Neither will they need to overcome local government resistance to their strategic policy direction since the local sector is unlikely to have the capacity to mobilize and mount this resistance.

The situation may, however, be different in countries where local government accounts for a larger share of government spending and is seen as a significant source of resistance to the macroeconomic imperative of reducing or at least controlling total public spending in both real terms and in relation to GDP. The approach to local government reform by a central government whose policy direction is being steered by a strong leadership coalition (SLC) that seeks to impose a more disciplined fiscal regime must now be considered.

6.3 RESTRUCTURING AND MINIMALIST INITIATIVES UNDER STRONG POLICY LEADERSHIP

Effectively to advance its macroeconomic stabilization goals by placing sustained downward pressure on public sector spending (hereafter referred to a strategy of 'fiscal decrementalism'), an SLC will clearly benefit from the cooperation of actors at lower levels of government who enjoy an element of agent discretion in three important areas. These are the discretion to raise their own revenue, to adjust the level and range of the services they provide and to select the mix of resources and governance mechanisms they can use to provide them. In many countries, local authorities stand out from other government agencies in terms of the significant discretion they can exercise in all three areas. They are therefore in a position cooperatively to make a significant contribution to a strategy of fiscal decrementalism. They can take the initiative to downsize, shedding services that can be more efficiently and cost effectively provided and/or funded by other organizations. They can restructure their operations, seeking more efficient ways to combine and coordinate their resources so that they can cut the cost without reducing the quality of the services they continue to supply. In this way they can minimize the public backlash to cuts in central government funding to local government. They can also disseminate local information to control agencies to enable them to reshape more rationally the allocation of public functions and responsibilities to different levels of government and types of organization.

Unfortunately, the theories of local government failure discussed in previous chapters must raise doubts about whether this cooperation will be forthcoming from a sufficient number of local authorities to ensure that decrementalist goals are achieved within the local sphere of the public sector. In particular, these theories highlighted the probability that an excess spending bias would be maintained in authorities where local discretion is exercised by the type of 'iron triangle' described in Chapter 3 or the stable, insulated 'policy community' described in Chapter 5. Rather than cooperate with control agencies in their drive to reduce government spending, the members of these associations may have a strong incentive to cooperate with one another in the maintenance of programs in respect of which 'micro-decoupling' (Wolf 1989, p. 41) arises such that the benefits mainly accrue to the interests they represent whereas the costs are dispersed amongst all other groups. It may thus be to the mutual benefit of 'vote-buying' local politicians, 'empire-building' local bureaucrats and rent-seeking local interest groups to expand, or at least resist, the contraction of these programs.

There are a number of non-cooperative strategies these actors can deploy in response to a cut in central funding to the local government. In the first place, they can compensate for the reduction in central funding by using their discretion to raise revenue from other sources. In particular, they can either increase locally levied rates or taxes or they can hike upwards the user charges on services supplied by local natural monopolies owned by local authorities. Clearly their capacity to use these revenue-raising options will be limited by the strength of the 'voice' and 'exit' options referred to in Chapter 3. Local citizens can thus voice their dissatisfaction with the higher financial burden these options impose although this voice mechanism may be weakened by the factors that make local politics susceptible to voter apathy and fiscal illusion that have also been analyzed in Chapter 3. Alternatively they can take the exit option either voting with their feet and moving to jurisdictions that are better able to contain the local tax burden or switching to alternative suppliers. The capacity of local government to absorb the impact of central funding cuts may thus be related to the degree to which they are exposed to the types of competitive pressures set out by Boyne (1998).

Second, in some countries, local authorities have the discretion to borrow. The degree to which they can offset reduced central funding by borrowing is obviously limited if this option fails to increase their asset base and thereby expand their capacity to repay the debt.

A third non-cooperative response to a central funding cut would be for local authorities to cut services strategically in a way that intensifies the public backlash to top-down decrementalism. If 'iron triangles' are not to cut off their noses to spite their faces they may be able to target these cuts to those less visible (Lindsay 1976, p.82) aspects of local government services that benefit local consumers as a whole more than the particular groups they represent and then attribute the blame for reduced service quality to the decrementalist policies being pursued by central government. Alternatively, they can bias local government spending to consumption rather than investment, deliberately allowing infrastructure to run down to the point where it can only be upgraded with a significant injection of central government funding.

There are two broad strategies that an SLC can deploy to overcome, or at least minimize, these types of local resistance to its decrementalist strategy. The first is the potentially minimalist strategy of restructuring local government through territorial amalgamation and internal rationalization according to the principles of the NPM. Second, there is a more explicitly minimalist approach that combines measures that reduce the scope for agent discretion at the local level while at the same time strengthening the voice and exit mechanisms that can be activated in response to the fiscally irresponsible use of this discretion. Both strategies need to be considered in more detail.

Restructuring to Overcome Local Resistance to Decrementalism

A characteristic trait of strong policy leaders is the way they eschew accommodation or compromise with groups that they identify as potential sources of resistance to the advancement of their goals. Through strategic restructuring an SLC can attempt to ensure that collaboration with other actors is more likely to take place on its own terms. In countries where there has been an incremental proliferation of local authorities, territorial amalgamation can become an important element of a restructuring strategy.

Amalgamation

The literature on market and government failure at the local level, surveyed in Chapters 2 and 3, suggests that it is difficult to determine, *a priori,* whether amalgamation will make a positive or negative contribution to the advancement of decrementalist goals. This ambiguity may surround the increase in the revenue-raising capacity of local authorities that often results from amalgamation. The consequent reduction in local government dependence on central government grants may, on the one hand, reduce the 'flypaper effect' – or the hypothesized tendency for these grants to increase public expenditure by more than an equivalent increase in income from other sources, as outlined in Chapter 3. On the other hand, local governments may have more discretion to increase their own revenue to maintain their spending even where central government is trying to make them reduce it by cutting their level of intergovernmental assistance.

On the negative side of the ledger, amalgamation may reduce the competitive pressure that authorities in different local jurisdictions place on one another to contain costs and make their localities more attractive in terms of the financial burden they impose on ratepayers.   In particular, amalgamating existing small local governments into larger units can raise the costs of migration and thus diminish the mobility of the citizenry. Moreover, in these larger units it may be more difficult for citizens to access council officials to voice dissatisfaction about fiscally irresponsible ways in which they can exercise their revenue-raising discretion.

From a more positive perspective, it is possible that amalgamation can help local authorities realize economies of scale and thereby reduce the per capita costs of local government.   Indeed, in Chapter 3 some suggestions were made about how amalgamation may actually strengthen the voice mechanisms that can be activated in response to fiscal irresponsibility.   In general, the fact that for citizens the 'stakes are higher' with respect to the policies of larger municipal entities means that they are likely to be subject to greater voter interest, oversight by elected politicians and media attention than the smaller units they replace.

However, from the point of view of SLCs, the most significant impact of amalgamation and the factor that is most likely to tip them in its favor, is the way it breaks up the iron triangles and policy communities that form around local authorities and make them a source of resistance to top-down pressure to contain their spending. Following amalgamation new councils will be elected and new council managers appointed who might not have the same links with the rent-seeking interest groups that made up the old local establishment. This can provide an opportunity for internal rationalization to take place according to principles of NPM.

New Public Management in Local Government

NPM is shorthand for the 'set of broadly similar administration doctrines' (Hood 1991) which combined insights from public choice, the 'new institutional economics' and 'generic managerialism' to strengthen the management capacity of public servants and reduce the scope for non-market failure in that residual core of the public sector which could not be contracted out. Notwithstanding its controversial and ill-defined character, NPM can be viewed as the second great wave of radical reform in the administration of the modern state (Barzelay 1992).   The first revolution in public administration, said to have occurred initially in Britain in the nineteenth century and termed 'Progressive-Era' Public Administration (PPA) (Hood

1994, p. 125), sought to 'professionalize the public service in the sense of ensuring that selection and promotion were on merit rather than patronage, rule rather than discretion governed how public bureaucratic process and decisions operated, and public service was oriented by norms of impersonality, correct procedure and consistency' (Yeatman 1997, p. 175). Hood (1994, p. 126) has argued that exponents of PPA stressed two basic features of organizational design: the public sector should be starkly distinguished from the private sector in terms of its operations, and rules of procedure should be developed to limit discretionary behavior by bureaucrats and politicians. By contrast, NPM can be seen as diluting these two ingredients of PPA. Hood (1994, p. 129) has argued that NPM:

> [S]trikes directly at the heart of the two basic doctrines of PPA described above. One of its themes is the doctrine of lessening or removing organizational differences between the public and private sector, to reduce avoidable public sector inefficiency. The doctrine is that methods of doing business in public organizations need to be shifted away from heavy emphasis on general rules of procedure and be focused more on getting results.

Hood (1994) proposes that the rise of NPM over the recent past should not be seen as an isolated phenomenon but rather viewed as part of at least four other megatrends, notably: attempts to constrain the growth of government in western democracies, a shift away from public production towards corporatization and privatization, the extensive use of information technology in the public sector, and the internationalization of public administration into a generic management philosophy.

Although there are variations in the way NPM has been applied in different countries, it generally moves away from the procedurally-based management framework of PPA by emphasizing the importance of hands-on professional management and the freedom to manage, the introduction of performance appraisal with explicit performance standards, and a greater use of output controls with their stress on results rather than procedures. Implicit in these strategies is a specific view on the nature of management which is held to be generic on the assumption that 'management is management, no matter where it takes place' (Peters 1996, p. 28). This, in turn, leads to an emphasis on a 'professional management', which is 'portable', 'paramount', 'discretionary', 'central', and 'indispensable' (Hood 1991, p. 6).

From the perspective of an SLC, territorial amalgamation can afford the opportunity for a cadre of professional managers who hold to NPM doctrines to take over the management of the new councils. According to Hood (1991, p. 11) such managers are likely to engage on a quest to advance what he calls the 'sigma-type' cluster of administrative values that highlight 'economy', and 'parsimony' even where this makes it more difficult to realize the 'theta-type' of 'honesty' and 'fairness'; and 'lambda-type' values of 'security' and 'resilience'. Table 6.1 summarizes the content of these three different clusters of values:

Table 6.1 Hood's three sets of core administrative values

	Sigma-type values KEEP IT LEAN AND PURPOSEFUL	Theta-type values KEEP IT HONEST AND FAIR	Lambda-type values KEEP IT ROBUST AND RESILIENT
STANDARD OF SUCCESS	Frugality (matching of resources to tasks for given goals)	Rectitude (achievement of fairness, mutuality, the proper discharge of duties)	Resilience (achievement of reliability, adaptivity, robustness)
STANDARD OF FAILURE	Waste (muddle, confusion, inefficiency)	Malversation (unfairness, bias, abuse of office)	Catastrophe (risk, breakdown, collapse)
CURRENCY OF SUCCESS AND FAILURE	Money and time (resource costs of producers and consumers)	Trust and entitlements (consent, legitimacy, due process, political entitlements)	Security and survival (confidence, life and limb)
CONTROL EMPHASIS	Output	Process	Input/Process
SLACK	Low	Medium	High
GOALS	Fixed/Single	Incompatible	Emergent/ Multiple
INFORMATION	Costed, segmented (commercial assets)	Structured	Rich exchange, collective asset
COUPLING	Tight	Medium	Loose

Source: Hood (1991)

Where council managers are given the discretion to redesign the management and organization of local authorities to advance sigma-type values they should be able to realize efficiency gains that contribute to decrementalist goals by enabling these organizations to provide services of the same quality at lower cost. Perhaps the best way of appreciating this possibility is to view NPM as a means of removing, or at least mitigating, the effects of each of these attributes of non-market supply identified by Wolf (1989).

In the first place, the difficulties associated with defining, evaluating and monitoring the range of outputs typically provided by a local authority can be reduced as a result of the organizational restructuring associated with the application of NPM. To implement its doctrines, new council managers will usually seek to break up bureaucratic structures into manageable units dealing with one another on an arm's length basis with each focused on achieving clearly defined single objectives and producing specified outputs. The underlying rationale holds that the closer these units approach the ideal of being 'single-objective, trackable and manageable' (Hood 1991, p. 12), the easier it is to match resources to defined tasks and to shift from controlling input to monitoring output. Such restructuring can make it possible to assign the responsibility for managing these units to named persons and, where feasible, can also be accompanied by the development of output-based accounting systems which make intensive use of information technology. With their greater freedom to manage, council managers move quickly to cut inefficient services and reduce overstaffing.

Organizational restructuring can also make it possible to mitigate the non-contestability of government supply which Wolf (1989) identified as the second attribute of non-market production. Thus, even in the case of those public services which cannot be contracted out, it has been possible to create an internal or quasi-market for these services within the public sector through the separation of the purchasing and provision of public services.

The shift toward a system of output monitoring would also help mitigate the problems associated with the uncertain or ambiguous technology which Wolf (1989) identified as the third attribute of nonmarket supply. By emphasizing the distinction between inputs, outputs and outcomes, council managers can assert their freedom and responsibility to press their staff into searching for greater efficiencies in combining inputs to produce clearly defined outputs, while at the same time seeking to clarify with elected councilors the outcomes they expect these outputs to generate. Both councilors and managers therefore have an incentive to develop the policy making capacity of their advisory staff so that they have a clearer understanding of the relationships between agency outputs and social outcomes.

Finally, NPM has sought to address the problems associated with the lack of bottom-line and termination mechanisms by establishing a framework within which the supply of management to the public sector can be made more contestable. This reflects the influence on NPM of the 'managerialist' notion of 'professional management expertise as portable, paramount over technical expertise, requiring high discretionary power to achieve results ("free to manage"), and central and indispensable to better organizational performance' (Hood 1991, p. 6). If organizational performance is linked to management expertise, and if the latter is viewed as a generic, portable skill, then it follows that no specific asset will be lost if the manager of a poorly performing agency is replaced. Council managers can therefore be placed on fixed-term contracts to make the management of local authorities more contestable.

Problems an SLC Might Have with the Application of NPM at Local Level

From the perspective of an SLC seeking to advance decrementalist goals, the main problem with the extension of NPM to the local government level is that it might actually increase the discretion and capacity of the managers of new larger councils to steer them in an activist rather than a minimalist direction. Thus rather than using the information the new accounting and management systems give them about the resource requirements of their different outputs to streamline their operations and reduce productive inefficiency, the council managers may seek to expand the range of services they offer within their budget constraints.

For those local authorities that seek to take advantage of their enhanced capacity to pursue a more activist course, the adoption of NPM may actually exacerbate at least two of the factors that were identified in Chapter 3 as making these bodies particularly susceptible to government failure. By concentrating administrative authority in the hands of managers, giving them greater freedom to manage and enhancing their capacity to monitor and evaluate the performance of the disaggregated single-goal units under them, a move to NPM may increase the information asymmetries that allow managers to 'capture' elected councilors. An empire-building manager may thus be able to steer a council in an activist direction that makes it more difficult for it to contain its total spending, by filtering and screening the information it receives in a way that biases it toward the development and extension of its services to the local community.

Moreover, to the degree that NPM improves the strategic quality of the information held by council managers, it can also increase their bargaining power in the multi-organizational partnerships they forge with private and voluntary organizations. Their influence over the direction of community development may thus expand as they are better able to leverage the resources of these organizations. What might be of concern to an SLC, however, is the possibility that these new IBNs might have an even greater spending bias than the 'iron triangles' that formed around the old councils before they were restructured. In particular, the voluntary and community organizations that are drawn into partnerships with activist councils may represent a disproportionate number of non-rate paying citizens. This could mean that they have a relatively weak incentive to pressure the council into fiscally responsible behavior. Indeed, they could offer to deliver to activist councils the votes of the groups they represent in return for an extension of services to these citizens that are cross-subsidized out of rates levied on property owners.

Once a local government restructuring process has been completed, the SLC who may have initiated it is likely to be primarily concerned with the extent to which they can trust the new cadre of council managers to pursue the minimalist course of seeking greater productive efficiencies rather than the activist approach of striving to develop new avenues of council service to their communities. Unfortunately, the basis for this trust may be weaker with respect to managers at the local than at the central level where the 'change agents' appointed to executive positions in control agencies and restructured government departments may be trusted members of the HBN through which strong policy leadership is collectively supplied (Kelsey 1995; Wallis and Dollery 1999). This is because it is unlikely that this HBN can be extended to include the new council managers. There may simply be too many of them and they may be too geographically dispersed to enable them to engage in the dense, bounded interaction through which the internal cohesion and shared commitment of this HBN is built up.

Moreover, in many countries, council managers are primarily accountable to the elected councils who appoint them. While these bodies are likely to be concerned with their effectiveness in realizing agreed goals, this concern will go beyond a narrow focus on their success in making efficiency gains. In any case the impact these managers have on overall efficiency may be difficult to assess since, even after restructuring, local authorities will continue to be multi-purpose organizations. With their control over information flows managers may be able to conceal slack in some areas while highlighting selective efficiency gains in others as we argued earlier in Chapter 3.

The influence an SLC can have over new councils and their managers will tend to be indirect. They may have to infiltrate and attempt to take over the national associations of local authorities and local government managers within which local actors tend to interact. However, even if these networks are receptive to NPM doctrines–perhaps because they see them as providing an impetus for the professionalization of local government management – the SLC can have no assurance that they will not be used to push local government development in an activist rather than a minimalist direction.

A situation of central–local mistrust will, of course, be exacerbated where there are different political parties in control at central and local levels. This situation may, to some degree, be avoided in countries where political parties have a tradition of not contesting local elections, although local electors may still look to their non-partisan representatives to countervail and balance the top-down initiatives of an SLC to impose greater fiscal discipline. It was, however, particularly pronounced in the UK during the 1980s and early 1990s when a right-wing Conservative government seeking to exercise strong policy leadership to 'roll back the frontiers of the state' confronted strong resistance from a preponderance of Labour-led local governments that generally sought to expand municipal socialism via an enlarged local welfare state. The Thatcherite 'attack on local government' (Jones and Stewart 1985; Newton and Karran 1985) thus provides a useful case study of the link between a strong leadership style and a minimalist approach to local government reform that combines measures which seek to make councils more accountable for their 'fiscal irresponsibility' with those which try to reduce their ability to behave in this way by curtailing their discretion over revenue-raising and service provision. This approach must now be considered in more detail.

A Minimalist Approach to Increasing the Accountability and Reducing the Discretion of Local Government

There is an apparent irony in the tendency of an SLC, like that which formed around the Thatcher government, to combine a policy of reducing state intervention in the market with one that, at the same time, steps up central intervention in local government affairs. This irony does, however, fade away in the light of the arguments that local bodies are more susceptible to government failure than their central counterparts. Constraining local government may thus be seen as part of a general drive to reduce the scope for government failure in the public sector. This would, of course, be highlighted where local governments are seen, as they were in the UK in the 1980s, as a significant source of resistance to a macroeconomic strategy of government expenditure restraint.

There are a number of ways in which an SLC that controls central government can intervene to address its concern with the potential for fiscal irresponsibility at the local level. Table 6.2 distinguishes these intervention-ist measures according to their intended effect on local government discretion.

Table 6.2   *Interventionist measures according to their effect on local*
              discretion

Type of Measure	Effect on Local Discretion
Measures to Increase Transparency	Low
Accrual accounting	
Annual plans	
Funding policy statements	
Long-term financial strategy statements	
Measures to Strengthen 'Voice'	Low/medium
Access to meetings	
Public consultation	
Complaints procedures	
Citizen charters and juries	
Incentives to vote	
More frequent elections	
Citizen initiated referenda	
Proportional representation	
Measures to Reduce Local Service Discretion	Medium
National standards	
Direct central funding of service units	
Discretion to opt-out of local control	
User charges and voucher schemes	
Devolution to non-elected agencies	
Recentralization of local responsibilities	
Compulsory competitive tendering	
Compulsory privatization	
Measures to Reduce Local Financial Discretion	High
Move to lump sum central grants	
Capping local tax rates	
Nationalization of business rates	
Poll Tax	

Measures to Increase Transparency

The form of central intervention that probably has the least impact on local
government autonomy would comprise a range of measures designed to
make the financial implications of the discretionary element of local policy
more transparent. A number of local government reforms introduced in New

Zealand since 1989 appear to have led the way in this regard. While the detail of these reforms will be discussed in the next chapter, it will suffice to point out at this stage that these types of transparency requirements can be expected to strengthen both the voice and exit mechanisms that may be activated in response to information about how councils have exercised their discretion. Those councils that impose a relatively heavier burden on business ratepayers can, in principle, be disciplined by the exit mechanism as business investment is drawn to localities that have demonstrated a capacity to focus their spending on core services to property. Moreover, those groups who advocate a minimalist approach to local government can use the information disclosed through the transparency requirements to campaign for the election of more fiscally conservative councils or push for the replacement of activist council managers.

Measures to Strengthen 'Voice'

As Table 6.2 indicates, there are, in addition, a number of ways in which the range and frequency of voice mechanisms can be increased. For example, in New Zealand the imposition of transparency requirements has been combined with a drive to establish a more open form of local government as the public has been given free access to council meetings and the opportunity to make submissions before annual plans and long-term financial strategies are adopted. More generally, central governments may attempt to address factors that contribute to low turnout at local elections by requiring that, for instance, polling booths be made more accessible, postal balloting be introduced and voters be offered a wider selection of candidates by expanding electoral assemblies or implementing a ward system for local elections. To the degree that these measures counter voter apathy they may reduce tendencies toward organizational slack in local government.

Measures to strengthen voice mechanisms may also focus on some of the shortcomings of representative democracy. Where representatives are selected on the basis of the package of policies they promise to advocate, citizens may not have a sufficient opportunity to voice their dissatisfaction at the cost and/or quality of specific services provided by the local authority. The institution of complaints procedures, the mandatory appointment of ombudsmen, the requirement that consumer rights be specified in 'Citizens Charters' and that provision be made for citizen juries to hear legal actions taken with regard to these rights might all provide additional and more effective channels for consumer dissatisfaction to be voiced. Local representative democracy might also be supplemented by establishing the conditions for citizen-initiated referenda (on the basis on a minimum number of signatories to a petition) or by the replacement of a first-past-the-post system with proportional representation. It should be pointed out that while the latter measure may provide more representation for minority interests at local level, an SLC may resist its implementation at the national level since it can increase the strength of the legislative relative to the executive branch of government and increase the likelihood of policy paralysis and incoherence (Bates 1996).

It may thus be possible for central governments to enhance local governments' accountability by requiring them to make their decisions more transparent and give citizen-consumers more opportunity to exercise voice without significantly curtailing their discretion over services and revenue-raising. However, an SLC may consider that these measures may not suffice to contain the susceptibility to government failure at the local level. It may therefore embark on a range of minimalist initiatives that can significantly impinge on the two main areas of local government discretion.

Measures to Reduce Local Service Discretion

In general, central government is more capable of reducing local discretion in respect of those services that are either contracted out to local governments by its agencies or that must be provided by these bodies as a statutory duty compared to those that are provided on the basis of purely permissive powers (such as leisure). While there has long been a tendency for centralizing welfare states such as the UK to limit local discretion through the imposition of nationally uniform, legally prescribed minimum service standards, the more recent shift to NPM has, by facilitating more precise output specification and monitoring, given central government agencies the capacity to make local authorities contractually accountable for providing specified services. It has also given central agencies more scope to circumvent local government intermediaries and to allocate funds directly to organizations providing specific services in local areas.

The Thatcher government made this an important feature of its education policy when it introduced legislation that allowed individual schools to 'opt-out' of local government control and be funded directly by central government. The intention was that, in response to financial inducements, the majority of schools would become 'grant-maintained' with central government effectively purchasing school places and requiring schools to provide minimum education standards. Bailey (1999, pp. 274–5), however, reports that by 1997 when the newly-elected Labour government announced that no more schools would be allowed to opt-out of local authority control, less than 3 per cent of primary schools and 18 per cent of state secondary schools had actually availed themselves of this option.

More generally, this type of exit mechanism can be strengthened when local authorities are required to extend, as far as feasible, the practice of financing service provision through user charges rather than compulsory local rates and taxes since this gives individual consumers the freedom to 'opt-out' of specific services if they are dissatisfied with their cost and/or quality. Similarly, the introduction of vouchers exchangeable both within and without the jurisdiction, like school vouchers, allow citizens to switch to alternative providers and place pressure on local authorities to be more efficient and responsive.

The centralizing aspect of an SLC may also be reflected in its tendency to establish non-elected agencies (NEAs) to advance single, well-specified goals that fall within the wider range of concerns of local governments. Since these NEAs operate alongside local authorities a 'polycentric policy terrain' (Rhodes 1997, p.37) can emerge that places these two types of organization in a situation of 'structural dependence' on one another. From the perspective of an SLC this may be a welcome development since it opens up a new channel of influence and leverage over local government. It may, however, be less welcome by local authorities since, as Bailey (1999, p. 269) has observed 'the increasing fragmentation of UK public decision-making during the 1980s through specially appointed central government agencies with explicit remits and special boundaries (especially for local economic development initiatives) was in direct and uneasy contrast with the consolidating, over-arching corporatist approach of local government'.

An SLC may, however, seek to diminish local discretion over services more directly through a reassignment of responsibilities. It could relieve local government of some services and provide them directly from the center or reassign their provision to NEAs or voluntary organizations or profit-making businesses. This reassignment may be based on an reassessment of comparative institutional advantage that takes into account the presumed greater susceptibility of local authorities to government failure.

With the extension of NPM principles to the local public sector, it may become increasingly feasible for local authorities to decide unilaterally to contract out some of the services they provide and privatize trading enterprises they own. An SLC may, however, be unwilling to allow these decisions to remain subject to the discretion of local governments. In the UK, for example, the Thatcher government introduced compulsory competitive tendering (CCT) in 1980 for local government's construction-related activities, including new building and renewal, building repairs and maintenance, and highways construction and maintenance. It later extended CCT to the internal cleaning of buildings, refuse collection, street cleaning, school and welfare catering, vehicle maintenance, grounds maintenance and management of sports and leisure services. It is easy to see that a similar compulsory approach could be applied with respect to the privatization of local government-owned trading enterprises. As Chapter 7 will describe, compulsory privatization has become an important component of the local government reform package that a minimalist advocacy coalition is urging central government to adopt in New Zealand.

Measures to Reduce Local Financial Discretion

The concerns an SLC has about local governments are likely to revolve mainly around the ways in which they finance their activities since these bodies can thwart top-down pressures to cut their spending by simply offsetting any reduction in central grants with an increase in local rates and taxes. Any attempt to curb or limit the tax-raising powers of local government does, however, strike at the very basis of local government autonomy since, as Bailey (1999, p. 177) points out 'the economic rationale for local governments to have their own tax-raising powers is grounded in Oates's decentralization theorem ... Local governments without tax-raising powers are effectively agencies of central government.'

Minimalists would tend to argue that any decline in local autonomy resulting from their proposals to reform local government finance is a price that needs to be paid to advance their goal of strengthening local accountability by 'introducing a clear link between the provision of services, paying for them and voting in local elections' (Marsh and Rhodes 1992, p. 51). The Thatcher government clearly took the public choice theoretic view that this led to 'an in-built tendency for voters to vote for excessive local government spending' (Bailey 1999, p. 267). The successive reforms of local government finance by the Thatcher government culminated in a 1990 package that addressed the three main areas where the system was thought to weaken accountability for fiscal irresponsibility at the local level.

The first area related to the grant system that British central governments have used since 1966 to equalize the taxable resources of local authorities while taking account of the various demographic, geographic, social, environmental and other factors that were thought to affect their need to spend. The Thatcher government considered that this system provided too strong an incentive for high-spending authorities to increase their spending further so as to gain larger grants and, accordingly, replaced it in 1980 with a new block grant that was designed to increase financial pressure on local authorities to bring their expenditure into line with targets set by central government. Expenditure in excess of the 'Grant-Related Expenditure Assessment' (GREA) thus attracted an additional block grant at a diminishing or 'tapered' rate so as to increase the cost to local taxpayers of such excess spending. As a result of its increasing unease with the way the complexity of this system blurred local accountability, the Thatcher government replaced it in 1990 with a new 'Revenue Support Grant'. This comprised two main elements: a standard grant paid as an equal fixed sum per head of adult population in all local authorities in support of the generality of services; and a lump sum needs grant that varied according with differences in the assessed need to spend per head. In general, reforms of the grant system in the UK reflected a minimalist concern with reducing fiscal illusion and ensuring that grants are mainly lump sum so that they have only an income and not a substitution effect since they do not change the relative price of the grant-aided service.

A second major area of concern for the Thatcher government was with the property tax system local authorities used to raise general revenue. The tenuous link this system allowed to develop between tax liability and voting was thought to be most problematic with respect to the property tax levied on businesses since local businesses usually have no vote. Moreover, this government came to see relatively high local business taxes as a significant supply side constraint on the efficiency of local economies. Bailey (1999, p. 174) points out in this regard that:

> Despite the lack of clear empirical evidence about the impact (if any) of locally variable business property taxes on the location of firms, during the 1980s and 1990s, the UK government believed that relatively high rates for the local business property tax caused significant crowding-out at the local level by deterring investment by locally-indigenous firms, by causing local firms to exit the locality, and by deterring inward investment by firms from outwith the jurisdiction.

Although the Thatcher government had taken on powers to cap local tax rates, it eventually decided to remove this business property tax from local government control in 1990 by introducing a single uniform tax rate on business properties, the proceeds of which were paid into a national pool that was, in turn, distributed as an equal amount per head of population. The local business tax was thus transformed into an 'assigned revenue' that was in practice not markedly different from the other grants made to local authorities. The base on which local authorities could raise their own tax revenue outside of the control of central government was thus significantly narrowed by this measure.

Perhaps the most radical and controversial component of the 1990 package was the replacement of the local residential property tax with a local poll tax– a flat-rate, locally variable tax payable by all adults resident within a local authority's jurisdiction. Poll taxes are generally thought to come closest to the type of lump sum tax that avoids the substitution effects associated with most other feasible forms of taxation. However, their implementation at the local level in the UK was mainly designed to establish a tight correspondence between tax liability and vote eligibility. The greater incentives voters would have under this system to reinforce central pressures on local authorities to restrain their spending were augmented by the very high 'gearing effects' that arose from the dependence of these bodies on central grants. As Bailey (1999, p. 92) explains:

> On average, about 80 per cent of British local government's income net of charges is financed by central government grants ... This creates a *gearing effect* whereby, on average, British local governments would have to have to raise the tax by 5 per cent or so in order to increase their net expenditure by 1 per cent. (original emphasis)

Despite these purported advantages the Thatcher government soon encountered strong resistance in its drive to implement this tax. Its poll tax proposals had attracted little support in the local government policy community due to 'its distributional consequences, its deleterious effects on local government and local democracy, its impracticability and the high administrative costs, especially those of trying to trace all adults in order to raise tax payments from them' (Bailey 1999, p. 164). Recalcitrant councils were thus able to enlist the support of the large numbers of predominantly urban citizens who were made worse off by this tax to put pressure on government to reverse this component of its reform package. The effectiveness of this campaign is, however, not just reflected in the replacement of the poll tax by a new form of local residential property tax (council tax) in 1993 but in the part it has been claimed to play in the replacement of Thatcher by Major as Prime Minister in the Conservative Cabinet.

SLCs in other countries might not be able to go as far as the UK in limiting local financial discretion since this country stands out in terms of the narrowness of the local government tax base and the control over local finance central government is able to exert through its comprehensive equalizing grant system. Indeed the experiments in implementing a uniform business property tax rate and a local poll tax appear to be unique in recent experience to this country. The UK experience in this regard does, however, illustrate the inherent tendency of an SLC to over reach itself and create a climate within which there can be a growing demand for a change in leadership style. The direction this shift in style is likely to take and the possible tendency that can emerge for a more activist approach to be taken in local government policy must now be considered.

6.4 EMPATHETIC POLICY LEADERSHIP AND A MORE ACTIVIST APPROACH TO LOCAL GOVERNMENT REFORM

It is possible to make a number of generalizations from our earlier discussion of the conditions under which a demand for strong policy leadership will emerge, the relationship between the stages of a paradigmatic reform process and the path according to which different styles of policy leadership are likely to succeed one another. Firstly, following Hall (1993) and Howlett and Ramesh (1995), it would seem that a paradigmatic reform process is likely to go through the four stages of 'erosion', 'fragmentation', 'implementation' and 'consolidation' described in the first column of Table 6.3. Secondly, as the second column of this table indicates, the accumulation of disappointment with the style of leadership that tends to prevail at each stage may produce an emotional climate that makes the public receptive to a change in leadership style. Finally, the most likely successor style of leadership (shown in the third column) will be that style that most effectively counters this emotional climate and facilitates the transition to the next stage of the paradigmatic reform process.

We have already argued that a strong leadership style can, through its commitment to advance a quest for policy coherence by reconstructing policy according to a narrow set of principles derived from a new paradigm, both counter the climate of puzzlement produced by the inspirational leadership style that tends to prevail during the fragmentation phase and facilitate a transition to the implementation phase of a paradigmatic reform process. As a strong leadership style comes to prevail during the implementation phase, its characteristic inflexibility may, however, cause disappointments to accumulate in a way that eventually causes a pervasive climate of anxiety to surround the policy process.

This inflexibility may be reflected in the narrow range of goals an SLC deems to be consistent with the new paradigm. Thus, for example, the narrow pursuit of price level stability through monetary policy may cause real GDP and employment to fluctuate more in response to 'supply shocks' than is necessary to preclude a resurgence of inflationary expectations.

Similarly, a commitment to use the budget surpluses generated by a prolonged policy of restraining government expenditure exclusively to reduce debt and tax burdens may cause the perpetuation of supply side rigidities that could be alleviated through selective strategies that government agencies are too resource-constrained to initiate. The anxiety that is generated by the belief that an SLC is allowing a country's producers and

Table 6.3   A paradigmatic reform process and the succession of leadership styles

Stage of Paradigmatic Reform Process	Emotional Climate Produced by Prevailing Leadership Style	Successor Leadership Style
1. Erosion of Authority Anomalies accumulate and efforts are made to stretch the reigning paradigm to account for them	*Frustration* Disappointments accumulate with the unwillingness of pragmatic leaders to rethink established ideas or challenge established interests	*Inspirational Leadership* Counters climate of frustration by engaging actors on a quest for *policy innovation*
2. Fragmentation of Authority A number of incommensurable paradigms are proposed as alternatives to the existing paradigm	*Puzzlement* Disappointments accumulate with the unwillingness of inspirational leaders to commit themselves to a new policy paradigm	*Strong Leadership* Counters climate of puzzlement by engaging actors on a quest for *policy coherence* through the imposition of a new paradigm
3. Implementation of New Paradigm The advocates of a new paradigm secure positions of authority and alter existing organization and decision-making arrangements according to principles derived from the new paradigm	*Anxiety* Disappointments accumulate with the inflexibility of the strong leader's commitment to a narrow set of goals and to denying opponents the opportunity to mobilize resistance to reform	*Empathetic Leadership* Counters climate of anxiety by engaging actors on a quest for *policy flexibility* within the boundaries of the new paradigm
4. Consolidation of New Paradigm A new political consensus against reversing the reform process emerges due to the sunk costs incurred in structural adjustment and the establishment of institutional 'fire alarms' against reversal	*Fatigue* Disappointments accumulate with the tendency of empathetic leaders persistently to challenge actors to adjust to change and reinterpret their goals according to the new paradigm	*Pragmatic Leadership* Counters climate of fatigue by engaging actors on a quest for *policy stability* that takes for granted a standardized interpretation of the new paradigm

workers to be exposed to the harsh realities of a dynamic and volatile global environment without providing them with adequate assistance to adjust to its exigencies may be compounded by the commitment the members of this coalition typically have to use the positions of authority they secure to exclude, marginalize and overcome any source of resistance to their reform initiatives.

This climate of anxiety is likely to be most effectively countered by an empathetic style of policy leadership. The members of the coalition that seeks to supply this style of leadership will be characteristically engaged on a quest for greater policy flexibility within the boundaries of the new paradigm that has been imposed by the SLC. At the same time they will engage in expression games that differentiate their leadership style from that of both inspirational and strong leaders. Unlike inspirational leaders they will not challenge the authority of the new reigning paradigm. Rather they will tend to challenge its narrow interpretation by the SLC. They will typically argue that it permits a broader range of goals to be pursued through a wider range of instruments, institutions and participating actors than those which were deployed the SLC they are seeking to succeed. They will further differentiate themselves from strong leaders by their active concern for groups that have been disadvantaged by the adjustment process. Their quest for flexibility will thus also encompass a search for policies that facilitate the adjustment of these groups to the new realities. Moreover, empathetic leaders are more likely to collaborate with these groups and attempt to encourage and empower community-based leadership that can function as the catalytic focus of initiatives to enhance their adjustment capacity.

Empathetic policy leaders will tend to take an activist approach to local government, being concerned with enhancing their capacity as part of their drive to consolidate and broaden the gains from the most recent political and economic changes. The emergence of a more activist approach to local government during the consolidation of a paradigmatic reform process is observable in countries undergoing a transition from authoritarian to democratic governance. Although local government has historically tended to be weak in these countries, there has been a rapidly growing interest in the decentralization of previously highly centralized governments and a broadening and strengthening of local governance capacity. As Cheema (1996, p. 16) has observed:

From Bolivia, where a new popular participation law is designed to encourage the movement of the poor into the nation's political mainstream through the development and strengthening of local institutions, to the Peoples Republic of China, where the granting of substantial degrees of municipal autonomy to selected local governments has produced, for example, in Shanghai, a major economic boom that includes the largest amount of new construction activity in a single urban area in human history, one witnesses the stirring of new leadership and creativity at the local level.

This development has been particularly marked during the course of the last fifteen years in Latin America which 'has moved from having major governments dominated by dictatorships of one kind or another to a situation where almost every country in the hemisphere has elected its leaders through democratic processes. Coincident with this major movement to democracy has been a major movement toward decentralization of national governance, strengthening of local government, the enhancement of citizen participation and even increasing transparency in government' (Cheema 1996, p. 18).

A 'Third Way'?

The tendency for a shift from a strong to a more empathetic leadership style to lead to a more activist approach to local government is also evident in advanced countries, particularly those that have recently elected left-wing governments that have committed themselves to the pursuit of a 'Third Way' between the new classical neo-liberalism of their predecessors and old-style Keynesian interventionism. The Clinton administration in the US, the Schroeder government in Germany and the Blair government in the UK have all presented themselves as exponents of Third Way policies. Their claims that that this marks a distinctive approach have been disputed by critics such as Reich (1999) who typically suggest that it is 'nothing more than a watered down version of the neo-liberal policies pursued by Thatcher and Reagan' (Eichbaum 2000, p. 38) or as Faux (1999) puts it 'a deftly crafted slogan designed to make the capitulation to a conservative agenda intellectually and morally respectable'. Giddens (1998), however, has argued strongly that the Third Way needs to be taken seriously as a program in the making. Eichbaum (2000, pp. 46–8) has summarized the main features of this program as follows:

> For Giddens ... a Third Way program ... includes the refurbishment, if not the remaking, of a democratic state some reform and reinvention of government, the measured use of market mechanisms, and upwards and downwards devolution of government consistent with the challenges of globalization (and supranational institutions) on the one hand, and greater local governance on the other. The program also includes a refurbishment of civil society, largely by means of partnerships between local communities and the government ... Education and training become key ingredients in a public policy mix designed to facilitate access to paid work, participation in the labor market being viewed as the basis for economic and social participation ... Therefore, within the domestic context the role of the state, as an investment state, is a facilitative one. The state becomes a broker for a new relationship between the public and the private sector, a relationship largely predicated on making the market work not only more efficiently, but more effectively as well. The welfare state is also a facilitative state, a redesigned, more responsive, and clearly somewhat smaller state targeting

supply-side assistance to those on the margins of the labor market. Such assistance is couched in terms of notions of reciprocity in which the recipients of 'welfare' accept the obligation to address the 'personal' determinants of their exclusion from work.

A Third Way program can thus be seen as part of a move to supply a more empathetic style of policy leadership that seeks to build on the historic achievement of strong predecessors in implementing a paradigmatic reconstruction of public policy while, at the same time, focusing on the facilitative functions of the state that are likely to assume particular importance as the reform process moves into its 'consolidation' phase.

Third Way governments such as those of Clinton and Blair have claimed to have been influenced by 'New Keynesian' economists such as Taylor (1986), Akerlof and Yellen (1986), Mankiw and Romer (1991), Greenwald and Stiglitz (1993) and Romer (1993) who have sought to develop an approach to macroeconomic policy making through which monetary policy could reduce instability in GDP and unemployment without destroying the credibility of inflation targets and fiscal policy could allow a more flexible use of budget surpluses. These governments have, however, sought to differentiate themselves from their predecessors not so much in terms of their approach to macroeconomic policy but in terms of their supply side agenda and their 'modernizing' claims to have shifted from 'government' to 'governance'. With regard to their supply side agenda, British Prime Minister, Tony Blair, and German Chancellor, Gerhard Schroeder asserted in a joint statement that 'changes in interest rates and tax policy will not lead to increased investment and employment unless the supply side of the economy is adaptable enough to respond' and that 'the most important task of modernization is to invest in human capital: to make the individual and businesses fit for the knowledge-based economy of the future' (Blair and Schroeder 1999, p.2). It should be pointed out, though, that the two main items on this agenda reducing the taxation burden on companies and other taxpayers and facilitating an acceleration in the accumulation of the human and social capital stocks required by the 'knowledge economy' have been made achievable, within conservative fiscal policy settings, by the budget surpluses generated over long periods of positive growth and spending restraint by their predecessors. However, unlike their predecessors, Third Way governments advocate 'reinventing government' (Osborne and Gaebler 1992, p.132) rather than 'rolling back the state'. This shift in focus has been conceived as 'a shift from government to governance'. The main dimensions of this shift have been outlined by Bailey (1999, p. 271) as follows:

It is in this context that current use of the term *'government'* implies a standardized form of polity, a highly organized and coordinated form of civil government. The term '*governance*' refers to the act, manner or function of governing and does not have the modern connotation of uniformity, comprehensiveness or standardization of 'government'. 'Governance' suggests a multiplicity of ways in which representation is achieved and services are delivered. (original emphasis)

In studying this shift other writers have emphasized the catalytic role that state actors can play in engaging societal actors in network relationships through which they can strive to steer the policy process toward the realization of shared goals (Rhodes 1996; Stoker 1998; Jessop 1998). Chapter 5 highlighted the key role local authorities could play in these networks. We must now focus on the specific initiatives the Blair government has taken to strengthen the capacity of local governments to enable them to contribute to its overall governance since this would seem to be a key area in which its program mix and style of leadership have built upon, and yet been differentiated from, that of its predecessor.

The Activist Approach to Local Government of the Blair Government

Following its election in the UK in 1997, the Blair-led Labour government wasted little time in announcing its intention to co-opt local authorities into making a significant contribution to the delivery of its domestic policy agenda. The stream of consultation documents issued by this government in 1998 and the main provisions of the legislation it enacted in 1999 did, however, indicate that its local government policy would combine elements of continuity and change in a number of ways that we consider to be characteristic of a government seeking to shift from a strong to a more empathetic style of policy leadership.

In the first place, the Blair government has sought to capitalize on the organizational changes that have occurred in the local sector as councils have sought to restructure themselves to cope better with the top-down pressures placed on them by the previous government. It has not only endorsed a modernization process that encompasses 'a shift away from monolithic, hierarchical, highly standardized bureaucratic production technologies to microcorporatist networked organizations dominated by meeting the needs of consumption rather than of production' (Bailey 1999, p. 262). It has also sought to make modernization a condition for the devolution of new powers and responsibilities. Second, this government has sought to broaden the model of the enabling authority that its predecessor had identified as emerging from its drive to separate the purchasing and provision of local public services. Its view was that a model local authority would enable persons and communities as well as businesses to have a role in shaping and providing these services (Bailey 1999, pp. 270–71). Third, the Blair government sought to 'continue the trend, developed by the previous administration, of promoting solutions derived from the ethos of the New Public Management' (Brooks 2000, p. 598). It does, however, attempt to broaden the focus of NPM from a drive to cut the costs of delivering tightly specified outputs to an approach that attempts to make local authorities, along with all other public agencies, responsible, first of all, for the outcomes of 'citizen-centered services'. According to Blair (1998), his declared ambition was to lead 'a government that focuses on the outcomes it wants to achieve, devolves responsibility to those who can achieve those outcomes and then intervenes in inverse proportion to success'.

The cornerstone of this outcomes-focused approach appears to be the 'Best Value' regime that is to be implemented through the Local Government Act of 1999. Table 6.4 compares this regime with the Compulsory Competitive Tendering (CCT) system it replaced.

By extending its regulations to all rather than just defined activities of local government, by requiring continuous improvement rather than just periodic market testing, by deploying a wider range of tests of competitiveness, by promoting partnerships in which collaboration rather than competition is promoted, by emphasizing the need to improve service standards as well as drive down costs and by introducing regular inspections of all local authority services, the Blair government appears to be pioneering an approach to local government regulation that is more comprehensive and flexible than what existed before.

A major lesson this government appears to have drawn from the Thatcherite experience in reforming local government is that an adversarial central–local relationship can make it more difficult to achieve top-down effectiveness in policy implementation (Marsh and Rhodes, 1992). The new government's commitment to improve central–local relations was initially signaled by its signing in 1997 of the European Charter on Local Self-Government and by its formation of the central–local partnership as a forum for discussion between ministers and local authority leaders. It has relied more on persuasion and exhortation than the detailed legislation and prescription that characterized its predecessor's approach and it has sought to work with the policy networks that surround the Local Government Association (LGA) in promoting the modernization of British local government. It has also sought to allocate the auditing and inspection functions required by the Best Value regulatory framework to intermediary organizations such as the Audit Commission and the LGA.

This collaborative approach has also characterized a number of recent central government initiatives that have the activist goal of enhancing the capacity of local authorities to implement the new regime. These include its active support of the establishment by the LGA of an Improvement and

Development Agency (IDeA) to promote peer review of authorities' existing

Table 6.4   From CCT to Best Value

CCT	Best Value
Applied to 'defined activities'.	Applies to all local authority services.
Episodic market testing to establish cost and performance standards for the next contract.	Authorities are able to use a range of tests of competitiveness including benchmarking, joint ventures and voluntary competitive tendering.
Encouraged autonomous business units, executive agencies and competition between public service providers.	Designed to encourage collaboration between service providers to 'lever in' capital investment and address 'cross-cutting' issues.
Focused largely on the costs of service provision.	Emphasizes the importance of cost savings and improving service standards.
Limited role for service users.	Councils have a legal duty to consult with all those appearing to have an interest in any area within the authority which carries out functions.
Councils required to maintain trading accounts and satisfy external auditors.	Authorities have to satisfy auditors, Best Value inspectors and be more directly accountable to the public.
Councils required to publish Audit Commission performance indicators (PIs).	Authorities required to publish annual performance plans reporting past performance and future targets in terms of local PIs, national statutory PIs and measures of organizational health.
No inspection in CCT services. Intervention triggered by failure to follow the rules.	Inspection of all local authority services. Intervention triggered by failure to follow procedures and/or where service standards fall below national minimum requirements.

Source: Adapted from Martin (2000, p. 211).

capabilities and to assist them in acquiring the skills needed to provide local community leadership and deliver high quality services. They have also involved the Beacon Council Scheme' under which those authorities that are judged to have provided 'excellent services' and that have shared their expertise with other councils are rewarded with greater freedom and flexibility when setting their council tax, planning capital expenditure and undertaking initiatives that are currently *ultra vires*. Brooks (2000) has pointed out that while, on the one hand, 'rewarding those local authorities that excel in meeting their objectives with special privileges is a departure from the punitive methods of previous regimes' (p. 399), the scope of this regulatory framework has been significantly enlarged since 'in the past, statutory duties were mostly confined to local government functions, whereas the present administration plans to regulate the political practice and management of local authorities' business' (p. 398).

Generally, the Blair government appears to have taken the activist view that, once they have been modernized, local authorities can be allowed to realize their comparative institutional advantage in the provision of community governance. Through its Department of the Environment, Transport and the Regions (DETR), the government has announced that it intends to, first, impose a new obligation on councils 'to promote the economic, social and environmental well-being of their areas', and second 'strengthen councils' powers to enter into partnerships' (DETR 1998, p. 80). With regard to this new obligation, Brooks (2000, p. 604) has commented that:

> This new duty will require local authorities to place sustainable development of their localities at the center of their activities. By considering economic, social and environmental factors, local authorities will act as a catalyst to develop a strategy for the area and to co-ordinate organizations and bodies which operate in a locality. With planning partnerships and development strategies, local authorities will use community consultation and scrutiny to highlight issues that are of concern to the locality. This is a departure from previous models of local government, which were preoccupied with the structure and functions of institutions.

To some degree, it reflects the possibilist approach described in Chapter 5 that highlights the potential that exists for local authorities to play a catalytic role in community development through their ability to network with other organizations and groups to advance shared goals. The Blair government proposes to enhance the capacity of local authorities to play this role in two main ways: by encouraging new forms of executive leadership; and by insisting that new forms of participatory democracy be introduced.

With regard to the executive direction of local authorities, this government is proposing to replace the council committee structure that has traditionally performed both executive and legislative functions in local government with three forms of executive leadership. Councils will thus be allowed to choose whether their executive structure will comprise one of the following: a directly elected mayor with a cabinet of senior councilors; a cabinet with a leader appointed or elected from councilors; or a directly elected mayor with a council manager. The so-called 'backbench councilors' that emerge under these arrangements will be expected to function as scrutineers of the executive with scrutiny arrangements being decided by the whole council (DETR 1998). The arguments that have been presented in support of these proposals reflect both an agency-theoretic focus on strengthening accountability and a possibilist emphasis on allowing scope for the emergence of transformational leadership (Burns 1978). Thus, on the one hand, it is argued that a small, identifiable executive will produce more coherent and transparent decisions and may ameliorate voter apathy (DETR 1998; 1999). On the other hand, it has been pointed out that the new executive may have opportunities to act as transformational leaders or civic entrepreneurs, promoting the interests of constituents, working in partnership with other organizations, engaging previously excluded groups and providing an inclusive vision for local development (McGovern 1997; DETR 1998; Leadbetter and Goss 1998).

With regard to revitalizing local democracy, the Blair government has focused on encouraging local authorities to introduce new forms of participatory democracy rather than seeking to make local government more representative by, say, introducing some form of proportional representation. It has thus continued the trend, initiated by the previous administration, toward making local authorities more responsive to consumers by strengthening various voice mechanisms. In particular, it has signaled its intention to introduce a new statutory duty on local authorities to consult with their localities on service delivery. Moreover, the 'Beacon awards' for excellence have taken into account council innovations in democratic practice such as the use of referenda and 'deliberative forums' that seek 'to overcome the difficulties of exclusion evident elsewhere in society' (Brooks 2000, p. 608).

Although the Blair government sees improving leadership and revitalizing local democracy as the two main prongs of its modernization quest, it tends to downplay the potential for conflict between the goal of making decision making more effective and immediate, on the one hand, and increasing opportunities for democratic participation, on the other. However, as Brooks (2000, p. 607) has argued, the tensions between these two goals may become more apparent when the new system actually comes into operation:

> The community leadership role proposed for local authorities implies that there are common interests which transcend all spatial and interest derived differences. However, few localities display such high levels of homogeneity. By streamlining the decision-making process, the opportunity for those who disagree to oppose new policies will be curtailed. Although opposition and backbench councilors will have the opportunity to scrutinize the actions of the (executive), with few meaningful sanctions (the executive leaders) could bring forward controversial policies to be decided and implemented other than by periodic elections.

This pinpoints what may be the fatal flaw of an empathetic leadership style: its tendency persistently to challenge policy actors to adapt to the new and broader goals it sets them while minimizing the tensions and conflicts this pressure to change is placing them under. The types of tensions and conflicts associated with a Blair-style activist approach to local government reform will now be considered as being symptomatic of the species of disappointment that can accumulate in relation to empathetic policy leadership.

Potential Disappointments

The Blair government's modernizing agenda for local government contains a number of pressures and tensions that are likely to become more apparent as it is put into practice. It seeks to promote greater local autonomy and enhance community governance and citizen participation at the local level while, at the same time perpetuating the trend of a government-led reform agenda that extends the central regulatory framework that manages local government. A potential tension can thus arise between 'those who believe that reform in councils should be experimental and administered primarily from within the local government community and those who doubt whether local authorities can be modernized without central regulation' (Brooks 2000, p. 593). The introduction of a new community leadership role for local authorities could, if anything, exacerbate this tension as councils come under greater pressure from local interests to lobby for increased government funding while, at the same time, being expected by central government to cooperate in its drive to maintain overall fiscal discipline. Questions will inevitably arise about whether the relationship between the two levels of government is primarily one of a genuine partnership between equals or is essentially one in which local authorities are co-opted into advancing policy initiatives that are entirely centrally determined. Brooks (2000, p.598) is in no doubt about where the Blair government stands on this issue:

> By reiterating that local authorities are a creation of Parliament, the government is reminding local authorities of the unequal nature of intergovernmental relations. It also serves as a reminder of the powerlessness of local authorities to resist the actions of government intent on intervention and the willingness of labor to act against miscreant councils.

Brooks (2000) points out that although the proposal to award some Councils 'Beacon Status' may indicate a preference for incentives and rewards, the Blair government 'by retaining reserved powers and threatening councils which are labeled as "failing" (with the risk that they lose powers) ... indicates that sanctions ... are (also) part of its preferred strategy' (p. 599).

These pressures and tensions can be related to a fatal flaw that empathetic leaders are prone to when they succeed strong policy leaders in positions from which they can steer policy development in a particular direction. This flaw arises from their excessive optimism that they dispense with the tunnel vision of their predecessors and persistently challenge policy actors to pursue a broader range of goals without placing in jeopardy the historic achievements effected under the previous regime. To understand how this can cause disappointments to accumulate in a way that eventually produces a climate of reform fatigue that precipitates another shift in leadership style, it will be helpful to assume that the policy sub-systems in which this climate becomes most pervasive are those in which actors are engaged in the type of coping activities described by Wilson (1989).

The local government policy sub-system would seem to have this characteristic since the actors involved in the implementation of its policies typically have to cope with the pressures and expectations of a multiplicity of stakeholders.   They may thus seek to attain the type of satisficing equilibrium' described by various economic revisionists such as Simon (1975), Leibenstein (1978) and Etzioni (1988).   In this equilibrium no stakeholder is willing to exert the effort required to place pressure on the implementing actors to change their behavior.   However, to assess the stability of this equilibrium these actors may actively canvas the opinion of stakeholders to confirm whether their observed 'effort inertia' can be attributed to a satisfactory (but not optimal) attainment of their goals. The increasing tendency of local authorities to undertake surveys to establish whether citizens are satisfied, as a whole, with their performance would seem to be explicable in these terms (John and Block 1991).

This kind of effort equilibrium can be disrupted when a governing coalition stakes its claim to be an effective supplier of a particular style of policy leadership on its capacity to achieve particular reform goals in this sub-system.   As we have seen, local authorities may engage in a radical restructuring to cope with the pressures an SLC places on them to become more fiscally responsible.   While they may at first welcome the greater appreciation a successor empathetic leadership coalition (ELC) has of the enhanced local government capacity to provide community governance that results from this restructuring, they may experience disappointment when they realize that the goalposts have once again been shifted and the emerging effort equilibrium has once again been disrupted by a new set of top-down pressures to change.   Indeed, the demands by Third Way governments for continuous improvement and reinvention at the local level would seem to be antithetic to the coping behavior associated with the quest for a satisficing equilibrium.   Disappointments with the empathetic leadership style of these governments can be compounded when their tendency to minimize the conflict between different goals, in principle, leads to a shifting of the responsibility for resolving these conflicts on to implementing institutions, in practice.

In the climate of reform fatigue that may be produced by the accumulation of disappointment with empathetic leadership, a demand is likely to arise for policy leaders to disengage from policy sub-systems, such as those surrounding local government, so that a satisficing equilibrium can be worked out by a stable new policy community of the type described by Rhodes and Marsh (1992). As this pattern of disengagement spreads across policy sub-systems, there may be a return to the conditions of paradigm stability that preceded the shift from one policy paradigm to another. The new policy paradigm may become increasingly implicit and taken for granted as it comes to underlie a new policy consensus. Governing coalitions will become less concerned with identifying themselves with a particular style of leadership as they become generally pragmatic, adopting an incrementalist approach to policy reform and allowing policy communities within particular policy sub-systems to shape policy according to a process of mutual partisan adjustment (Lindblom 1959). In a sense the paradigmatic reform process and the path of leadership succession would have come full circle. The implications of this cyclical perspective must now be considered by way of conclusion to this chapter.

6.5 CONCLUSION

The Blair government is not alone in its claim that that its local government reforms can advance the modernization of this sector. As Hood (1998, pp. 194–5) has observed:

> One of the most powerful themes in the rhetoric of contemporary public management is the idea of 'modernization'. [It] is used extensively to explain and justify contemporary changes in the structure and operation of public services with 'modernization' plans appearing for the public services in many European countries ... The idea of 'modernization' is appealing, because it can be linked metaphorically to universal themes in nature changes in generations, the vigor of youth, the feebleness of age, the truism that in human affairs, 'nothing is true but change, nothing abides'.

This metaphor is readily discernable in the view of administrative modernization as 'a relatively linear, institutional evaluatory process of constant differentiation and performance improvement on the part of 'modern' administrations: from feudal authoritarian counselors to the Weberian type of bureaucracy as rational administration to modern client-oriented and results-centered forms of organization' (Naschold 1997, pp. 5–6). Three trends in administrative restructuring would seem to reflect the advancement of modernization from this perspective:

> The first focal point relates to the internal modernization of local government, involving results steering, budgeting, and the flexibilization of the organization of work and personnel policies; a second broad-based trend is to be seen in the democratization of local government in the sense of democratizing decision-making processes and, above all, in the devolution of tasks back to civil society; a third area concerns the increasingly strong orientation towards market forces, and involves instruments such as market testing, legal-organizational autonomy, principal-agent models and, as the 'strongest' measure, privatization. (Naschold 1997, p. 9)

Although the local government reforms described in this chapter seem to have prompted all three types of restructuring, the process does not appear to have been as linear as the proponents of the modernization thesis seem to be suggesting. We have argued that in countries such as the UK where local government reform has been chosen as an arena where successive governments can demonstrate their capacity to supply a particular style of policy leadership, the succession of leadership styles that occurs over the course of a paradigmatic change process have caused marked shifts from minimalist to activist approaches to reconstructing this sector. The fact that NPM doctrines are susceptible to both minimalist and activist interpretations has clearly helped make this type of oscillation possible.

Where the direction of local government reform is shaped by the prevailing style of policy leadership, it is possible to relate the disappointments that accumulate in this policy sub-system with those that can more generally produce a climate that is receptive to a change in leadership style. This process has been particularly striking in the UK where policy failures in local government appeared to symptomize the shortcomings of Thatcher's strong leadership style and precipitated her downfall while the areas of incoherence in the Third Way espoused by the more empathetic leader, Blair, are being highlighted in his drive to modernize the local sector. This does, however, raise the question of whether the link established in this chapter between different approaches to local government reform and different styles of policy leadership can break down in countries where governing coalitions are less engaged with what happens in the local sector. We will consider this question in Chapter 7 by undertaking a case study of local government reform in a country where it has historically played a relatively insignificant role in the delivery of public policy and accordingly has never figured that highly on the agenda of reforming governments.

7. A Case Study of Local Government Reform in New Zealand

7.1 INTRODUCTION

Any attempt to draw lessons from case studies of local government reform in particular countries must start by recognizing the considerable cross-country diversity in these institutions. Both the functions undertaken by local government and the sources of local government revenue vary significantly from country to country. In some countries local authorities are involved in the delivery of a comprehensive range of social welfare and regulatory functions while in others their capacity to meet, at even a most basic level, the local demand for road, refuse collection and water services is very limited. In some countries, the principal revenue source is income tax and/or user fees; while in other countries, it is the tax on property or block and/or special-purpose grants from the central government. Moreover, the relations between the state and local government are based on very different fundamental principles from country to country. Indeed, it is difficult to find two nations with precisely the same organizational structures for local governance.

Castles (1993) has, however, suggested that it may be possible to discern similar patterns of policy making in various families of nations. He has been particularly interested in the similar patterns of public sector reform that have emerged in the last two decades in the English-speaking family of nations – Australia, Canada, New Zealand, the UK and the US – where 'economic crisis occasioned a major reappraisal of the role of the state and an attempt, either in the arena of the welfare state and/or economic regulation, to diminish the degree of public intervention that had become customary in the post-war period' (p. 6).

The common language and close educational, cultural and institutional ties between these countries clearly facilitate the transmission of policy-related ideas between them and ensures that their policy advising institutions routinely seek to draw lessons from policy innovations undertaken by any one of these countries. Thus when Australia and New Zealand undertook disinflationary monetary policies during the mid-1980s they avoided the experimental targeting of monetary aggregates undertaken by the US and the UK between 1979 and 1981 since these monetarist experiments had clearly run into implementation problems largely because they were accompanied by a deregulation of financial markets that had caused a parametric shift in the relationship between these aggregates and economic activity. Conversely, the apparent success New Zealand enjoyed in establishing credible inflation targets after making its independent central bank accountable for them through the Reserve Bank Act of 1989 is reflected in the way similar monetary policy regimes have been introduced during the 1990s in Canada, Australia and the UK.

There have also been considerable similarities in the public sector reform programs followed in these countries over the last two decades, with their typical mix of commercialization, corporatization, privatization, deregulation of public sector management, devolution of management responsibility, performance monitoring and contracting out. Some differences in application and style nevertheless remain. Hood (1991) has, for example, pointed out that while NPM principles were applied in a pragmatic way that drew mainly from the latest wave of managerialist doctrine in Australia and the UK, in New Zealand economic theories of government failure have been packaged together to produce 'an analytically driven reform movement of unusual coherence' (p. 6).

Schick (1998) has observed that the enormous number of public management reforms implemented in New Zealand since 1988 'add up to an integrated concept of how government should work', a concept that can be encapsulated in the phrase 'government by contract' (p. 124). A wide range of contractualist instruments have been introduced in New Zealand to establish and strengthen contract-like relationships in which bureaucrats function as agents either of elected officials, funding agencies or civil servants placed further up the hierarchy of government. These have included performance agreements between departmental heads and their portfolio ministers, contracts between funders and purchasers, purchasers and providers, funders and regulators, and so on (Boston 1995). Although the legal status of these contracts varies, with only some being legally binding, their general aim has been to specify as precisely as possible the resources that one side will provide and the performance the other side will produce.

Interest in this model of contractualist governance appears to have spilled outside the ESNs. It has been showcased at international conferences, and studied in detail by delegations sent to New Zealand by 'dozens of countries' while the architects of the reforms have 'crisscrossed the globe' extolling its 'virtues and portability' (Schick 1998, p. 123). This interest has, however, largely been focused on the reforms undertaken in New Zealand's central

government in the late 1980s. Much less attention appears to have been paid
to the Local Government Act of 1989 that radically reshaped the structure
and management of local government in this country. This probably reflects
the view that this legislation simply extended the model of contractualist
governance embodied in the State Sector Act of 1988 and the Public Finance
Act of 1989 to the second tier of government (Boston 1996).

We, however, take the view that the policy developments that surrounded
and followed New Zealand's local government reforms should be of
significant interest in their own right. In the first place, they were undertaken
within an institutional context that would seem be closer to that within which
the British local government reforms discussed in Chapter 6 were
implemented than would be the case with the other ESNs. Like the UK, New
Zealand is a parliamentary democracy that has only two levels of government
with local government being 'a creature of statute' (Bush 1995, p. 104) that
has never been conferred a 'power of general competence'.

There are, however, also significant differences between the two
countries. Although they are of similar size, New Zealand is geographically
more isolated and has a much smaller population of only 3.4 million. For a
country of its size, New Zealand has historically had numerous local
governments (with over 700 authorities existing before the 1989 reforms).
However, by comparison with the United Kingdom and most of the OECD
area, the functions of local government have been very limited.   This is
reflected in the fact that its local authorities have never had primary
responsibility for health services, income redistribution, justice, police or
education.   Table 7.1 indicates that, as a result of the smaller role local
government plays in public policy in New Zealand, it absorbs relatively less
resources but is also less dependent on central government funding than is
the case in the UK.

*Table 7.1   Comparative local government statistics for 1994 in New Zealand
and the UK*

Local Government	New Zealand %	United Kingdom %
Expenditure relative to GDP	2.4	11.0
Expenditure relative to gross government expenditure	13.4	27.0
Central grant funding relative to total revenue	10.0	76.0

Sources: Council of Europe (1997) and Statistics New Zealand (1994).

We would argue that the relatively limited scope of, and resource commitment to, local government in New Zealand means that its local government reforms can be treated as solutions to problems specific to this sub-system. This makes it easier to draw lessons for local government policy from these reforms than in countries where the greater size and importance of local government means that reforms in this sector are directed toward system-wide fiscal and democratic imperatives. In particular, recent governments in New Zealand have not seen the local government policy sub-system as an important arena within which their claim to supply a particular style of leadership can be tested in terms of their capacity to steer policy in this area in either a minimalist or activist direction. The question of whether the link between styles of policy leadership and approaches to local reform that we discussed in relation to the UK in Chapter 6 can also be observed in countries like New Zealand where there seems to be less at stake with local government reform would seem to merit exploration.

A further reason for undertaking a case study of local government reform in New Zealand is that the reformers in this country appear to have followed a reform strategy that sought to address the types of implementation problems that the Thatcher government experienced with many of its reform initiatives, particularly those in the area of local government (Marsh and Rhodes 1992).

This chapter is divided into five main sections. Section 7.2 examines the main features of the New Zealand model of strategic reform. Section 7.3 then describes how between 1987 and 1989, two key policy entrepreneurs were able to exploit a unique window of opportunity to break the historical pattern of effective resistance to local government modernization in New Zealand. Section 7.4 looks at how the reforms implemented through the 1989 Act were designed to establish the conditions for a post-reform consensus by reconciling the potential conflict between efficiency and democratic values by engaging the policy sub-system on a quest for greater accountability that was further advanced through the provisions of the 1996 Amendment to this Act. Section 7.5 then explains how areas of incoherence in the concept of government failure held by the reforming coalition contributed to the emergence of divergent minimalist and activist perspectives on the comparative institutional advantage of local government that have eroded the post-reform consensus. The chapter concludes with some brief remarks in Section 7.6.

7.2 THE NEW ZEALAND MODEL OF STRATEGIC REFORM

Overseas interest has not just been directed toward the New Zealand model of contractualist governance. It has also been directed toward the strategy the reformers used to implement these reforms. Table 7.2 sets out the staged approach to consensus-building that characterized this strategy.

Table 7.2   The New Zealand model of consensus-building

Stage of Policy Cycle	Type of Consensus Sought
1. Agenda-setting and policy formulation.	Narrow consensus within network of key technopols and technocrats concerning the system-wide direction of the reform process.
2. Decision-making and implementation	Narrow consensus within group of change agents concerning the sub-system implementation of reform.
3. Evaluation and reformulation	Broad post-reform consensus about the core policy objectives of the sub-system.

In general, this strategy sought to ensure that particular reform initiatives sustained and strengthened the coherence of policy development at both the system-wide and sub-system levels. It thus sought to advance the type of quest for policy coherence that we identified with a strong style of policy leadership in Chapter 6. As Table 7.2 indicates, at the agenda setting and policy formulation stage, a narrow consensus was established on the policy paradigm that was to be applied in developing and screening the stream of neo-liberal reform initiatives undertaken by successive Labour and National administrations between 1984 and 1993. This was sustained within an elite reformist network that comprised reformist factions in both Cabinets, technocrats in the key control agencies, such as the New Zealand Treasury, the Reserve Bank and the State Services Commission and the influential 'Business Roundtable', a self-selected lobby group that includes in its membership (which is by invitation only) the chief executives of some of New Zealand's largest companies (Kelsey 1995; Easton 1997; Wallis 1999). The policy paradigm they applied was constructed from a number of economic theories (public choice, agency theory, the new institutional economics and new classical macroeconomics) that tended to highlight problems of government failure. Its imposition was facilitated by a 1985 overhaul of the machinery through which Cabinet received policy advice.

This saw a Cabinet Policy Committee being established with the task of ensuring the clarity and coherence of all policy. Since this structure was serviced by the Treasury, this control agency could perform a gatekeeper function, screening policy proposals according to whether or not they were consistent with the government failure paradigm. In general, it sought to encourage bold, radical initiatives within particular policy sub-systems (Easton 1997, p. 99) provided that they did not impair the coherence of the system-wide reform process.

Once reform proposals had passed Treasury scrutiny and secured Cabinet approval, 'blitzkrieg' tactics were typically used during the second stage of decision-making and implementation to drive them through the various 'veto points' at caucus and parliamentary level and radically to restructure the institutions that were to be involved in their implementation. No attempt was made to deepen and broaden the consensus beyond the Cabinet minister and 'change agents' selected to advance the legislation and implementation process since, in the view of the reformers, this would simply give opponents the opportunity to mobilize resistance and slow down, or perhaps stall, the reform process. They anticipated that this resistance would subside once the reforms were implemented. This concern with overcoming resistance to centrally-initiated reform initiatives was, of course, mirrored by the Thatcher government and would seem to be generally characteristic of a coalition seeking to supply strong policy leadership.

The New Zealand reformers would, however, argue that the greater top-down effectiveness of the strategy they followed should not only be assessed in terms of its capacity to effect rapid and significant change, but also according to the nature of the consensus that emerged during the third stage of evaluation and policy reformulation that followed the radical structural reform. It seems that the New Zealand reformers were looking to use a radical reform process to reconcile potentially conflicting policy values that might be held by participants in the policy sub-system so that a new consensus could be established on its core objective. This would then ensure that policy could develop in a coherent manner as the participants in the sub-system concerned sought to evaluate and reformulate the reform according to the degree to which it realized this objective.

The way in which this model of strategic reform was applied in the area of local government must now be considered.

7.3 OVERCOMING RESISTANCE TO THE RADICAL REFORM OF LOCAL GOVERNMENT

From 1876 (when the two tier, central-local government structure was established in New Zealand) until 1989, local government was allowed to develop in a way that perpetuated its institutional weaknesses.   The proliferation of small authorities and the *ad hoc* formation of special authorities meant that 'the more authorities there were, the more their overlapping functional boundaries were a recipe for weakness and the stronger central government became' (Bassett 1996, p. 30).   The issue of amalgamation did, from time to time, rise to prominence on the policy agenda but supporters of the status quo were invariably able to mount sufficient resistance to block this first step to modernizing this level of government.   This resistance was effective not just because it reflected the pressures of local parochialism but also because 'the functions of local government were so limited relative to central government that there was little to be gained from a more rational structure' (Easton 1997, p. 187). Thus despite the emergence of reasonably broad bipartisan support for local government amalgamation following the formation of the Local Government Commission (LGC) in 1946 neither major political party was prepared to take the risk of pushing through this reform.

This situation changed with the election of a reformist Labour Government in 1984.   Amalgamation not only featured in its election manifesto but also appeared to be the 'pet' reform initiative of Michael Bassett, its Minister of Local Government, and Brian Elwood who was appointed in 1985 to chair the LGC.   Both Bassett and Elwood had a background in local politics and soon exhibited the qualities of policy entrepreneurship described by Kingdon (1984).   According to Kingdon policy entrepreneurs perform the function of coupling solutions, problems and politicians together at the time when policy windows open. As brokers they seek to build support within key committees in favor of proposals. As advocates they must have their pet proposals or concerns ready to be pushed when the opportunity arises. They may spend years lying in wait for such propitious moments to arrive. During this time they will ensure that their pet problems, solutions and theories survive in conflict and competition with alternatives, and that the policy-making community is softened up to a state of receptivity to them.

This softening-up process was undertaken between 1985 and 1987 over which period Bassett and Elwood worked closely together to refine their amalgamation proposals. The Minister gave Elwood a free rein to soften up the local government policy community through a carefully staged consultation process. He contacted councilors from every local authority to engage them in the process of reviewing their boundaries, functions, powers and relationships. By making clear to respondents that 'no change was not going to be an acceptable response' (Bassett, 1996, p. 33), Elwood was able to flush out those councilors whose resistance to reform could be anticipated and overcome as well as identify potential supporters who were willing to constructively contribute to proposals for change.

Meanwhile Bassett was able to couple the issue of amalgamation to the broader issue of public sector management reform. This latter issue was highlighted in Treasury briefing papers to the Labour government after it was re-elected in 1987. These recommended that public management reform be developed from a broad system-wide perspective derived primarily from agency theory and public choice that focused on 'the lack of management incentives' that lay at root of pervasive government failure rather than on 'the symptoms of dysfunctionality ... such as financial waste, excessive rules and poor performance' (Bale and Dale 1998, p. 107). Cabinet consideration of these briefing papers gave Michael Bassett, the Minister of Local Government, the opportunity to point out those aspects of local government structure and management that were inconsistent with the model that the Treasury was seeking to apply to core government departments. In particular, the following weaknesses were identified:

> the confusion between councilors and senior management about their roles; a built-in bias towards inefficiency resulting from the absence of contestability in the provision of council services, most of which were provided 'in-house'; confusion between the commercial and non-commercial objectives in the management of council trading activities; the lack of appropriate incentives and accountability arrangements to enable elected representatives to hold managers accountable for resource use; and the diseconomies of scale - in resource use and recruitment of quality management - of too many small authorities. (McKinlay 1994, p. 6)

Accordingly, when the Cabinet responded to the shock market crash by introducing an urgent economic reform package in December 1987, Bassett succeeded in having a proposal to reform local government to address these problems included in this package.

Realizing that 'delay had defeated all previous attempts at reform' (Bassett 1996, p. 34), Bassett and Elwood adopted a number of tactics to 'fast track' local government reform after 1987. First, they worked to a timetable that required the changes to be in place within the Labour government's second term since 'to let the reforms spill beyond another general election in 1990 risked turning restructuring into a national election issue' (p. 34). Second, as a result of the preparatory work done between 1985 and 1987, they now knew what they wanted to achieve and could afford to minimize the time available for further consultation. A Local Government Bill was drawn up and introduced in parliament on 22 March 1988 which announced that new structures would be in place before local election day on 14 October 1989 and gave the body sweeping powers to achieve this goal. This body could then proceed with its task of establishing new boundaries for local authorities while the officials working under Bassett could craft legislation specifying the principles under which these authorities were to be managed and made publicly accountable for their decisions.   The third tactic the reformers deployed thus involved the simultaneous formulation of proposals for legislative and structural changes.   Basset was able to push through the Local Government Amendment Bill specifying new management and accountability mechanisms on 23 May 1989, 15 days before he received from the LGC their proposed boundary changes that were to apply from the October elections.

For Bassett and Elwood, then, the reform process was like a military campaign in which speed, control of the commanding heights of the policy process and a refusal to be deflected from the achievement of clear objectives were of the essence.   Such 'blitzkrieg' tactics have been severely criticized for their tendency to circumvent and undermine public trust in the democratic policy process in New Zealand   (Kelsey 1995; Easton 1997).   Both Bassett and Elwood appear, however, to take the view that the ends justified the means if the reforms could be designed 'to balance democratization of process and the efficient and effective use of limited resources' (Elwood 1996, p. 312).   The ways in which the reformers pursued this design goal and thereby established the conditions for an *ex post* decline in resistance and the emergence of a post-reform consensus must now be considered.

7.4   THE QUEST FOR GREATER ACCOUNTABILITY THROUGH LOCAL GOVERNMENT REFORM

The Restructuring Requirements of the 1989 Act

The 1989 Act set in motion a process of restructuring that rapidly and radically reshaped the territorial configuration and internal organization of local government in New Zealand.   By using the tactics described in the previous section, Bassett and Elwood succeeded where their predecessors failed in rationalizing local government so that a structure emerged in which economies of scale could be realized that would enable regional councils (reduced in number from 22 to 13) and city and district councils (designated 'territorial authorities' and reduced in number from 200 to 74) to perform their separate but complementary functions more effectively.   Boston (1996, p.184) pointed out that, in terms of this legislation, regional councils and territorial authorities 'should be regarded as an entity ... rather than as two levels of sub-national government where one is subordinate to the other'. Regional councils were set up to perform mainly regulatory functions, particularly the environmental regulation functions that were later set out in the Resource Management Act of 1991. By contrast, territorial authorities were given a much broader mandate to contribute to the social, economic and infrastructure development of their communities. Territorial amalgamation was thus achieved in New Zealand in one 'big bang' rather than the more gradual process observed in the UK (Bailey 1999, p. 34). The New Zealand reformers could thus place a relatively greater reliance on this measure to break up the iron triangles that tended to form around old councils.

The internal structure of local authorities was also changed to ensure (i) the separation of regulatory functions from other functions through the structuring of committees and the allocation of management responsibilities; (ii) the encouragement of corporatization through the transfer to 'Local Authority Trading Enterprises' (LATES) of commercial activities; and (iii) the concentration of administrative authority in the new post of chief executive (CE). The 1989 reforms sought to differentiate the roles of the elected council on the one hand and the appointed CE on the other by decoupling the council from the day-to-day management of the authority and empowering the CE to perform a comprehensive range of implementation, advisory and management functions. Like their counterparts in central government departments, these CEs were appointed for fixed terms of up to five years, renewable for a further three years depending on performance criteria specified in the performance agreements they negotiated with their principals – the members of the elected councils. By failing to separate the executive and legislative functions of the council and provide for executive authority to be vested in the elected mayor or a local Cabinet, as has been proposed in the UK (as we discussed in Chapter 6), the New Zealand reformers may, however, have allowed the balance of power in local government to tilt toward unelected CEs whose informational advantages are, if anything, enhanced by the reforms.

Resistance to restructuring of this magnitude could only be expected to subside after it was undertaken if the reforms established the conditions for a post-reform consensus on the core objective according to which the reforms were to be evaluated. The completion of the restructuring process would then remove the *ex ante* uncertainty about the identity of winners and losers that Rodrik (1996) argues provides much of the political support for groups opposing structural reform. It would also reconfigure the policy networks surrounding local governments so that they could be closed as a channel for post-reform resistance. By this stage decision makers in the restructured local authorities would be more reluctant to reverse the process since they would have already incurred the sunk costs of complying with the reforming legislation. In addition, they may have begun to experience unforeseen benefits from reform such as the increased capacity for community governance that can arise from efforts to comply with the restructuring and managerial disciplines imposed by this legislation.

Bassett and Elwood appear to have appreciated that this anticipated decline in resistance may not have materialized if the restructuring had advanced the value of efficiency in local governance at the expense of the value of strengthening local democracy in the sense of making it more responsive to the preferences of local citizens.   An advocacy coalition structure could then have emerged in which resistance to the ascendancy of an efficiency coalition would have coalesced within a coalition committed to strengthening local democracy. Jenkins-Smith and Sabatier (1993 p. 179-80) have proposed that a stable line-up of opposing advocacy coalitions can emerge under the following conditions: (i) the participants in a policy sub-system should come to have a hierarchy of beliefs reflected in their unwillingness to revise policy core as distinct from secondary beliefs in response to new information; (ii) advocacy coalitions should come to be identifiable by the policy core beliefs which their members share in common; (iii) the main controversies in a policy sub-system should involve disputes about the core beliefs of opposing coalitions; and (iv) these disputes should typically not be capable of uncontestable resolution through scientific methods or according to the standards of independent professional forums but should tend to be perpetuated as each side buttresses its position by using substantive policy information in an advocacy fashion. The emergence of this structure in New Zealand local government would signal the breakdown of the post-reform consensus the reformers were striving to establish. Moreover, as Jenkins-Smith and Sabatier (1993, p. 194), point out, 'significant perturbations external to the sub-system (e.g. changes in socio-economic conditions, system-wide governing coalitions or policy outputs from other sub-systems)' could alter the distributions of resources between these rival coalitions and give the local democracy coalition the opportunity to effect a significant change (or even reversal) in the direction of local government policy.

The Quest for Greater Accountability

To prevent the future emergence of this type of advocacy coalition framework, Bassett and Elwood sought to design the reforms to reconcile the conflicting values of efficiency and democracy by engaging the restructured local authorities on a quest for greater accountability. These architects of local reform were very conscious of the criticism that is frequently directly toward any amalgamation initiative which is that larger authorities can weaken local democracy by increasing the potential distance between citizens and their representatives on elected councils. To counter this criticism they were careful to ensure that the boundaries of the new councils encompassed identifiable communities of interest as well as devising various institutional mechanisms to safeguard the localness in local government and strengthen the democratic accountability of the new bodies. In particular, community boards (with an advisory role only) were established within larger territorial authorities to give smaller communities a voice in local government; a system of postal voting and ward elections in areas with a population above 20000 was introduced; and open government at the local level was promoted through legislation which required that the meetings of councils and their committees be open to the public and, in what was a major innovation, stipulated that councils consult with, and respond back to, their ratepayers and electors about their annual plans and performance.

The internal restructuring of local authorities established clear vertical lines of accountability between the CE and those functionally distinct council departments and business units placed under this officer's management. In addition, the capacity of elected councils to hold CEs accountable for their managerial performance was arguably strengthened by the legislative requirement that there be a shift to an accrual basis for financial statements, the budget and appropriations. This represented a dramatic change from the situation that typified most local authorities before 1989 where 'accounts were prepared on a cash basis for the entity as a whole, and were virtually meaningless as a source of information on its activities' (McKinlay 1994, p. 21).

Despite the significant compliance costs these consultative, accountability and reporting requirements predictably came to impose, particularly on smaller authorities, the reformers appear to have believed that these would not only be offset by the incentive they would give CEs to seek greater efficiency in the provision of council services but also in the opportunity they gave citizens to participate in local decision making and to hold officeholders to account for their performance. Thus, while the establishment of a internal organization structure made up of single objective, manageable units with a clear linear accountability made it easier for local authorities fully to privatize those commercial activities that had been transferred to LATES and to contract out, through a tendering process, those activities which it would continue to fund but not provide in-house, the discretion to take these privatization and contracting-out options was nevertheless left with elected councils.

In stark contrast to the drive by the Thatcher government to reduce council discretion over revenue and services, New Zealand local bodies were not only given a greater revenue-raising capacity through territorial amalgamation, but the 1989 Act also left elected councils with the discretion to determine the level and structure of their property rates, the mix of services they would provide, the methods of delivery and their stake in the ownership and provision of these services. This framework therefore allowed scope for significant variation to emerge in the degree to which councils retained their stake in LATES, provided services in-house, or used their rates revenue to expand into new areas of service provision or to cross-subsidize the users of some services from the differential rates applied on residential or business properties. It seemed to be entirely consistent with the central intent of these reforms which was to make local government more democratic and efficient by making it more accountable, if council decisions in these areas could be made more transparent.

The additional reporting requirements imposed by the Local Government Amendment Act of 1996 were apparently directed toward this end. The 1996 Act sought to advance the quest for greater accountability initiated by the 1989 Act. Accountability was thus established as the core objective of the policy sub-system surrounding local government so reform in this area could unfold in the coherent direction that Schick (1996, p. 73) observed in central government where 'accountability has not been an afterthought; it was designed into the system at the outset, and as gaps in accountability have been identified, additional requirements have been imposed'.

The Local Government Amendment Act of 1996

The 1996 Act requires local authorities to prepare two major policy documents: a long-term financial strategy and a funding policy. Through their long-term financial strategies, councils are now required *inter alia* to specify, for at least the next ten years, the estimated expenses to fund the range of activities in which they expect to be involved, the justification for undertaking them and the cash flow they expect to receive from all sources. The intent was to discipline the authorities to reflect carefully on the options for undertaking particular activities including whether they need to be involved in some of them at all.

The other major requirement of the 1996 Act – that authorities prepare a funding policy document – did not proscribe cross-subsidization by subjecting funding to the benefits principle of taxation but did require authorities to go through the discipline of reflecting on how far this principle could be applied by setting out the steps according to which funding policy documents were to be prepared. Essentially this document requires local authorities to ascertain the extent to which particular goods and services are public goods, private goods or some mixture of the two. Private goods should be paid for by end-users while the rates applied to finance public goods are to be allocated in proportion in proportion to the benefit which different groups in the community derive from the service. Once local authorities have made their judgment, 'on economic principles', as to the nature and distribution of the benefits of their activities, they are required to make transparent any further adjustments with respect to matters such as fairness or equity or the policy of the local authority.

It could be argued that the 1996 Act is a tribute to the success of the reformers in establishing a consensus on the principles that should guide local government policy development since it represented a logical extension of the concept of accountability contained in the 1989 Act. Conversely, it could also be argued that the Act advanced the quest for greater accountability to the point where it called attention to the issue of central – local government trust; an issue that had much greater potential to divide this policy sub-system along the lines suggested by the advocacy coalition framework. This tendency was, to some degree, latent due to aspects of incoherence in the understanding of government failure held by different elements in the 1989 reforming coalition. On the one hand, the policy entrepreneurs advocating the 1989 reforms appear to have viewed them as the crucial first step in the process of modernizing local government by increasing its capacity 'to deal with complex issues and meet local expectations' (Reid 1999, p. 168). On the other hand, the gatekeepers who sought to maintain the system-wide coherence of the New Zealand reform process, were essentially economic rationalists who allowed the proposals to advance because they saw them to be consistent with a reform model that sought to minimize the scope for agency failure and fiscal irresponsibility at all levels of government. The lines along which these divergent views developed during the 1990s must now be considered.

7.5 THE MINIMALIST–ACTIVIST DEBATE ABOUT THE COMPARATIVE INSTITUTIONAL ADVANTAGE OF LOCAL GOVERNMENT

Beneath the surface of the post-reform consensus on accountability, divergent views on the comparative institutional advantage of the restructured local authorities have developed that could eventually divide the local government policy sub-system into minimalist–activist advocacy coalitions. Some key differences between the proponents of the minimalist and activist policy lines are set out in Table 7.3.

The Minimalist Policy Line

The key proponent of the minimalist line that 'local authorities should be required to focus on the public good activities that are the proper business of government at the local level, and prohibited from engaging in the provision of private goods and services' (Kerr 1999, p. 5) is the New Zealand Business Roundtable (NZBR). Since setting up an office in Wellington in 1986 under the direction of a former Treasury official, Roger Kerr, the NZBR has persistently advocated a downsizing of the role of government in the economy beyond that achieved between 1984 and 1993 and has sought to act as a fire alarm alerting the policy community to instances of slippage, incoherence and reversal in those sub-systems that were subject to radical reform during this period. Local government is one of the policy areas it has singled out for special attention. The extraordinary interest this body has shown in local government issues is indicated in Table 7.4.

Table 7.3   Minimalists vs. activists in the local government policy sub-system

	Minimalist	Activist
Key proponents	Business Roundtable	Policy analysts in local government New Zealand
Underlying theories	Public choice and agency theory	Bottom–up theories of governance; social capital theory
Assumptions about agents	Fiscally irresponsible when accountability is weak	Responsibly concerned with coping capacity
Institutional preferences	Local authorities ranked behind public companies, SOES and government departments	Democratically elected local body in horizontal partnership with a range of government agencies and non-government organizations
Assessment of expenditure trends	Indicative of weak accountability of local government	Indicative of local government modernization
Proposed policy directions	1. 'Residuality' principle 2. Commercialization of road and water services	1. Subsidiarity principle 2. Predictable funding as the basis for central–local trust
Sources of support	Economic rationalists in control agencies, 'New Right' politicians, Manufacturers Federation	'Social capital' advocates in the center, the Labour–Alliance Coalition, voluntary organizations

In these documents the NZBR typically advances arguments derived from the same theories of government failure from which the Treasury constructed its blueprint for public sector reform in its 1987 briefing papers. Underlying these theories is the core belief that people can be assumed to act in ways that best advance their own interests. If the public sector is then viewed as vertical 'chain of principal-agent relationships' (Moe 1984, p. 765), this means that the agents in this chain will behave in a fiscally irresponsible way when weak accountability arrangements allow them scope to do so. The NZBR has thus sought to prod central government into an ongoing process of evaluating the institutional arrangements through which it performs and devolves its functions to ensure that they minimize the scope for agency failure and fiscal irresponsibility.

Table 7.4   References to local government in NZBR Publications (1990 –99)

References	Number
Media releases	17
Speeches	217
Submissions	58
Publications	37
Total	329

A clear hierarchy of institutional preferences is usually applied with local authorities being ranked below privately owned public companies and single-purpose government agencies respectively. Where feasible, the privatization of the commercial activities of both central and local government is invariably recommended. This recommendation is not typically based on empirical evidence. Rather it is rests on the logic of agency theory that leads to the conclusion that significant business assets are best held in public company form since individual shareholders (the principals) can sell their shares to new owners if they consider that managers (the agents) are not acting in their best interests. Where ownership remains in public hands, there is more scope for agency failure, since ministers within central government or councilors within local government have to act as proxy for the true owners, taxpayers or ratepayers, who, in turn, have no right to exit from their investment by selling to a third party.

The New Zealand model of contractualist governance does, however, limit the scope for further agency failure in single-purpose agencies where a designated CE can be made contractually accountable for the delivery of a specific output. Unfortunately, despite radical restructuring effected through the 1989 local government reforms, the NZBR would hold that the potential for agency failure remains greatest at this level of government. In a stream of submissions and publications this organization has highlighted the way multi-purpose authorities remain susceptible to the types of local government failure (associated with voter apathy, information asymmetry, rent-seeking and empire building by iron triangles and spending bias engendered by fiscal illusion) described in Chapter 3.

To limit the scope for agency failure at the local level, the NZBR (1995, pp.19 – 20) considers that local government policy should be shaped by the residuality principle 'that local government should be selected only where the benefits of such an option exceed all other institutional arrangements'. It is prepared to concede that local authorities may have a comparative institutional advantage in 'administering necessary local regulations' and in funding (but not typically providing) genuinely local public goods such as library services and garbage collection. However, it points out that even where councils possess better information on the value that their communities place on such goods, relatively weak accountability arrangements may not give them sufficient incentive 'to use that knowledge to the benefit of their communities'. In essence, the NZBR is calling on central government to move beyond its reliance on the transparency mechanisms set in place by the 1989 and 1996 Acts toward a 'minimalist approach' that advances Thatcher-type initiatives to curb local discretion to raise rates and expand services in a fiscally irresponsible way.

The Activist Policy Line

This somewhat pessimistic view of the role of local government has been countered by the proponents of an activist policy line. They have sought to endorse and encourage the tendency some local councils, particularly in urban areas, have shown since 1989 to move from a traditional focus on providing infrastructure and other core activities towards playing 'a lead role in working with their communities to define the economic and social outcomes they seek, and to develop the means for achieving them' (McKinlay 1999, p. 99). Although the national association of local bodies, Local Government New Zealand (LGNZ), is less identifiable by its advocacy of a particular policy line than the NZBR since it seeks to represent the collective interests of its members, it has provided an important forum for the advancement of this line by individuals such as Mike Reid, its Strategy Leader, Governance, and Peter McKinlay, a frequently used consultant on local government issues. The core beliefs of their activist policy line are based on the autonomist view of local government as a sphere of government in its own right that derives its legitimacy from its effectiveness in meeting community expectations and local needs. This can be contrasted with the functionalist perspective the NZBR derives from agency theory that regards 'local government as an agency of the state drawing its authority and mandate from the center' (Reid 1999, p. 168).

Governance is thus seen from the activist perspective as the primary role of local authorities. In an earlier article, Reid (1994, p. 2) proposed that the four elements of 'local governance' be the 'guardianship of difference'; 'the protection of future selves'; the advancement of 'positive rights'; and the provision of 'civic leadership'. He writer argues that 'good local governance' will be based on the 'participatory model' which recognizes that there is more than one 'public' and thus seeks to take account of the diversity of interests in a geographic community (including those of citizens beyond the current generation), by bringing groups (including those under-represented by the political process) together in deliberative forums where issues and concerns are sought out and given full expression. The governance role can thus be seen as being synonymous with a catalytic, participatory style of leadership described in Chapter 5 that forges a common vision for the community in a way that cannot be 'contracted out, delegated to appointed boards of management or ultimately privatized' (Reid 1994, p. 5).

From an activist perspective, local councils can be seen as having a comparative institutional advantage in the supply of local governance since they are multi-purpose agencies who interact with other local agencies and groups on issues that cross sectoral boundaries and which are defined by the needs of localities or places. The public sector reforms implemented in New Zealand since the late 1980s have in their view strengthened this institutional advantage, particularly with respect to the coordination and advocacy roles of local government. The CEs of local authorities came to be distinguished from the CEs of government departments in that they were given a holistic responsibility for the entire range of their institution's activities and could thus play an increasingly important role in coordinating the activities of central agencies whose narrow, contractually determined focus could otherwise lead to fragmentation and overlap in their provision of public services to local citizens. In addition, the dismantling by the 1993 health reforms of other locally-based democratic structures, such as Area Health Boards, has increased the importance of local government as a vehicle for articulating local concerns since it has become 'the only democratically accountable body representing geographic communities' (Reid 1999, p. 168).

This view of local government appears to be based on fundamentally different assumptions about the motivation of local authority decision makers to those derived from public choice and agency theory. Instead of presuming them to be agents who will take advantage of weaknesses in the accountability system to behave in a fiscally irresponsible way, the autonomist view sees them as trying to cope responsibly with a number of conflicting pressures, demands and expectations and focuses on factors such as social capital that can enhance their coping capacity.

Activists such as Reid acknowledge that their emphasis on the role local authorities can play in community governance and social capital formation is reflected in some features of government policy in this area. Section 598 of the 1989 Act does, for example, give councils powers to promote community welfare either themselves, or by making grants to any organization or group who shares this goal within their community of interest. In addition the central government has since 1996 sought to cooperate with local authorities in a number of community-based initiatives. Of these only the Safer Community Council (SCC) Program, through which local authorities can apply for capped central grants to establish SCCs to work with community groups, voluntary organizations and government agencies (most commonly police, corrections and social welfare) to devise local solutions to local problems of crime prevention, constitutes a genuine partnership initiative. Other instances where government departments have sought some involvement by local authorities in the delivery of services include a community 'workfare scheme' and the 'Welfare to Well-being' and 'Strengthening Families' initiatives of the Department of Social Welfare (DSW). In these cases devolution is pursued through co-option rather than partnership with councils being co-opted into a local liaison role in the case of the DSW initiatives and having to make work available for those former beneficiaries who qualify for the community wage program. There are also numerous cases of unintended devolution that have arisen where councils have sought to fill gaps created by central government withdrawal from their communities. Most notably local authorities have, throughout the 1990s, become increasingly involved in health services advocacy and planning while some have even sought to keep hospitals and clinics open in the face of central decisions to close them down.

The major concern from an activist perspective is that this process of devolution is occurring in an *ad hoc* manner in the absence of any overarching policy framework to organize and structure central–local governance relations. Reid (1999) has proposed that the devolution of government functions to the local level should be governed by the subsidiarity principle. The most notable international application of this principle is by the European Union in its relations with individual nation states. In New Zealand, however, the 1988 Royal Commission on Social Policy's recommendation that no organization should be bigger than necessary and nothing should be done by a larger and higher unit than can be done by a lower and smaller unit has had little influence on government policy. Reid (1999) argues, nevertheless, that this subsidiarity principle can be used to formulate a checklist of the key criteria for determining the location of accountability - not only between different spheres of government, but also between governments and communities. Specifically he contends that any checklist 'needs to address the distribution of benefit; information needs and complexity; the relative importance of local knowledge and national consistency; the degree of national significance; the importance of critical mass and value of local discretion' (Reid 1999, p. 180). Thus while this principle can be contrasted with the residuality principle advocated by the NZBR in that it implies a presumption for rather than against the devolution of responsibilities to local government, its application would require an empirical assessment of the capability of different levels of government to undertake particular activities. The implication for local government autonomy of moving toward the British system where the degree of council 'modernization' is assessed through regular inspections and audits does not, however, appear to have been considered by the New Zealand local government activists.

In general, these activists appear to favor a gradualist approach to devolution, that would focus, first of all, on rebuilding relationships of trust between central and local government. While the member councils of the LGNZ may vary in their degrees of activism, they tend to share a common concern with the need to form and preserve relationships of mutual trust with the center with predictable funding being the basis for this trust.

The theories and assumptions underlying the activist policy line clearly give rise to fundamentally different perspectives on central–local government relations from those that shape the minimalist line. The way in which these divergent perspectives have been applied to the evaluation of post-reform expenditure trends must now be considered.

Minimalist vs. Activist Perspectives on Expenditure Trends

McDermott and Forgie's (1999) findings about shifts in the real value, relative size and functional composition of New Zealand local government spending as shown in Tables 7.5 to 7.7 are representative of the empirical background against which both minimalists and activists have sought to evaluate the impact of the 1989 reforms.

Table 7.5 indicates that while public sector reforms appear to have induced a downward (albeit modest) trend in the rate of increase of central government expenditure, the same cannot be said of local government in respect of which spending increased by 2.7 per cent in real terms over the 1990s after falling 0.9 per cent in the period immediately preceding the reform of this sector.

Table 7.5   Average percentage shifts in final expenditure, 1978–97

	1978–84	1985–90	1991–97
Central government	3.0	1.5	-0.11
Local government	6.1	-0.9	2.7
Households	1.9	1.9	2.4

Table 7.6 nevertheless shows that the impact of these trends on the relative size of local government has been negligible, with local government's share of GDP rising 0.4 per cent between 1978 and 1984 and remaining stable at around 2.4 per cent thereafter.

Table 7.6   Percentage changes in final expenditure in relation to GDP, 1978–97

	1978	1984	1990	1997
Central government	15.5	16.4	17.2	15.0
Local government	2.0	2.4	2.3	2.4
Household consumption	67.0	65.9	71.1	73.6
Saving	14.2	14.2	7.2	7.5
Non-profit services	1.0	0.9	1.2	1.5
GDP	100.0	100.0	100.0	100.0

These aggregate trends do, however, conceal significant changes in the functional composition of expenditure shown in Table 7.7.

Although Table 7.7 is based on McDermott and Forgie's (1999) analysis of the annual reports of fifteen councils covering both urban and rural areas in the Lower North Island over the period 1993–97, it is representative of a nation wide trend that has been highlighted by both minimalists and activists. While the increases in the costs of democracy and expenditure on regulation would reflect the additional reporting, monitoring and consultation imposed on councils and their greater responsibility for environmental regulation, the most dramatic expansion in spending has been on services to the community which has more than offset the reduction in spending on property services 'confirming the proposition that any potential for contraction of local government has been offset by a realignment of functions' (McDermott and Forgie 1999, p. 254).

Table 7.7 Patterns of functional change, Lower North Island 1993/4 -1997

Functions	1993/4 $NZ millions (%)	1997 $NZ millions (%)	Shifts 1993/4-97
Democracy	19.0 (3.3)	20.9 (3.6)	1.9 (10.0)
Regulation	49.9 (8.7)	52.6 (9.0)	2.7 (5.4)
Services to property	339.9 (59.7)	315.5 (53.8)	-24.4 (-6.7)
Services to community	161.7 (28.3)	196.7 (33.6)	35.0 (21.6)
Total	572.5 (100%)	585.7 (100%)	13.2 (2.3%)

For minimalists the positive spin that activists such as McDermott and Forgie place on these trends is itself a source of concern. While these writers view as an achievement the fact that local authorities have been able to absorb the costs of complying with the accountability requirements of the 1989 reforms and the increased statutory responsibilities for environmental regulation imposed by the Resource Management Act of 1991, without significantly increasing their spending or the burden on ratepayers, the NZBR position is that this is simply not good enough. Central government departments also underwent a radical restructuring and had to cope with the burden of complying with the demands of what Schick (1996) termed a 'hard-edged contractualism' after 1989. However, the tendency for local government spending to creep upward over a period (1991–97) in which tight fiscal discipline reversed the upward drift of central government spending may be attributable, at least in part, to the fact that local authorities were under less pressure to seek efficiency gains to offset additional compliance costs since they continued to have the discretion to pass these costs on in the form of rate increases.

Minimalists also view the trend toward a functional realignment of local government spending in a way that is diametrically opposed to that of activists.   On the one hand, McDermott and Forgie (1999) suggest that the impact of the 1989 reforms should be positively evaluated in terms of the way they enhanced the capacity of local authorities to take on more functions and thereby play a more activist role in the social and economic development of their communities rather than in terms of any overall contraction in the size of this sector.   On the other hand, the NZBR has become increasingly concerned that this trend could place more publicly funded services outside the control of the center and diminish the capacity for activist councils to meet the demand for traditional local public goods.   It suggests that some of those urban councils who 'continue to engage in a wide range of activities that should be left to the private sector or central government' may have 'neglected their traditional activities, such as roading, sewage disposal and drainage, to such an extent that inadequate services are limiting growth and development' (Kerr 1999, p. 2).   Through such arguments the NZBR may have cultivated the climate of mistrust in local government that shaped recent proposals for the reform of road and water service provision.

Minimalist Reform Proposals and the Mobilization of Rival Advocacy Coalitions

The breakdown of the two-party coalition formed after the first election under mixed member proportional representation (MMP) rules in 1996 gave a minority National Cabinet the opportunity to shake off the reform fatigue that had characterized New Zealand governments since 1993 and embark on some bold reform initiatives along the minimalist lines advocated by the NZBR.   In 1998, two of these initiatives – the government recommendations for road reform, 'Better Transport Better Roads', and the announcement of a water review by the Minister of Commerce – appeared to threaten community involvement in two areas that had traditionally been regarded as the 'core business' of local authorities.   This threat was more explicit in the case of the roading reform, the proposals of which were set out in a white paper which recommended, *inter alia*, that: four to eight regionally-based state-owned road companies would take over running local roads from New Zealand's 74 territorial local authorities; rates would no longer be used to fund roads; and the road companies would be able fully to fund regional roading needs through a road levy imposed at the point of sale on transport fuels.

The extent to which the provision of roading services constitutes a core function of local government is indicated by the finding that 'roading is the single largest expenditure item for many local authorities, accounting for up to 60% in some jurisdictions.   On average, 27% of locally sourced funds are spent on roading' (Hutchings 2000a, p. 2).   The signal these proposals sent to local authorities was that they were not trusted sufficiently to provide even their core services in an efficient manner and that a National Cabinet and their Treasury advisors had joined the NZBR in its drive to find institutional alternatives to their ownership and management of these services. This signal was reinforced when the announcement of a review of water services that are currently supplied to '85% of the population' by local authorities 'came hard on the heels of these recommendations'. By drawing attention to 'the degree to which competition and competitive neutrality may be established between alternative suppliers, including from the private sector', the terms of reference of this review made clear that some rolling back of local government involvement in this sector was to be considered. (Hutchings 2000b, p. 3).

These proposals constituted a significant departure from the core objective of making local democracy more effective by making it more accountable that had formed the basis of the post-1989 consensus on local government policy. Activists within LGNZ were able to find a common cause with its other members in lobbying to modify these proposals to allow local authorities to retain their stake in the governance of road and water services. At issue was the extent of trust central government was prepared to place in local councils to manage 'competing interests', preserve citizen rights of access to basic services and 'determine future ownership and service delivery arrangements' (Hutchings 2000b, p. 8) in respect of assets that it argued 'play a fundamental role in promoting efficient and cohesive communities' (Hutchings 2000a, pp. 5–6).

The issue of central-local trust therefore appears to have replaced the issue of accountability as the primary focus of the local government policy debate. While a consensus developed on the desirability of strengthening accountability, the debate over roading and water reforms has produced a policy sub-system that is more sharply divided. The NZBR, the Treasury, the Manufacturers Federation and 'New Right' politicians would all appear to be lined up against the LGNZ in its efforts to preserve local autonomy and build trust-based relations with the center. Nevertheless the balance of power appears to be shifting toward the LGNZ. By aligning itself with the 'social capital movement' it has been able to gain a sympathetic hearing from those government agencies and left of center politicians who have sought to 'bring back balance to policy development' (Robinson 1997) through taking into account the impact of policies on social capital and social cohesion. This became evident after the election of a Labour–Alliance Coalition in 1999 when the new government moved quickly to fulfill its pre-election commitment to rebuild relations of trust by initiating a regular forum 'to identify policy issues requiring debate and further work and to develop a long term coherent strategy for local government as a whole' and by indicating that the 'Better Transport, Better Roads Proposal' is 'well and truly dead' (Hutchings 2000a, pp. 11–12). However, although this Labour-led government has used similar language to its counterpart in the UK, there is no indication that it is to attach the same importance to establishing a coherent basis for central–local relations or to rely as much on modernized local authorities in the delivery of its domestic policy agenda.

7.6 CONCLUSION

The evolution of local government policy in New Zealand after the radical restructuring set in motion by the 1989 Act suggests that effective consolidation may be more difficult to achieve than effective implementation, even where the central governing coalition remains more disengaged from this policy sub-system than was the case in the UK. While the resistance to the reforms subsided significantly once the restructuring process was completed, sources of conflict that were latent within the reforming coalition have surfaced as the quest to reconcile efficiency and democratic values by making local government more accountable appears to have exhausted itself. These areas of conflict that relate to diverging core beliefs on the comparative institutional advantage of local government have come to reflect the ideological divisions between parties to the left and right of center and mirror, in orientation if not in intensity, those that characterized UK local government policy under Conservative and Labour governments during the last two decades. They may therefore have the potential to cause more abrupt shifts in local government policy direction after changes in the composition of governing coalitions than would occur if the coherence of policy development was maintained by the effective consolidation of core reform principles.

8. Conclusion

8.1 WHAT CONTRIBUTION CAN ECONOMICS MAKE TO LOCAL GOVERNMENT POLICY MAKING?

The main purpose of this book has not been to trace the emergence and development of local government economics as a distinct branch of public sector economics. Rather, it has been to ascertain the contribution which economic theories can make to local government policy making. We have thus tended to view local government in the way recommended by Sabatier (1988), as a distinct 'policy sub-system' that draws together actors who have sufficient specialized information about this area of policy to be able to understand substantive debates, at a relatively technical level, about the comparative merits and significance of the solutions and problems that are being advanced for consideration. As local government has become more complex, particularly in advanced industrial countries, these actors have had to look increasingly to the social sciences, in general, and economics, in particular, to provide them with the conceptual tools to engage constructively in this policy sub-system.

The point of departure for this book has been the view that, for all its elegance and rigorous elaboration and refinement, the theory of fiscal federalism is not, by itself, adequate to this task. This is because it is too narrowly concerned with the assignment of responsibility for the provision of various public goods to different tiers of government. Participants in a local government policy sub-system are likely, however, to be concerned not just with the localness of public goods but with the incidence within local jurisdictions of all types of market failure. In this regard they might find the more general market failure paradigm, discussed in Chapter 2, helpful since it can be adapted to help them formulate an optimal response to local manifestations of market failures arising from externalities, non-competitive markets, asymmetric and uncertain information and incomplete markets as well as those equity issues that impinge on local government policy making.

However, as we discussed in Chapter 3, it appears that the various lines of criticism of the market failure paradigm that have gained momentum over the last three decades can be drawn together into a distinct government failure paradigm. In general, there has been a presumption in the literature on local government economics that the decentralization of government responsibilities to the local level can help ameliorate the inefficiencies associated with government failure by increasing the scope for competition within and between local authorities. In our view this presumption neglects the distinctive insights the government failure paradigm can bring to bear on local government policy making. We have sought to extend the logic of public choice and agency theory, in particular, to highlight the ways in which specific local government structures can be even more susceptible to voter apathy, asymmetric information, rent-seeking and fiscal illusion than central government agencies. The question of whether these types of local government failure can combine to produce a bias toward excessive spending by local governments is obviously an important one for the members of this sub-system since it can shape their views about whether or not the center should intervene to more tightly circumscribe local discretion. It is somewhat ironic that the advocates of increased central intervention to curb local government discretion are often 'minimalists', committed at the same time to pushing for the downsizing of the role of the state in the market economy so that its functions can be more closely matched with a (they would argue) more realistic assessment of the limitations in its capacity to efficiently perform these functions.

In principle, theoretical debates about the economic efficiency of local governments, which are implicit in both the market failure paradigm and the literature on government failure, should be amenable to resolution by recourse to the empirical literature which has sought to measure local government efficiency. But as we saw in Chapter 4, although the empirical analysis of economic efficiency in local government is not only abundant, but also technically advanced, important caveats should hold in the interpretation and application of this literature to real-world systems of local governance. For example, the existence of non-discretionary variables which cannot be controlled by local government managers, the divergence between effectiveness and efficiency in municipal service delivery, amongst many other factors, limit the usefulness of this empirical literature to local government policy making.

While the government failure paradigm may help to broaden the theoretical vision of participants in local government policy sub-systems, it nevertheless fails adequately to grasp some of the complexities and potentialities of modern local government. The structure of local government has significantly changed in many countries with there being 'a shift away from monolithic, hierarchical, highly standardized, bureaucratic production technologies to microcorporatist networked organizations dominated by meeting the needs of consumption rather than production'

(Bailey 1999, p. 262), and local policy makers have had to look to social sciences, such as economics, to provide them with theoretical frameworks that can elucidate the new options and possibilities they face after this restructuring.

In Chapter 5 we argued that the 'new institutional economics' (NIE) can go a long way toward comprehending these emerging complexities. As local bodies have sought to address cross-cutting issues and lever-in outside resources by forging collaborative partnership arrangements with other government agencies and local businesses, voluntary associations and community groups, they have had to decide whether horizontal coordination between these parties should be achieved by market, hierarchy or network mechanisms. NIE can be helpful in this regard since it identifies the factors affecting the transactions costs associated with deploying each governance mechanism. In particular it draws from strategic game theory to show that in situations where both market and hierarchical modes of governance are incomplete or subject to high transaction costs, trust and cooperation can develop in the absence of formal safeguards through the process by which network interactions become embedded within each other so that non-cooperation in any one area can lead to an unraveling of cooperation in other areas. While these networks are often seen as substitutes for markets and hierarchies they may also function as complements in the sense that networking may be a feature of the collaborative activity that precedes the formation of multi-organizational partnerships that come to be governed by more formal market and hierarchy mechanisms.

The scope and range of the partnerships a local authority is able to form would therefore seem to depend on its capacity to network with other actors in the local area. We suggested that recent developments in the theory of social capital can shed light on the nature of the resource that crucially affects this capacity. While the seminal thinkers on this subject appear to have been somewhat skeptical about the ability of either central or local governments to influence the accumulation of social capital, some recent research has found that local authorities can shape the political opportunity structure in ways that affect the access to, and formation of, social capital in their localities.

The literature on networks and social capital tends to cross the boundaries between economics and political science although it is still largely based on a game theoretic perspective that is founded on the same rational choice assumptions of mainstream economic theory. Having examined how far conventional economics can go in analyzing the issues facing local government policy makers, we sought to examine whether this was another field where 'something is sometimes to be gained by making things more complicated' (Hirschman 1985, p. 5). In particular, we sought to examine how economics can be revised to take into account the expressive dimension of policy-related behavior.

We suggested that this complication may be required to understand the behavior of networks whose members are bound together not so much by structures of resource dependence as by the hope they place in the advancement of common goals. In Chapter 5 it was argued that the cohesion of these networks and the trust their members place in one another can be conceived as being developed through repeated expression games that restrict the benefits, in terms of increased emotional energy, to those members whose passion crosses the threshold at which they can enjoy successful interaction rituals with other members. The emergence of hope – rather than interest-based networks in a local area does, however, place greater demands on the governance capacity of local authorities in the sense that they need to develop transformational leadership skills to bring these potentially conflicting groups together in the pursuit of a shared vision for the development of their community.

Economic theories that take into account the different types of network interaction and social capital can provide a rationale for the relatively open-minded approach to the capabilities of particular local authorities that we associate with an activist orientation by central government to local government policy. Rather than simply presuming that local authorities, in general, have an excess spending bias due to their susceptibility to various types of local government failure, this approach would recognize the networking capacity some local authorities might have as a result of the area-based resources of social capital they can draw on. From this perspective the question of whether particular local authorities may have a comparative advantage in coordinating and steering multi-organizational partnerships is essentially an empirical one. An activist approach to local government policy would thus not involve the center conferring a *carte blanche* on all local authorities. Rather it would foster and develop central–local trust-based relationships in which those authorities that satisfy the performance expectations of the center are rewarded by being entrusted with more functions and a greater degree of local autonomy. Eventually, the most trusted authorities could come to play a significant activist role in the supply of local governance and the development of their communities.

It would thus seem that distinct streams of economic theory can be adapted to lend support to minimalist and activist lines in local government policy respectively. To understand the factors that can lead to either line being ascendant, we sought to adopt a broader political economy perspective that took into account the context in which some recent local government reform initiatives have been undertaken.

8.2 THE POLITICAL ECONOMY OF LOCAL GOVERNMENT REFORM

Contemporary local government reform initiatives have generally taken place within the context of a much broader process of public sector reform. In Chapter 6 we suggested that in many countries public sector reforms have both reflected a shift from a policy paradigm that generated interventionist solutions to problems of market failure to one that has given rise to reforms designed to address the root causes of pervasive government failure and the macroeconomic imperative of restraining public expenditure as a key component of a strategy to control inflation and alleviate national tax and debt burdens. We relate Hall's (1993) conception of a paradigmatic reform process going through the four stages of erosion, fragmentation, implementation and consolidation to a theory that explains the succession of leadership styles and the endogenous accumulation of disappointment with the style of policy leadership that is likely to prevail during each of these stages. This theory thus treats the expression dimension of collective disappointment along similar lines to Hirschman's (1982) account of the 'shifting involvements' in private *vis-a-vis* activist lifestyles.

We direct our attention to the strong leadership style that may be necessary to establish the credibility of the inflation and debt objectives of macroeconomic policy and to overcome the resistance to reform that can arise during the implementation phase of a paradigmatic reform process. A demand for this style of leadership is likely to gain momentum within the climate of puzzlement that often prevails after the erosion and fragmentation of authority of a previously hegemonic policy paradigm. We show how this style can be collectively supplied by a reformist coalition that plays an expression game directed toward differentiating strong from both inspirational and empathetic leadership styles by giving a stable impression that they are resistant to alternative ideas and the claims of groups that stand to lose from the reform process.

While the restructuring produced by territorial amalgamation and the application of NPM principles to local government may help break up the policy communities that can seek to contain and ride out top-down pressures to change at this level, a strong leadership coalition may seek other ways to address its concern that local authorities can exercise their discretion over service quality and financing to counteract the intended impact of central funding cuts. This tendency was strikingly exemplified by the series of initiatives the Thatcher government launched to limit local discretion and place local governments under increasing pressure to cut costs by providing their services more efficiently. These culminated with the politically disastrous imposition of the poll tax, and not only illustrate the link between strong leadership and a minimalist mistrust of local government as being particularly prone to government failure, but also the climate of anxiety an SLC can produce through its intransigent refusal to work with the groups affected by change.

We would suggest that this climate of anxiety can produce an increasing demand for the empathetic style of leadership reflected in the Third Way policies of the Clinton, Blair and Schroeder governments. Our claim that a change in the style of policy leadership may involve more than a change in rhetoric without any substance is investigated with reference to the substantive changes in the direction of local government policy that have occurred in the UK under the Blair government. In essence this would seem to represent a definite shift toward a more activist approach to local government reform that seeks to both engage local policy communities in implementing this government's modernization agenda and reward those authorities that make the most exemplary contribution to this agenda by entrusting them with a greater degree of local autonomy. The pressures and tensions that are inherent to this more flexible approach can, however, be expected to surface within the local government policy sub-system the longer it is pursued. The resulting climate of reform fatigue may induce the governing coalition to disengage from this sub-system – a process that may be repeated in other sub-systems as this climate comes to prevail and create the conditions for a shift toward the more pragmatic style of policy leadership we associate with the consolidation and stabilization of the new policy paradigm.

The connection between the direction of local government reform and prevailing styles of policy leadership would seem to be so apparent in the UK since local government is one of the policy sub-systems in which recent governments have staked their claims to be suppliers of particular leadership styles on their capacity to move local policy in either a minimalist or activist direction. In Chapter 7 we examine whether a similar minimalist –activist divide can emerge in a country where governments have tended to remain relatively disengaged from the local government policy sub-system.

The comprehensive reform of the public sector that was undertaken in New Zealand after 1987 created a window of opportunity for two policy entrepreneurs to couple the extension of the principles embodied in these reforms to the local public sector with the radical territorial amalgamation proposal that they had taken almost three years to refine and develop. To implement this proposal they followed the model of strategic reform that was being applied by their government in other areas. This basically involved the use of 'blitzkrieg' tactics to deny opponents the opportunity to mobilize resistance and the explicit design of the reforms to establish a post-reform consensus on the objectives according to which the reforms were to be evaluated. The initial impression was that this strategy was very effective in the area of local government reform. The forces of local parochialism seem to have been marginalized and overcome by the reformers and the reforms implemented in 1989 appear to have committed the local government policy sub-system to a quest for greater accountability that seemed to reconcile the potential conflict between advocates of efficiency and democratic values. This impression of success has, however, given way to indications that this sub-system is becoming increasingly divided along minimalist and activist lines as the quest for accountability appears to have exhausted itself.

The New Zealand experience thus suggests that these are two distinct paths that can emerge from a similar set of basic reforms even when the local government policy sub-system does not become an arena for the demonstration of different styles of policy leadership. The restructuring of local government to match resources to tasks through, say, the separation of purchasing from provision can thus facilitate either a minimalist drive to downsize local government or an activist expansion of enabling authorities that capitalize on their enhanced capacity to network with other organizations to take on a more ambitious governance role in their communities. Our demonstration that economic theory can be used to rationalize either approach does raise questions about the relationship between theory and policy and the role of economists in the policy process.

8.3 THE ROLE OF ECONOMISTS IN THE POLICY PROCESS

Implicit in much of the discussion in this book has been the rejection of the image projected by traditional welfare economics of the economist as a progressive neutral expert (Nelson 1987, p. 55). Such a 'philosopher king' would be able to contribute to a comprehensively rational approach to public policy making. Our view, however, is that economists cannot really hope to remain disengaged from the fundamental social issues that divide the other actors in a policy sub-system, such as the issue of central–local trust that divides minimalists and activists in local government policy. Nevertheless, we would argue that while economists may not be able to avoid taking sides in these debates they can do so in a way that lifts them to a higher level of conceptual and analytical rigor and lays bare the assumptions and chains of logical reasoning on which the different policy positions are based. Moreover, we would recommend local government as a fertile field within which economists can not only make a worthwhile contribution to the evaluation, refinement and development of policy proposals, but also reflect back on the adequacy and relevance of their own tools to this task.

References

Akerlof, G.A. (1970), 'The Market for "Lemons": Qualitative Uncertainty and the Market Mechanism', *Quarterly Journal of Economics*, **84** (3), 488–500.

Akerlof, G. and Yellen, J. (1986), *Efficiency Wage Models and the Labor Market*, Cambridge: Cambridge University Press.

Alchian, A. and Demsetz, H. (1973), 'The Property Rights Paradigm', *Journal of Economic History*, **33** (1), 16–27.

Aldrich, J.H. (1997), 'When is it Rational to Vote?', in D.C. Mueller (ed.), *Perspectives on Public Choice*, Cambridge: Cambridge University Press, pp. 373–90.

Allen, D. (1991), 'What are Transactions Costs?', *Research in Law and Economics*, **14** (3), 1–18.

Ammons, D.N. (1986), 'Common Barriers to Productivity Improvement in Local Government', in M. Holzer and A. Halachmi, *Strategic Issues in Public Sector Productivity: The Best of Public Productivity Review 1975–1985*, San Francisco: Jossey–Bass, pp. 34–39.

Ammons, D.N. (1992), 'Productivity Barriers in the Public Sector', in Holzer, M., *Public Productivity Handbook*, New York: Marcel Dekker, pp. 119–143.

Arrow, K. (1970), 'The Organization of Economic Activity: Issues Pertinent to the Choice of Market Versus Non-Market Allocation', in R.H. Haverman and J. Margolis (eds), *Public Expenditure and Policy Analysis*, Chicago: Markham, pp. 43–51.

Axelrod, R. (1984), *The Evolution of Cooperation*, New York: Basic Books.

Bahl, R.W. and Linn, J.F. (1992), *Urban Public Finance in Developing Countries*, Oxford: Oxford University Press.

Bailey, S. (1999), *Local Government Economics: Principles and Practice*, London: Macmillan.

Balcerowicz, L. (1994), 'Common Fallacies in the Debate on the Transition to a Market Economy', *Economic Policy,* **4** (1), 18–30.

Bale, M. and Dale, T. (1998), 'Public Sector Reform in New Zealand and its Relevance to Developing Countries', *The World Bank Research Observer*, **13** (1), 103–121.

Banker, R.D. and Morey, R.C. (1986), 'The Use of Categorical Variables in Data Envelopment Analysis', *Management Science*, **32**, 1613–27.

Banker, R.D. Charnes, A. and Cooper, W.W. (1984), 'Some Models for Estimating Technical and Scale Inefficiencies in Data Envelopment Analysis', *Management Science*, **30**, 1078–92.

Barber, B. (1984), *Strong Democracy: Participatory Politics for a New Age*, Berkeley: University of California Press.

Barr, J.L. and Davis, O.A. (1996), 'An Elementary Political and Economic Theory of the Expenditures of Local Governments', *Southern Economic Journal*, **33** (1), 149–65.

Barry, B.M. and Hardin, R. (1982), *Rational Man and Irrational Society?*, London:

Sage Publications.

Barzel, Y. (1982), 'Measurement Costs and the Organization of Markets', *Journal of Law and Economics*, **25** (1), 27–48.

Barzelay, M. (1992), *Breaking Through Bureaucracy: A New Vision for Managing in Government*, San Francisco: University of California Press.

Bass, B.M. (1990), *Bass and Stogdills Handbook of Leadership*, New York: Free Press.

Bassett, M. (1996), 'The Context of Local Government Reform: The New Zealand Perspective', in P. McDermott, V. Forgie and R. Howell (eds), *An Agenda for Local Government*, Palmerstone North, Local Government Studies Occasional Paper, Massey University, pp. 29–38.

Bates, W. (1996), *Will a Coherent Economic Strategy Be Possible Under Proportional Representation*, Wellington: Business Roundtable.

Bator, F. (1958), 'The Anatomy of Market Failure', *Quarterly Journal of Economics*, **72** (2), 311–400.

Baumol, W.J., Panzar, J.C. and Willig, R.D. (1982), *Contestable Markets and the Theory of Industrial Structure,* New York: Harcourt Brace.

Bendor, J. (1990), 'Formal Models of Bureaucracy: A Review', in N. B. Lynn and A. Wildavsky (eds), *Public Administration: The State of the Discipline*, London: Chatham, pp. 373–417.

Bennis, W. and Nannus B. (1985), *Leaders*, New York: Harper Row

Bjurek, H. Hjalmarsson, L. and Førsund, F.R. (1990), 'Deterministic Parametric and Nonparametric Estimation of Efficiency in Service Production: A Comparison', *Journal of Econometrics*, **46**, 213–27.

Bjurek, H., Kjulin, U. and Gustafsson, B. (1992), 'Efficiency, Productivity and Determinants of Inefficiency at Public Day Care Centers in Sweden', *Scandinavian Journal of Economics*, **94**, 173–87.

Blair T. and Schroeder, G. (1999), *The Third Way/Die Neue Mitte*, London: British Labour Party.

Borzel, T.J. (1998), 'Organizing Babylon – On the Different Conceptions of Policy Networks', *Public Administration*, **76**, 253–73.

Boston, J. (1996), *Public Management: The New Zealand Model*, Auckland: Oxford University Press.

Boulding, K.E. (1978), *Ecodynamics*, New York: Sage.

Boyne, G.A. (1998), *Public Choice Theory and Local Government*, Basingstoke: Macmillan.

Bradrach, J. and Eccles, R. (1991), 'Price, Authority and Trust: From Ideal Types to Plural Forms', in G. Thompson, J. Frances, R. Levacic and J. Mitchell (eds), *Markets, Hierarchies and Networks: The Coordination of Social Life*, London: Sage, pp. 277–92.

Brennan, G. and Buchanan, J.M. (1984), 'Voter Choice', *American Behavioral Scientist*, **28** (10), 185–201.

Brennan, G. and Buchanan, J.M. (1985), *The Reason of Rules*, Cambridge: Cambridge University Press.

Breton, A. (1995), *Competitive Governments*, Cambridge: Cambridge University Press.

Breton, A. and Wintrobe, R. (1982), *The Logic of Bureaucratic Conduct*, New York: Cambridge University Press.

Bromley, D.W. (1989), *Economic Interests and Institutions*, Oxford: Basil Blackwell.

Brooks, J. (2000), 'Labour's Modernization of Local Government', *Public Administration*, **78** (3), 593 – 612.

Bryson, J. and Crosby B. (1992), *Leadership for the Common Good: Tackling Problems in a Shared Power World*, San Francisco: Jossey-Bass.

Buchanan, J.M. (1967), 'The Fiscal Illusion', in J.M. Buchanan (ed.), *Public Finance in the Fiscal Process*, Chapel Hill: University of North Carolina Press, pp. 135–48.

Buchanan, J.M. (1978), 'From Private Preferences to Public Philosophy: The Development of Public Choice', in *The Economics of Politics*, London: Institute of Economic Affairs, pp. 15–25.

Buchanan, J.M. (1980), 'Rent-Seeking and Profit Seeking', in J.M. Buchanan, R.D. Tollison and G. Tullock (eds), *Toward a Theory of a Rentseeking Society*, College Station: Texas University Press, pp. 36–61.

Buchanan, J.M. (1986), *Liberty, State and Market*, Brighton: Harvester Press.

Buchanan, J.M. (1994), *The Economics and the Ethics of Constitutional Order*, Ann Arbor: University of Michigan Press.

Buchanan J.M., Tollison R.D. and Tullock G. (eds), *Toward a Theory of a Rentseeking Society*, College Station: Texas University Press.

Burns, J.M. (1978), *Leadership*, New York: Harper and Row.

Bush, G. (1995), *Local Government and Politics in New Zealand*, Auckland: Auckland University Press.

Carter, N., Klein, R. and Day, P. (1995), *How Organizations Measure Success: The Use of Performance Indicators in Government*, London: Routledge.

Castles, F.G. (1993), *Families of Nations: Patterns of Public Policy in Western Democracies*, Aldershot: Dartmouth Press.

Chang, H.J. (1994), *The Political Economy of Industry Policy*, London: Macmillan.

Chang, H.J. and Rowthorn, R. (1995), 'Introduction', in H.J. Chang and R. Rowthorn, (eds), *The Role of the State in Economic Change*, Oxford: Clarendon Press, pp. 1–30.

Chang, K.P. and Kao, P.H. (1992), 'The Relative Efficiency of Public versus Private Municipal Bus Firms: An Application of Data Envelopment Analysis', *Journal of Productivity Analysis*, **3**, 67–84.

Charnes, A., Cooper, W.W. and Li, S. (1989), 'Using Data Envelopment Analysis to Evaluate Efficiency in the Economic Performance of Chinese Cities', *Socio-Economic Planning Science*, **23**, 325–44.

Charnes, A., Cooper, W.W. and Rhodes, E. (1978), 'Measuring the Efficiency of Decision Making Units', *European Journal of Operational Research*, **2**, 429–44.

Cheema, G. (1996), *Decentralization and the Strengthening of Local Government*, Gothenburg: United Nations Global Forum on Local Governance.

Chhibber, A. (1997), 'The State in a Changing World', *Finance and Development*, **34** (3), 17–20.

Coase, R.H. (1937), 'The Nature of the Firm', *Economica*, **4** (November), 386–405.

Coase, R.H. (1960), 'The Problem of Social Cost', *Journal of Law and Economics*, **3** (1), 1–44.

Coase, R.H. (1964), 'The Regulated Industries: Discussion', *American Economic Review*, **54** (4), 777–95.

Coase, R.H. (1992), 'The Institutional Structure of Production', *American Economic Review*, **82** (4), 713–19.

Coelli, T., Rao, D.S.P and Battese, G.E. (1997), *An Introduction to Efficiency and Productivity Analysis*, Boston: Kluwer.

Coleman, J. (1988), 'Social Capital in the Creation of Human Capital', *American Journal of Sociology*, **94**, 95–120.

Coleman, J. (1990), *Foundations of Social Theory*, Cambridge, MA: Harvard

University Press.

Collins, R. (1993), 'Emotional Energy as the Common Denominator of Rational Social Action', *Rationality and Society*, **5** (2), 203–20.

Cook, W.D., Kazakov, A. and Roll, Y. (1993), 'On the Measurement and Monitoring of Relative Efficiency of Highway Maintenance Patrols', in A. Charnes, W.W. Cooper, A.Y. Lewin and L.M. Seiford (eds), *Data Envelopment Analysis: Theory, Methodology and Applications*, Boston: Kluwer, pp. 231–52.

Cook, W.D., Kazakov, A., Roll, Y. and Seiford, L.M. (1991), 'A Data Envelopment Approach to Measuring Efficiency: Case Analysis of Highway Maintenance Patrols', *Journal of Socio-Economics*, **20**, 83-103.

Cook, W.D., Roll, Y. and Kazakov, A. (1990), 'A DEA Model for Measuring the Relative Efficiency of Highway Maintenance Patrols', *Informational Systems and Operational Research*, **28**, 113–24.

Cornes, R. and Sandler, T. (1996), *The Theory of Externalities, Public Goods and Club Goods*, New York: Cambridge University Press.

Council of Europe (1997), *Local Finance in Europe*, Strasbourg: Council of Europe.

Crain, W.M. and Tollison, R.D. (1993), 'Empirical Public Choice', in W.M. Crain and R.D. Tollison, *Predicting Politics: Essays in Empirical Public Choice*, Ann Arbor: University of Michigan Press, pp. 3–14.

Dahlman, C.J. (1979), 'The Problem of Externality', *Journal of Law and Economics*, **22** (1), 141–62.

De Alessi, L. (1983), 'Property Rights, Transactions Costs, and X-Efficiency: An Essay in Economic Theory', *American Economic Review*, **73** (1), 64–81.

De Borger, B. and Kerstens, K. (1996a), 'Cost Efficiency of Belgian Local Governments: A Comparative Analysis of FDH, DEA and Econometric Approaches', *Regional Science and Urban Economics*, **26**, 145–70.

De Borger, B. and Kerstens, K. 1996b, 'Radial and Nonradial Measures of Technical Efficiency: An Empirical Illustration for Belgian Local Governments using an FDH Reference Technology', *Journal of Productivity Analysis*, **7**, 5–18.

De Borger, B. Kerstens, K., Moesen, W. and Vanneste, J. (1994), 'Explaining Differences in Productive Efficiency: An Application to Belgian Municipalities', *Public Choice*, **80**, 339–58.

Deller, S.C. (1992), 'Production Efficiency in Local Government: A Parametric Approach', *Public Finance/Finances Publiques*, **47**, 32–44.

Deller, S.C., Chicoine, D.L. and Walzer, N. (1988), 'Economics of Size and Scope in Rural Low-Volume Roads', *Review of Economics and Statistics*, **70** (3), 459–65.

Deller, S.C. and Halstead, J.M. (1994), 'Efficiency in the Production of Rural Road Services: The Case of New England Towns', *Land Economics*, **70**, 247–59.

Deller, S.C. and Nelson, C.H. (1991), 'Measuring the Economic Efficiency of Producing Rural Road Services', *American Journal of Agricultural Economics*, **72**, 194–201.

Deller, S.C., Nelson, C.H. and Walzer, N. (1992), 'Measuring Managerial Efficiency in Rural Government', *Public Productivity and Management Review*, **15**, 355–70.

Deller, S.C. and Rudnicki, E.R. (1992), 'Managerial Efficiency in Local Government: Implications on Jurisdictional Consolidation', *Public Choice*, **74**, 221–31.

Demsetz, H. (1969), 'Information and Efficiency: Another Viewpoint', *Journal of Law and Economics*, **82** (4), 713–19.

Dillinger, W. and Fay, M. (1999), 'From Centralized to Decentralization Governance', *Finance and Development*, **36** (4), 19–21.

Dollery, B.E. and Singh, S. (1998), 'A Note on the Empirical Analysis of Wagner's Law', *Economic Analysis and Policy*, **28** (2), 245–57.

Dollery, B.E. and Wallis, J.L. (1997), 'Market Failure, Government Failure, Leadership and Public Policy', *Journal of Interdisciplinary Economics*, **8** (2), 113–26.

Dollery, B.E. and Worthington, A.C. (1996a), 'The Empirical Analysis of Fiscal Illusion', *Journal of Economic Surveys*, **10** (3), 261–98.

Dollery, B.E. and Worthington, A.C. (1996b), 'The Evaluation of Public Policy: Normative Economic Theories of Government Failure', *Journal of Interdisciplinary Economics*, **7**, 27–39.

Domberger, S., Meadowcroft, S.A. and Thompson, D.J. (1986), 'Competitive Tendering and Efficiency: the Case of Refuse Collection', *Fiscal Studies*, **7** (4), 69– 87

Dornbusch, R. and Fischer, S. (1990), *Macroeconomics*, New York: McGraw-Hill.

Dunham, D. and Kelegama, S. (1997), 'Does Leadership Matter in the Economic Reform Process? Liberalization and Governance in Sri Lanka, 1989-93', *World Development*, **25** (2), 179–90.

Dye, T. (1990), *American Federalism*, Lexington: Heath.

Easton, B. (1997), *The Commercialisation of New Zealand*, Auckland: Auckland University Press.

Eggertsson, T. (1990), *Economic Behavior and Institutions*, Cambridge: Cambridge University Press.

Eichbaum, C., (2000), 'The Politics and Economics of the Third Way', in S. Chatterjee (ed.), *The New Politics: A Third Way for New Zealand*, Palmerstone North: Dunmore Press.

Eisinger, P. (1973), 'The Conditions of Protest Behavior in American Cities', *Political Studies*, **67** (1), 11–28.

Elster, J. (1998), 'Emotions and Economic Theory', *Journal of Economic Literature*, **36** (1), 47–74.

Elwood, B. (1996), 'From Theory to Practice: The New Zealand experience', in P. McDermott, V. Forgie and R. Howell (eds), *An Agenda for Local Government*, Palmerstone North, Local Government Studies Occasional Paper, Massey University, pp. 158–71.

Epstein, P.D. (1992), 'Measuring the Performance of Public Services', in Holzer, M., *Public Productivity Handbook*, New York, Marcel Dekker, pp. 321–364.

Etzioni, A. (1988), *The Moral Dimension*, New York: The Free Press.

Faith, R.L. and Tollison, R.D. (1993), 'Expressive versus Economic Voting', in W.M. Crain and R.D. Tollison, *Predicting Politics: Essays in Empirical Public Choice*, Ann Arbor: University of Michigan Press, pp. 231–44.

Färe, R., Grosskopf, S. and Lovell, C.A.K. (1994), *Production Frontiers* Cambridge: Cambridge University Press.

Farrell, M.J. (1957), 'The Measurement of Productive Efficiency', *Journal of the Royal Statistics Society*, **120** (Part III), 253–82.

Faux, J. (1999), 'Lost on the Third Way', *Dissent*, **46** (2), 105–116.

Festinger, L. (1957), *A Theory of Cognitive Dissonance*, Stanford, CA: Stanford University Press.

Fried, H.O., Lovell C.A. and Schmidt, S.S. (1993), *The Measurement of Productive Efficiency: Techniques and Applications*, New York: Oxford University Press.

Frijda, N.H. (1986), *The Emotions* (1994), Cambridge: Cambridge University Press.

Fromm, E. (1968), *The Revolution of Hope: Towards a Humanized Technology*, New York: Harper and Row.

Fukuyama, F. (1995), *Trust: The Social Virtues and the Creation of Prosperity.* New York: The Free Press.

Furubotn, E.G. and Richter, R. (1992), 'The New Institutional Economics: An Assessment', in E.G. Furubotn (ed.), *New Institutional Economics*, Aldershot, UK: Edward Elgar, pp. 1–32.

Gambetta, D. (1988), *Trust: Making and Breaking Cooperative Relations*, Oxford: Basil Blackwell.

Ganley, J.A. and Cubbin, J.S. (1992), *Public Sector Efficiency Measurement: Applications of Data Envelopment Analysis*, Amsterdam: North Holland.

Giddens, A., (1998), *The Third Way: The Renewal of Social Democracy*, Cambridge: Polity Press.

Goffman, E. (1959), *The Presentation of Self in Everyday Life*, New York: Anchor Books

Golany, B. and Roll, Y. (1993), 'Some Extensions of Techniques to Handle Non-Discretionary Factors in Data Envelopment Analysis', *Journal of Productivity Analysis*, **4**, 419–32.

Gramlich, E.M. (1977), 'Intergovernmental Grants: A Review of the Empirical Literature', in W.E. Oates (ed.), *The Political Economy of Fiscal Federalism*, Lexington: Lexington Books, pp. 219–39.

Granovetter, M. (1985), 'Economic Action and Social Action: The Problem of Embeddedness', *American Journal of Sociology*, **91**, 481–510.

Greenwald, B. and Stiglitz, J. (1993), 'New and Old Keynesians', *Journal of Economic Perspectives*, **6** (1), 23-44.

Grindle, M. (1996), *Challenging the State: Crisis and Innovation in Latin America and Africa*, Cambridge: Cambridge University Press.

Grosskopf, S. and Yaisawarng, S. (1990), 'Economies of Scope in the Provision of Local Public Services', *National Tax Journal*, **43**, 61–74.

Hall, P.A. (1993), 'Policy Paradigms, Social Learning and the State', *Comparative Politics*, **25** (3), pp. 275–96.

Hall, P. (1998), 'Social Capital in Britain', paper presented at the American Political Science Association Meeting, Boston.

Hatry, H.P. and Fisk, D.M. (1992), 'Measuring Productivity in the Public Sector', in M. Holzer (ed.) (1992), *Public Productivity Handbook*, New York: Marcel Dekker, pp. 365–89.

Hawley, W. (1973), *Nonpartisan Elections and the Case for Party Politics*, New York: Wiley.

Hayes, K. and Chang, S. (1990), 'The Relative Efficiency of City Manager and Mayor-Council Forms of Government', *Southern Economic Journal*, **57**, 167–77.

Helm, D.R. (1986), 'The Economic Borders of the State', *Oxford Review of Economic Policy*, **2** (2), i–xxiv.

Helm, D.R. and Smith, R. (1987), 'The Assessment: Decentralization and the Economics of Local Government', *Oxford Review of Economic Policy*, **3** (2), i–xxi.

Henney, A. (1984), *Inside Local Government*, London: Sinclair Browne.

Hindmoor, A. (1998), 'The Importance of being Trusted: Transaction Costs and Policy Network Theory', *Public Administration*, **76**, 25–43.

Hirschman, A.O. (1970), *Exit, Voice and Loyalty*, Cambridge: Cambridge University Press.

Hirschman, A.O. (1971), *A Bias For Hope: Essays on Development and Latin America*, New Haven: Yale University Press.

Hirschman, A.O. (1976), Political Economy: Some Uses of the Exit-Voice Approach: Discussion', *American Economic Review*, **66** (2), 386–89.

Hirschman, A.O. (1982), *Shifting Involvements: Private Interests and Public Action*,

Princeton: Princeton University Press.

Hirschman, A.O. (1985), 'Against Parsimony', *Economics and Philosophy*, **1** (1), 7–21.

Hjalmarsson, L. and Veiderpass, A. (1992), 'Efficiency and Ownership in Swedish Electricity Retail Distribution', *Journal of Productivity Analysis*, **3**, 7–23.

Hjern, B. and Hull, C. (1982), 'Implementation Research as Empirical Constitutionalism', *European Journal of Political Research*, **10** (2), 105–16.

Hollis M. and Nell, E. J. (1975), *Rational Economic Man*, London: Cambridge University Press.

Holzer, M. (1992), *Public Productivity Handbook*, New York: Marcel Dekker.

Holzer, M. and Halachmi, A. (1986), *Strategic Issues in Public Sector Productivity: The Best of Public Productivity Review 1975–1985*, San Francisco: Jossey-Bass.

Hood, C. (1991), 'A Public Administration for all Seasons?', *Public Administration*, **69** (1), 3–19.

Hood, C. (1994), *Explaining Economic Policy Reversals*, Buckingham: Open University Press.

Hood, C. (2000), *The Art of the State*, Oxford: Clarendon Press

Howlett, M. and Ramesh, M. (1995), *Studying Public Policy: Policy Cycles and Policy Subsystems*, Oxford :Oxford University Press.

Hutchings, J. (2000a), 'Creating Solutions to Transport Concerns: The New Zealand Experience', National Rural Roads Congress, Moree.

Hutchings, J. (2000b), 'Progress on the Review of Water Facilities in New Zealand', Water 2000 Conference, Wellington.

Industry Commission (1997), *Performance Measures for Councils: Improving Local Government Performance Indicators*, Melbourne: AGPS.

Inglehart, R. (1994), *Codebook for World Values Surveys*, Institute for Social Research, Ann Arbor.

Inman, R.P. (1987), 'Markets, Governments, and the "New" Political Economy', in A.J. Auerbach and M. Feldstein (eds), *Handbook of Public Economics*, vol. III, Amsterdam: North-Holland, pp. 647–778.

Inman, R.P. and Rubinfeld, D.L. (1997), 'Rethinking Federalism', *Journal of Economic Perspectives*, 11 (4), 43–64.

Jenkins-Smith, H.C. and Sabatier, P.A. (1993), 'Evaluating the Advocacy Coalition Framework', *Journal of Public Policy*, **14** (2), 175–203.

Jensen, M.C. and Meckling, W.H. (1976), 'The Theory of the Firm: Managerial Behavior, Agency Costs, and Ownership Structure', *Journal of Financial Economics*, **3** (3), 305–60.

John, P. and Block, A. (1991), *Attitudes to Local Government: A Survey of Electors*, York: Joseph Rowntree Foundation.

Johnson, R.W. and Lewin, A.Y. (1984), 'Management and Accountability Models of Public Sector Performance', in T.C. Miller (ed.), *Public Sector Performance: A Conceptual Turning Point*, Baltimore: John Hopkins University Press.

Jones, G.W. and Stewart, J.D. (1982), 'Policy making in Central and Local Government Compared', *Local Government Studies*, **8** (1), 73–79.

Jones, P. and Stewart, J. (1985), *The Case for Local Government*, London: Allen and Unwin.

Jordan, G. (1990), 'Sub-Government, Policy Communities and Networks: Refilling the Old Bottles', *Journal of Theoretical Politics*, **2** (3), 319–38.

Jordan, G. and Richardson, J. (1979), 'Policy Communities: The British and American Style', *Policy Studies Journal*, **11**, 603–15.

Keating, M. (1988), 'Local Government Reform and Finance in France', in D.N.

King (ed.), *Local Government Economics in Theory and Practice*, London: Routledge, pp. 154–70.

Kelsey, J. (1995), *The New Zealand Experiment: A World Model for Structural Adjustment*, Auckland: Auckland University Press.

Kenis, P. and Schneider, V. (1991), 'Policy Networks and Policy Analysis: Scrutinizing a New Analytical Toolbox', in B. Marin and R. Mayntz (eds), *Policy Network: Empirical Evidence and Theoretical Considerations*, Frankfurt: Campus Verlag, pp. 182–204.

Kerr, R. (1999), *Toward More Efficient and Democratic Local Government*, Hamilton: New Zealand Business Roundtable.

King, D.N. (1984), *Fiscal Tiers: The Economics of Multi-Level Government*, London: George Allen and Unwin.

King, D.N. (1992), 'Current Issues in the Theory of Fiscal Federalism', in D.N. King (ed.), *Local Government Economics in Theory and Practice*, London: Routledge, pp. 23–42.

Kingdon, J. (1984). *Agenda, Alternatives and Public Policies*, Boston: Little Brown.

Knack, S. and Keefer, P. (1997), 'Does Social Capital have an Economic Payoff? A Cross-Country Investigation', *Quarterly Journal of Economics*, 72, 1250–81.

Kolm, S. C. (1977), *Modern Theories of Justice*, Cambridge: MIT Press.

Kolm, S.C. (1993), *Justice and Equity*, Cambridge: MIT Press.

Kreps, D. (1990), 'Corporate Culture and Economic Theory', in J. Alt and K. Shepsle (eds), *Perspectives on Positive Political Economy*, Cambridge: Cambridge University Press, pp. 144–68.

Kriesi, H. (1995), 'The Political Opportunity Structure of New Social Movements: Its Impact on Their Mobilization', in J. Jenkins and B. Dermans (eds), *The Politics of Social Protest*, London: UCL Press, pp. 167–98.

Krueger, A.O. (1993), *Political Economy of Policy Reform in Developing Countries*, Cambridge, MA: MIT Press.

Krugman, P. (1998), 'What Happened to Asia?', http://web.mit.edu/krugman/www. DISINTER.html.

Kuhn, T. (1962), *The Structure of Scientific Revolutions*, Chicago: University of Chicago Press.

Kuran, T. (1990), 'Private and Public Preferences', *Economics and Philosophy*, 6 (1), 1–26.

Kydland, F. and Prescott, E. (1977), 'Rules Rather Than Discretion: The Inconsistency of Optimal Plans', *Journal of Political Economy*, 85, 473–491.

Leibenstein, H. (1978), *The General Theory of X-Inefficiency*, London: Allen and Unwin.

Levinthal, D. (1988), 'A Survey of Agency Models of Organizations', *Journal of Economic Behavior and Organization*, 9 (1), 153–85.

Lindblom, C. (1959), 'The Science of Muddling Through', *Public Administration Review*, 14, 79–88.

Lindsay, C. (1976), 'A Theory of Government Enterprise', *Journal of Political Economy*, 84 (5), 31-7.

Lipsey, R.G. and Lancaster, K. (1956), 'The General Theory of the Second Best', *Review of Economic Studies*, 24 (1), 11–23.

Lipsky, M. (1973), *Street Level Bureaucracy*, New York: Russell Sage.

Little, G. (1988), *Strong Leadership*, Melbourne: Oxford University Press.

Loughlin, M. (1986), *Local Government in the Modern State*, London: Sweet and Maxwell.

Loury, G. (1994), 'Self-Censorship in Political Discourse', *Rationality and Society*, 6

(4), 428–61.

Lowndes, V. and Skelcher, C. (1998), 'The Dynamics of Multi-Organizational Partnerships: An Analysis of Changing Modes of Governance', *Public Administration*, **76**, 313–33.

Lowndes, V., Stoker, G., Pratchett, L., Leach, S. and Wingfield, M. (1998), *Enhancing Public Participation in Local Government*, London: Department of the Environment.

Lucas, R. (1972), 'Testing the Natural Rate Hypothesis', in Eckstein, O. (ed.), *The Economics of Price Determination*, Washington: Federal Reserve Board, pp. 50–59.

Lucas, R., (1973), 'Some International Evidence on Output-Inflation Trade-offs', *American Economic Review*, **63** (3), 326–34.

Mackintosh, M. (1992), 'Partnership: Issues of Policy and Negotiation', *Local Economy*, **7**, 3.

Magee, S.P., Brock, W.A. and Young, L. (1989), *Black Hole Tariffs and Endogenous Policy Theory*, Cambridge: Cambridge University Press

Majone, G. (1993), 'Wann ist Policy-Deliberation Wichtig', in A. Heritier (ed.), *Policy-Analyze, Kritik, and Neuorientierung*, Opladen, Westdeutscher Verlag, pp. 86–103.

Maloney, W., Smith, G. and Stoker, G. (2000), 'Social Capital and Urban Governance: Adding a More Contextualized 'Top-Down' Perspective', *Political Studies*, **48**, 802–20.

Mankiw, G. and Romer, R. (1991), *New Keynesian Economics*, Cambridge MA: MIT Press.

Mann, S.Z. (1986), 'The Politics of Productivity: State and Local Focus', in M. Holzer, and A. Halachmi, (1986), *Strategic Issues in Public Sector Productivity: The Best of Public Productivity Review 1975–1985*, San Francisco: Jossey-Bass, pp. 167–99.

Mark, J.A. (1986), 'Measuring Productivity in Government: Federal, State and Local', in M. Holzer, and A. Halachmi (1986), *Strategic Issues in Public Sector Productivity: The Best of Public Productivity Review 1975-1985*, San Francisco: Jossey-Bass, pp. 401–35.

Marsh, D. and Rhodes, R. (1992a), *Implementing Thatcherite Policies: Audit of an Era*, Buckingham: Open University Press.

Marsh, D. and Rhodes, R.A.W. (1992b), *Policy Networks in British Governments*, Oxford: Oxford University Press.

Mayntz, R. (1993), 'Modernization and the Logic of Interorganizational Networks', in J. Child, M. Crozier and R. Mayntz (eds), *Societal Change Between Market and Organization*, Aldershot: Avebury, pp.175–96.

McDermott, P. and Forgie, V. (1999), 'Trends in Local Government: Efficiency, Functions and Democracy', *Political Science*, **50** (2), 223–41.

McKinlay, P. (1994), 'Local Government Reform: What Was Ordered and What Has Been Delivered', Unpublished paper, Wellington.

McKinlay, P. (1998), *Public Ownership and the Community*, Wellington: Institute of Policy Studies.

McKinlay, P. (1999), *Devolution: Partnership or Ad Hocism?* Wellington: State Services Commission.

McManus, J.C. (1972), 'The Theory of the Multinational Firm', in G. Pacquet (ed.), *The Multinational Firm and the National State*, London" Collier-MacMillan, pp. 63–72.

McNeill, J. (1997), 'Local Government in the Australian Federal System', in B.E.

Dollery and N.A. Marshall (eds), *Australian Local Government: Reform and Renewal*, Melbourne: Macmillan, pp. 17–39.

Miller, G.J. (1992), 'Productivity and the Budget Process', in M. Holzer, *Public Productivity Handbook*, New York: Marcel Dekker, pp. 62–91.

Mitchell, W.C. and Simmons, R.T. (1994), *Beyond Politics*, Boulder: Westview Press.

Moe, T.M. (1984), 'The New Economics of Organization', *American Journal of Political Science*, **28** (4), 739–77.

Mueller, D.C. (1989), *Public Choice II*, Cambridge: Cambridge University Press.

Musgrave, R.A. (1959), *The Theory of Public Finance*, New York: McGraw-Hill.

Musgrave, R.A. (1969), 'Theories of Fiscal Federalism', *Public Finance*, **24** (4), 521–32.

Musgrave, R.A. and Musgrave, P.B. (1984), *Public Finance in Theory and Practice*, Singapore: McGraw-Hill.

Naschold, F. (1997), *The Dialectics of Modernising Local Government*, Berlin: Science Center.

Nelson, R. (1987), 'The Economics Profession and the Making of Public Policy', *Journal of Economic Literature*, **25** (1), 49–91.

New Zealand Business Roundtable (1995), *Local Government in New Zealand: An Overview of the Economic and Financial Issues*, Wellington.

New Zealand Treasury (1987), *Government Management: Briefing to the Incoming Government*, Wellington: Government Printer.

Newton, K. (1976), *Second City Politics*, Oxford: Clarendon Press.

Newton, K. and Karran, T. (1985), *The Politics of Local Expenditure*, London: Macmillan.

Niskanen, W.A. (1971), *Bureaucracy and Representative Government*, Chicago: Aldine-Atherton.

North, D.C. (1979), 'A Framework for Analyzing the State in Economic History', *Explorations in Economic History*, **16** (3), 249–59.

North, D.C. (1984), *Structure and Change in Economic History*, New York: Norton.

Nowland-Foreman, G. (1995), *Neither Mendicants nor Dealmakers*, Wellington: New Zealand Council of Christian Services.

O'Dowd, M.C. (1978), 'The Problem of "Government Failure" in Mixed Economics', *South African Journal of Economics*, **46** (4) 360–70.

Oates, W.E. (1968), 'The Theory of Public Finance in a Federal System', *Canadian Journal of Economics*, **1** (February), 37–54.

Oates, W.E. (1972), *Fiscal Federalism*, New York: Harcourt Brace Jovanovich.

Oates, W.E. (1988), 'On the Nature and Measurement of Fiscal Illusion: A Survey', in G. Brennan, B.S. Grewel and P. Groenewegen (eds), *Taxation and Fiscal Federalism: Essays in Honour of Russell Mathews*, Canberra: Australian National University Press, pp. 75–96.

Oates, W.E. (ed.) (1998), *The Economics of Fiscal Federalism and Local Public Finance*, Cheltenham, UK: Edward Elgar.

Olson, M. (1965), *The Logic of Collective Action*, Cambridge: Harvard University Press.

Olson, M. (1982), *The Rise and Decline of Nations*, New Haven: Yale University Press.

Osborne, D. and Gaebler, T. (1992), *Reinventing Government*, New York: Addison-Wesley.

Ouchi, W. (1991), 'Markets, Bureaucracies and Clans', in G. Thompson, J. Frances, R. Levacic and J. Mitchell (eds), *Markets, Hierarchies and Networks: The*

Coordination of Social Life, London: Sage, pp.246–55.

Painter, C., Isaac-Henry, K. and Rouse, J. (1997), 'Local Authorities and Non-Elected Agencies: Strategic Responses and Organizational Networks', Public Administration, 75, 225–45.

Pareto, V. (1909), Manual of Political Economy, Paris: Girard

Pauly, M.V. (1973), 'Income Distribution as a Local Public Good', Journal of Public Economics, 2, 35–58.

Peacock, A.T. (1977), 'The Political Economy of Devolution: The British Case', in W.E. Oates (ed.), The Political Economy of Fiscal Federalism, Lexington: Lexington Books, pp. 49–63.

Peltzman, S. (1976), 'Towards a More General Theory of Regulation', Journal of Law and Economics, 19 (2), 211–40.

Peters, G. (1996), The Future of Governing: Four Emerging Models, Lawrence, University Press of Kansas.

Pigou, A. C. (1920), The Economics of Welfare, London, Macmillan.

Polidano, C. (2000), 'Measuring Public Sector Capacity', World Development, 28 (5), 805–22.

Posner, R.A. (1977), Economic Analysis of Law, Boston: Little Brown.

Powell, W. (1991), 'Neither Market nor Hierarchy: Network Forms of Organization' in G. Thompson, J. Frances, R. Levacic and J. Mitchell (eds), Markets, Hierarchies and Networks: The Coordination of Social Life, London: Sage, pp. 265–76.

Putnam, R. (1993), Making Democracy Work: Civic Traditions in Modern Italy, Princeton: Princeton University Press.

Reich, R. (1999), 'We Are All Third Wayers Now', American Prospect, 43 (1), 23–35.

Reid, M. (1994), 'Local Government: Service Delivery or Governance?', Public Sector, 17 (2), 2–6.

Reid, M. (1997), 'A Local Government Perspective on Social Capital', in D. Robinson, (ed.), Social Capital and Policy Development, Wellington: Institute of Policy Studies, pp. 103–20.

Reid, M. (1999), 'The Central-Local Government Relationship: The Need for a Framework?', Political Science, 50 (2), 164–81.

Rhodes, R. (1988), Beyond Westminster and Whitehall, London: Unwin Hyman.

Rhodes, R. (1997), Understanding Governance, Buckingham: Open University.

Rhodes, R.A.W. and Marsh, D. (1992), 'New Directions in the Study of Policy Networks', European Journal of Political Research, 21 (3), 181–205.

Riddell, M. (1997), 'Bringing Back Balance to Policy Development' in D. Robinson, (ed.), Social Capital and Policy Development, Wellington: Institute of Policy Studies, pp. 21–38.

Robinson, D. (ed.) (1997), Social Capital and Policy Development, Wellington: Institute of Policy Studies.

Rodrik, D. (1996), 'Understanding Economic Policy Reform', Journal of Economic Literature, 34 (1), 9–41.

Romer, R. (1993), 'The New Keynesian Synthesis', Journal of Economic Perpsectives, 6 (1), 5–22.

Romer, T. and Rosenthal, H. (1978), 'Political Resource Allocation, Controlled Agendas and the Status Quo', Public Choice, 33 (4), 27–43.

Rouse, P. Putterill, M. and Ryan, D. (1995), 'Measuring the Performance of New Zealand Local Authority Maintenance Activities' in Roading Using Data Envelopment Analysis, paper presented to the New England Conference on

Efficiency and Productivity, 23–24 November, University of New England.

Rubinfeld, D.I. (1987), 'The Economics of the Local Public Sector', in A.J. Auerbach and M. Feldstein (eds), *Handbook of Public Economics*, vol. 3, Amsterdam: North-Holland, pp. 571–646.

Rubinstein, A. (ed.) (1990), *Game Theory in Economics*, Aldershot, UK: Edward Elgar.

Rutherford, M. (1996), *Institutions in Economics: The Old and The New Institutionalism*, Cambridge: Cambridge University Press.

Sabatier, P. (1986), 'Top-down and Bottom-up Approaches to Implementation Research', *Journal of Public Policy*, 6 (1), 21–48.

Sabatier, P. (1988), 'An Advocacy Coalition Framework of Policy Change and the Role of Policy-Oriented Learning Therein', *Policy Sciences*, 21 (2), 129–68.

Sargent, T. (1981), 'The Ends of Four Big Inflations', in R. Hall (ed.), *Inflation: Causes and Effects*, Chicago: University of Chicago Press.

Sargent, T. and Wallace, N. (1975), 'Rational Expectations, the Optimal Monetary Instrument and the Optimal Money Supply Rule', *Journal of Political Economy*, 83, 241–254.

Scharpf, F. (1992), 'Political Institutions, Decision Styles and Policy Choices', in R. Crada and A. Windhorff-Heritier (eds), *Political Choice, Institutions, Rules and the Limits of Rationality*, Frankfurt: Campus Verlag, pp. 134–59.

Schick, A. (1996), *The Spirit of Reform: Managing the New Zealand State Sector in a Time of Change*, Wellington: State Services Commission.

Schick, A. (1998), 'Why Most Developing Countries Should Not Try New Zealand's Reforms', *The World Bank Research Observer*, 13 (1), 123–31.

Schmidt, P. (1985), 'Frontier Production Functions', *Econometric Reviews*, 4, 289–328.

Schneider, M. (1989), 'Intermunicipal Competition, Budget-Maximizing Bureaucrats and the Level of Suburban Competition', *American Journal of Political Science*, 21 (2), 612–28.

Schumpeter, J. A. (1943), *Capitalism, Socialism and Democracy*, London: Allen and Unwin.

Shubik, M. (1975), 'The General Equilibrium Model is Not Complete and Not Adequate for the Reconciliation of Micro and Macroeconomic Theory', *Kyklos*, 28 (3), 545–73.

Simon, H. (1983), *Reason in Human Affairs*, Oxford: Basil Blackwell.

Simon, H.A. (1975), *Models of Bounded Rationality*, Cambridge: MIT Press.

Smith, A. (1759), *The Theory of Moral Sentiments*, reprinted in A.L. Macfie and D.D. Raphael (eds), *The Glasgow Edition of the Works and Correspondence of Adam Smith*, vol. I, Oxford: Oxford University Press.

Smith, A. (1776), *An Inquiry into the Nature and Causes of the Wealth of Nations*, reprinted in W.B. Todd (ed.) (1976), *The Glasgow Edition of the Works and Correspondence of Adam Smith*, vol. II, Oxford: Oxford University Press.

Snyder, C.R. (1994), *The Psychology of Hope*, New York: The Free Press.

Steering Committee for the Review of Commonwealth/State Service Provision (SCRCSSP) (1998), *Data Envelopment Analysis: A Technique for Measuring the Efficiency of Government Service Delivery*, Canberra: AGPS.

Stewart, J. and Stoker, G. (1989), *Local Government in the 1990s*, London: Macmillan.

Stigler, G.C. (1957), 'The Tenable Range of Functions of Local Government', reprinted in W.E. Oates (ed.) (1998), *The Economics of Fiscal Federalism and Local Finance*, Cheltenham, UK: Edward Elgar, pp. 3–9.

Stigler, G.C. (1971), 'The Economic Theory of Regulation', *Bell Journal of Economics*, **2** (1), 137–46.
Stiglitz, J.E. (2000), *Economics of the Public Sector* (third edition), New York: Norton.
Streek, W. and Schmitter, P. (1985), *Private Interest Government*, London: Sage.
Stretton, H. and Orchard, L. (1994), *Public Goods, Public Enterprise, Public Choice*, Basingstoke: Macmillan.
Sutherland, S. (1989), 'Hope', in G. Vesey, (ed.), *The Philosophy in Christianity*, Cambridge: Cambridge University Press, pp. 111–29.
Tanzi, V. and Schuknecht, L. (2000), *Public Spending in the Twentieth Century*, Cambridge: Cambridge University Press.
Tarrow, S. (1994), *Power in Movement*, Cambridge: Cambridge University Press.
Taylor, C. (1985), *Philosophy and the Human Sciences*, Cambridge: Cambridge University Press.
Taylor, J. (1986), 'An Appeal for Rationality in the Policy Activism Debate', in R. Hafer (ed.), *The Monetary and Fiscal Policy Debate: The Lessons From Two Decades*, Totowa: Rowan and Allenheld.
Ter-Minassian, T. (1997), 'Intergovernmental Fiscal Relations in a Macroeconomic Perspective: An Overview', in T. Ter-Minassian (ed.), *Fiscal Federalism in Theory and Practice*, Washington: International Monetary Fund, pp. 3–24.
The Royal Commission on Social Policy (1988), *Report of the Royal Commission on Social Policy*, Wellington: Crown Copyright.
Thompson, G., Frances, J., Levacic, R. and Mitchell, J. (eds) (1981), *Markets, Hierarchies and Networks: The Coordination of Social Life*, London: Sage.
Tiebout, C. (1956), 'A Pure Theory of Local Government Expenditure', *Journal of Political Economy*, **60**, 416–24.
Tollison, R.D. (1997), 'Rentseeking', in D.C. Mueller (ed.), *Perspectives on Public Choice*, Cambridge: Cambridge University Press, pp. 506–25.
Tresch, R.W. (1981), *Public Finance: A Normative Theory*, Plano: Business Publications.
Tulkens, H. (1993), 'On FDH Efficiency Analysis: Some Methodological Issues and Applications to Retail Banking, Courts, and Urban Transport', *The Journal of Productivity Analysis*, **4**, 183–210.
Vanden Eeckaut, P.J., Tulkens, H. and Jamar, M.A. (1993), 'Cost efficiency in Belgian municipalities', in H.O. Fried, C.A. Lovell and S.S. Schmidt, *The Measurement of Productive Efficiency: Techniques and Applications*, New York: Oxford University Press, pp. 91–112.
Vitaliano, D.F. (1997), 'X-Inefficiency in the Public Sector: The Case of Libraries', *Public Finance Review*, **25**, 629–43.
Vitaliano, D.F. (1998), 'Assessing Public Library Efficiency using Data Envelopment Analysis', *Annals of Public and Cooperative Economics*, **69**, 107–22.
Viton, P.A. (1992), 'Consolidations of Scale and Scope in Urban Transport', *Regional Science and Urban Economics*, **22**, 25–49.
Wallis, J.J. and Oates, W. (1988), 'Decentralization of the Public Sector: An Empirical Study of State and Local Government', in H.S. Rosen (ed.), *Fiscal Federalism: Quantitative Studies*, Chicago: University of Chicago Press, pp. 5–32.
Wallis, J.L. (1999), 'Understanding the Role of Leadership in Economic Policy Reform', *World Development*, **27** (1), 39–54.
Wallis, J.L. and Dollery, B.E. (1999), *Market Failure, Government Failure, Leadership and Public Policy*, London: Macmillan.
Wallis, J.L. and Dollery, B.E. (2001), 'Local Government Policy Evolution in New

Zealand: Radical Reform and the Export Emergence of Consensus or Rival Advocacy Coalitions', Public Administration (forthcoming)

Weimer, D.L. and Vining, A.R. (1999), *Policy Analysis* (third edition), Upper Saddle River, NJ: Prentice Hall.

Weisbrod, B.A. (1978), 'Problems of enhancing the Public Interest: Towards a Model of Government Failures', in B.A. Weisbrod, J.F. Handler and N.K. Komesar (eds), *Public Interest Law*, London: University of California Press, pp.30–41.

West, E.G. (1976), *Adam Smith: The Man and His Works*, Indianapolis: Liberty Fund.

Wildasin, D.E. (1986), *Urban Public Finance*, Chur: Harwood,.

Wilks, S. and Wright, M. (1987), *Comparative Government-Industry Relations*, Oxford: Clarendon.

Williamson, J. (1994), *The Political Economy of Policy Reform*, Washington: Institute for Economic Reform.

Williamson, O. (1975), *Markets and Hierarchies*, New York: Free Press.

Williamson, O.E. (1979), 'Transaction-Cost Economics: The Governance of Contractual Relations', *Journal of Law and Economics*, **22** (October), 233–61.

Williamson, O.E. (1985), *The Economic Institutions of Capitalism*, New York: Free Press.

Wilson, J.Q. (1989), *Bureaucracy: What Government Agencies Do and Why They Do It*, San Francisco: Jossey-Bass.

Wintrobe, R. (1997), 'Modern Bureaucratic Theory', in D.C. Mueller (ed.), *Perspectives on Public Choice*, Cambridge: Cambridge University Press, pp. 429–54.

Wolf, C. (1979), 'A Theory of Nonmarket Failure: Framework for Implementation Analysis', *Journal of Law and Economics*, **22** (10), 107–39.

Wolf, C. (1987), 'Market and Nonmarket Failures: Comparison and Assessment', *Journal of Public Policy*, **6** (1), 43–70.

Wolf, C. (1989), *Markets or Governments: Choosing Between Imperfect Alternatives*, Cambridge, MA: MIT Press.

World Bank Development Report (1997), *The State in a Changing World*, Oxford: Oxford University Press.

Worthington, A.C. (1999), 'Performance Indicators and Efficiency Measurement in Public Libraries', *Australian Economic Review*, **32**, 31–42.

Worthington, A.C. (2000), 'Cost Efficiency in Local Government: A Comparative Analysis of Mathematical Programming and Econometric Approaches', *Financial Accountability and Management*, **16**, 201–24.

Worthington, A.C. and Dollery, B.E. (1999), 'Fiscal Illusion and the Australian Local Government Grants Process: How Sticky is the Flypaper Effect?', *Public Choice*, **99** (1-2), 1–13.

Worthington, A.C. and Dollery, B.E. (2000a), 'Productive Efficiency and the Australian Local Government Grants Process: An Empirical Analysis of New South Wales Local Government', *Australasian Journal of Regional Studies*, **6**, 95–122.

Worthington, A.C. and Dollery, B.E. (2000b), 'An Empirical Survey of Frontier Efficiency Measurement Techniques in Local Government', *Local Government Studies*, **26**, 23–52.

Yeatman, A. (1987), 'The Concept of Public Management and the Australian State in the 1980s', *Australian Journal of Public Administration*, **46**(4), 339-53.

Young, S. (1999), 'Participation Strategies and Local Environmental Politics', in G. Stoker (ed.), *The New Politics of British Local Governance*, London: Macmillan,

pp. 181–97.
Zerbe, R.O. and McCurdy, H.E. (1999), 'The Failure of Market Failure', *Journal of Policy Analysis and* Management, **18** (4), 558–78.

Index

243